THE MAKING OF A GENERATION:
THE CHILDREN OF THE 1970S IN ADULTHOOD

Secondary school graduates of the late 1980s and early 1990s have found themselves coping with rising economic insecurity, social change, and workplace restructuring. Drawing on two major longitudinal studies of young people in Canada and Australia conducted over a period of fifteen years, *The Making of a Generation* offers unique insight into the hopes, dreams, and life journeys of a generation.

Although children of the 1970s attained higher education levels than their predecessors, as adults they entered new labour markets that were deregulated and precarious. Lesley Andres and Johanna Wyn discuss the consequences of education and labour policies in each country, emphasizing the long-term impacts on health, well-being, and family formation. The authors argue that these young adults, despite their modest expectations, bore the brunt of policies designed to bring about rapid changes in the nature of work. Highlighting similarities and differences between the Canadians and Australians, the book concludes that those born in the 1970s became a vanguard generation as they negotiated the significant social and economic transformations of the 1990s.

LESLEY ANDRES is a professor in the Department of Educational Studies at the University of British Columbia.

JOHANNA WYN is a professor in the Faculty of Education and director of the Youth Research Centre at the University of Melbourne.

LESLEY ANDRES AND JOHANNA WYN

The Making of a Generation

The Children of the 1970s in Adulthood

UNIVERSITY OF TORONTO PRESS
Toronto Buffalo London

© University of Toronto Press Incorporated 2010
Toronto Buffalo London
www.utppublishing.com
Printed in Canada

ISBN 978-0-8020-9258-8 (cloth)
ISBN 978-0-8020-9467-4 (paper)

∞

Printed on acid-free, 100% post-consumer recycled paper with vegetable-based links.

Library and Archives Canada Cataloguing in Publication

Andres, Lesley
The making of a generation : the children of the 1970s in adulthood / Lesley
Andres and Johanna Wyn.

Includes bibliographical references and index.
ISBN 978-0-8020-9258-8 (bound).   ISBN 978-0-8020-9467-4 (pbk.)

1. Young adults – Canada – Social conditions.   2. Young adults –
Australia – Social conditions.   3. Generation X – Canada.   4. Generation X –
Australia.   5. Canada – Social conditions – 1971–1991.   6. Canada – Social
conditions – 1991–.   7. Australia – Social conditions.   I. Wyn, Johanna, 1952–.
II. Title.

HQ799.8.C3A54 2010   305.2420971'09045   C2010-902912-7

This book has been published with the help of a grant from the Canadian
Federation for the Humanities and Social Sciences, through the Aid to
Scholarly Publications Programme, using funds provided by the Social
Sciences and Humanities Research Council of Canada.
University of Toronto Press acknowledges the financial assistance to its publishing program of the Canada Council for the Arts and the Ontario Arts Council.

 Canada Council   Conseil des Arts
for the Arts   du Canada

 ONTARIO ARTS COUNCIL
CONSEIL DES ARTS DE L'ONTARIO

University of Toronto Press acknowledges the financial support for its publishing activities of the Government of Canada through the Canada Book Fund.

Contents

Acknowledgments

This book would not have been possible without the generosity and dedication of the Canadians and Australians who participated in the multiple waves of surveys and interviews for the *Paths on Life's Way* and the *Life Patterns* research projects. To them we both owe a debt of gratitude.

Over the years, many student assistants have worked on every aspect of the *Paths on Life's Way* project. Special thanks go to Lorinda Coulter, Colleen Hawkey, Ellen Retelle, Michelle Pidgeon, and Maria Adamuti-Trache for their longstanding involvement in data collection and analysis. The Department of Educational Studies at the University of British Columbia has provided ongoing support and space for this project.

Since 1993 the *Paths on Life's Way* project has been funded by the British Columbia Council on Admissions and Transfer and the Social Sciences and Humanities Research Council of Canada.

We wish to thank Janine Jongbloed, Wendy Hartford, and Patrick Fick for their thoughtful comments on the manuscript, and Laura Vale for her expert proofreading abilities.

The *Life Patterns* project was initiated by Peter Dwyer, who led it through its first phase. Others at the Youth Research Centre at the University of Melbourne have also played a role: Graeme Smith, Debra Tyler, Dan Woodman, Helen Stokes, Hernan Cuervo, and Sally Beadle.

The *Life Patterns* project was supported by grants from the Australian Research Council 2005–2009, 2002–2004, and 1998–2000. It was also supported by a grant from the Australian National Training Authority in 1996.

This book has been published with the help of a grant from the Canadian Federation for the Humanities and Social Sciences, through the Aid to Scholarly Publications Program, using funds provided by the Social Sciences and Humanities Research Council of Canada.

Finally, we would like to thank our partners, Hans Pechar and Evan Willis, for living the writing process with us.

THE MAKING OF A GENERATION:
THE CHILDREN OF THE 1970S IN ADULTHOOD

1 Introduction

In this book we seek to provide answers to the overarching question 'of how a generation is made.' The formation of a generation is a multifaceted process that occurs over time and depends on the interplay of given characteristics of individuals and the demographic, economic, social, and cultural contexts through which they pass. The evolving sets of policies, practices, and institutional changes to which members of a given generation are exposed influence the shaping of that generation. This occurs through a dialectical dynamic process that involves changes over time. Members of a generation age, have relationships, get married, have children, and become workers, mature students, and caregivers of aging parents. As such, to understand the making of a generation requires an examination of the double helix of structures and related policies and of individual lives.

In order to detect the impact of evolving sets of social forces on a given cohort at both the micro and the macro levels, it is essential to conduct analyses across time. To do so requires the availability of databases that lend themselves to analyses of the impact of policies on educational and occupational outcomes in relation to both the factors affecting those outcomes (for example, gender, academic capital, and socio-economic status) and the adult-life events that are affected by these factors (for example, relationships, family, and home ownership).

Two such data sets currently exist that permit detailed longitudinal comparative analyses of the lives of today's young adults: the 'Paths on Life's Way' project in the province of British Columbia, Canada, and the 'Life Patterns' project based in the state of Victoria, Australia. They were developed independently, but the similarities between the two data sets are striking. Both studies have survey and interview components, contain representative province- and state-wide samples, and span fifteen and fourteen years, respectively. Both of the studies are informed by the body of research on the life course and youth transitions, and therefore these data allow us to examine the lives of individuals from multiple perspectives and to address theoretical, policy, and practice-based questions. In the mid 1990s we began to share survey questions, and so in many instances we have directly comparable data. We have seized the opportunity that the two data sets provide and have undertaken the first longitudinal comparative analysis of Canadian and Australian young adults. The detail contained in these studies has enabled us to gain unique insights into the effects of the educational and labour market policies of our respective countries in relation to the many other dimensions of young Canadians' and Australians' lives. The data also provide an opportunity to further reflect on the usefulness of different theoretical approaches and to develop new understandings of this generation.

To date, the majority of research on young people has focused on transitions. Young people's transitions through education and beyond have become of increasing importance in educational research in both Canada and Australia. In both countries, interest has been sparked by the increasing complexities of the transition process from school to work, leading to a new literature on young people's transitions (Andres and Wyn 2008; Bynner 2005; Krahn and Lowe 1999; Wyn and Woodman 2006). Educational research on transition processes has also been a focus in educational policy in which education is positioned as crucial to the production of highly skilled labour markets that meet the needs of post-industrial economies (McLaughlin 1999).

However, transitions research is fraught with limitations. Investigations of educational transitions or school-to-work linkages often use single, snapshot studies with retrospective questions to impute temporal causation (for example, Ainley and McKenzie 1999). Alternatively, when longitudinal research has been conducted, frequently it has relied on data sets targeted for single purposes (for example, Finnie 2004), and while adequate for describing patterns, it is usually not rich enough to provide explanatory details. Moreover, transitions research is usually delimited to a single-type transition – for example, the transition from high school to post-secondary education or the transition from education to work.[1] These analyses neglect the other dimensions and related transitions occurring simultaneously and over time in young people's

---

1 Throughout this book the term *post-secondary education* refers to all formal education that young people participate in beyond secondary school. The term *higher education*, which is used in policy documents in Australia, tends to refer to the university sector.

lives. Many researchers interested in youth transitions have drawn attention to the need for theoretical and analytical complexity when considering transitions (Andres 1999; Dwyer and Wyn 2001; Furlong, Cartmel, Biggart, et al. 2003). Principally because of funding limitations, research that spans significant time periods in the individual lives of young adults has been very rare. In addition, most studies do not combine quantitative and qualitative data to portray the full flavour of young people's lives.

In our examination of the making of a generation, we resist the temptation to use existing labels and stereotypes as shorthand to describe our generation of young adults. We heed the warning in Pomerantz (1999, 21) that generations exist as populations, 'not as a neatly packaged concept.' Pomerantz contends that when labels such as Generation X are blindly and uncritically accepted, they become 'tools of dehumanization, offering us little in the way of information. Labels are excuses not to know someone. They make us lazy and promote the unconscious use of language. They help us ignore complexity and glorify simplicity' (132). Also, she points out that one generation does not live in isolation from, and without influence by, other generational groups:

> Each generation bears the stamp of the one before it and will be visible in the ones to come. Each generation is not fully present, but is constantly differing and deferring. Thinking of a generation as autonomous and separate from other generations, then, becomes impossible ... Each generation is linked to every other generation, not just through genealogy, but by our mutual dependence on one another for societal development. Several generations inhabit the same historical space at one time. Therefore, each generation shares the society with the generations before and after, but never occupies it completely. Full presence is always tainted by the past and by the future, by differing and deferring. Our society is characterized by borrowed space, not permanent ownership ... Interdependence or intergenerational unity is one way to move past labels and into the limitless possibilities of play. If we see ourselves as a part of the whole, instead of segregated units, then it becomes rather difficult to draw rigid boundaries around various age classifications. It simply ceases to matter. Similarities are emphasized instead of distinctions and the 'other' becomes not so other at all. In fact, the 'other' becomes us. (134)

Further education is also used in policy documents and tends to refer to non-university education beyond secondary school.

Our data sets contain information that allows us to carry out detailed comparative work. With such complex data we are able to entertain the following questions in a comparative perspective:

- How do young people anticipate their lives to unfold? How do their lives unfold in relation to their hopes and dreams?
- To what extent do the effects of cultural and social capital acquired (or not acquired) earlier in life endure over time?
- How does the structure of the post-secondary system and labour market in each country affect the choices and educational outcomes of young adults? How do individuals act in relation to existing structures?
- Are the participants shaping new identities and new understandings of 'adulthood' as they respond to their circumstances?
- How do young women and men juggle education, work, and family responsibilities? How do these responsibilities change over time?
- What is the impact of governmental policy (for example, paid parental leave, availability of publicly subsidized day care) on labour force participation by young women and men?
- How do young people view the choices they have made? How do their views change over time?
- What are the distinctive experiences of the 'post-1970 generation' in each country?

As reflected in this set of questions, data generated from our longitudinal projects focus on both processes and outcomes from multidimensional perspectives. As final outcomes are often contingent on earlier events and outcomes, we unravel these interrelationships by analysing the life paths travelled by the individuals in our samples. Below, we describe the *Paths on Life's Way* and *Life Patterns* projects.

The Data Sets

Paths on Life's Way

The *Paths on Life's Way* project is a fifteen-year longitudinal study of young people in British Columbia, Canada, who graduated from high school in 1988. The project began in 1989 as one of a series of 'Access for All' initiatives by the British Columbia Ministry of Advanced Education and is still ongoing.[2] This study of the transitions of young people was launched in response to low post-secondary participation rates, particularly of high school graduates. The two ministries responsible for education in the province collaborated by sending survey questionnaires to a stratified random sample of ten thousand British Columbia Grade 12 graduates of the 1988 cohort (Phase I). Respondents, representing 23 per cent of the entire cohort of 1988 high school graduates, included both non-participants and participants in the post-secondary system. High school and post-secondary records provided demographic information such as sex, geographic location, achievement in high school, and post-secondary institutions attended. Also, in 1989, to complement the questionnaire data, Andres conducted the first of a series of in-depth interviews with students who were currently in Grade 12. A purposive or judgment sampling strategy was used to select three British Columbia schools (one metropolitan, one urban/rural, and one remote school) in which to conduct the interviews. Face-to-face, semi-structured interviews were conducted in November 1989 and again in May 1990. In October 1990 interviewees were again contacted, by telephone, to ascertain their actual post-high-school destinations.

In 1993 Andres converted the original baseline study into a longitudinal project by carrying out a second follow-up of the 1989 survey sample (Phase II). At this point the study was named the 'Paths on Life's Way' project. Survey questionnaires were sent to respondents to the 1989 study. In 1993 the third in a series of semi-structured interviews was conducted. Two subsequent phases of data collection occurred in 1997–8 (Phase III) and 2003 (Phase IV). In total, 733 survey respondents have participated in all four waves of the study, and the same thirty interviewees have participated in all six sets of interviews between 1989 and 2003. A detailed description of the data set and related research reports are described elsewhere (Andres 2002a, 2002b, 2002c).

Life Patterns

The University of Melbourne Youth Research Centre's (YRC's) *Life Patterns* project is a fourteen-year, ongoing longitudinal study of young people in Victoria, Australia, who left secondary school in 1991 at about the age of eighteen years. Drawing on a commitment to explore issues

---

2 A twenty-two-year follow-up is currently underway.

of youth transitions, the *Life Patterns* research was designed to provide a critical perspective on current post-compulsory education and training-policy formation (Dwyer, Wilson, and Woock 1984; Dwyer and Wyn 2001; Wilson and Wyn 1987). The pathways metaphor, derived from Organisation for Economic Co-operation and Development (OECD) policy programs and goals, became widely used in Australian educational policies of the 1980s. These policies were directly concerned with the relationship between educational participation, attainment, and employment outcomes. Although initially guided by this metaphor, the early findings of complex and non-linear trajectories led to the adoption of the term *Life Patterns* instead.

The research has involved two phases and several waves of data collection. Phase I followed the students annually through the years 1991 to 2000, generating a ten-year record of young people's transitions into adult life. This phase focused on their pathways through further education and employment and documented their responses and adaptations to changing labour-market conditions. The concept *post-1970 generation* was coined in an attempt to characterize the ways in which this cohort of young people was evidently shaping new life patterns and understandings of adulthood. Phase II (2002 to 2004) was developed in response to issues developed at the end of Phase I and involved rethinking careers and mixed patterns of life priorities. In 2004, 625 individuals remained in the study. As we describe later in this chapter, most of the analyses herein are based on waves of data collection up to and including 2004. Phase III data collection began in 2005 and has continued through to 2009. In 2006, 344 survey respondents remain in the study, a subset of whom are interviewees. The sample includes both urban and rural youth, covering a representative range of schools, ethnic groups, and parental educational attainment.

In Australia the Longitudinal Surveys of Australian Youth (LSAY) provide national data on the transition processes of young Australians.[3] They were initiated with a survey of young Australians who were in Year 9 (aged sixteen) in 1995, augmented with a group of young people who were in Year 9 in 1998, and again in 2003 with a sample of fifteen-year-olds (who were part of the Programme for International Student Assessment [PISA], an international comparative study of

---

3 See http://www.acer.edu.au/lsay/study.html.

young people aged about fifteen in OECD countries who were tested for literacy and numeracy). This LSAY data set can be seen as complementary to the *Life Patterns* study. However, the data set is focused almost exclusively on school and employment issues, and this focus has been strengthened in recent years through the inclusion of the PISA cohort (Rothman and Hillman 2008). The data set emphasizes quantitative analyses that describe patterns of educational and employment participation,[4] and while this can be used as a backdrop to the *Life Patterns* data, it does not provide the breadth of analysis nor the depth of qualitative data that enables researchers to take a critical perspective on the changing meanings of education, employment, and life to young people.

Given the similarities in the *Paths on Life's Way* and *Life Patterns* projects, the purpose of this book is to extend the insights further through comparative analyses. By comparing their experiences and outcomes over the fourteen- to fifteen-year time span of these two studies, we reveal how Australian and Canadian young adults have negotiated the life course in specific cultural, social, and economic contexts and in relation to federal and provincial or state educational and employment policies.

In independent analyses of our respective data sets we have drawn on current theoretical perspectives to explain the patterns and relationships in the data. A number of approaches have been found to be relevant in explaining these patterns and outcomes. Although neither study has rested entirely on one theoretical approach, the emphasis in each study has been different. The analysis of the Canadian research has drawn extensively on theories of reproduction developed by Pierre Bourdieu, with a particular focus on the ways in which cultural capital is transmitted and used. By contrast, the Australian research has tended to draw on theories of individualization, risk, and identity formation through the work of Ulrich Beck and Anthony Giddens in order to explore the development of new patterns of life and identity. Also, both studies have been informed to some degree by the life course literature and in particular by moving away from the notion of *normal biographies* of previous generations in which a transition involved a simple passage from one social institution to

---

4 See http://www.acer.edu.au/lsay/research.html.

another (for example, school to work; school to marriage). In both studies the non-linear nature of the young people's pathways has a strong degree of resonance with these theoretical approaches. The complexity of their transitions contrasts with the linear transition models of government policies. The studies have also highlighted the extent to which young people have had to negotiate their own pathways.

In the analyses contained in this book we continue to employ these concepts to provide a multifaceted portrayal of the ways in which the agency-structure nexus has evolved over time for these individuals (see chapter 2). However, rather than being used simply as explanations, these concepts will be used to 'interrogat[e] the data' (Reay 2004, 432) to reveal *whether* and *how* they work together to produce different forms of agency and outcomes across different domains of life. We take advantage of the empirical richness of these extensive data sets together with the theories described above to gain unique insights into the effects of educational and labour-market policies of our respective countries in relation to young people's lives. Through comparative analyses we are able to determine how complementary and competing macrosocial structures and cultural forces shape the way these two cohorts experience the transition from one life phase to the next; how life trajectories of Canadian and Australian young adults unfold in relation to the cumulative impact of earlier conditions and events in each country; what constitutes 'agency' for these two groups; how structural changes and educational and labour-force policies have shaped participation in post-secondary education and the workforce over time; and the extent to which social class and gender still affect the life chances of Canadian and Australian young adults.

Uniqueness of the Study

The data sets themselves are key products of the *Paths on Life's Way* and the *Life Patterns* projects. These studies are the only comprehensive longitudinal research projects on the transition of youth to adulthood in British Columbia and Victoria and are two of the few longitudinal studies of young adults in Canada and Australia. Although other national longitudinal studies contain data on individuals, they are limited by less inclusive mandates and shorter time spans. No other currently active longitudinal study in Canada combines extensive qualitative and quantitative data, on 763 individuals over a fifteen-year time period.[5] Similarly, the *Life Patterns* project contains both quantitative and qualitative data on 640 individuals over a twelve-year time period (and 344 individuals over a fourteen-year time period). Other comparative studies exist (for example, Shannon and Kidd 2001; Tempier et al. 2009), but they do not employ longitudinal quantitative and qualitative data.

Our analyses allow us to determine the extent to which exposure to the specific social, cultural, and historical contexts of each country influences the construction of biographies by individuals who bring with them various levels of capital or resources, who are driven by aspirations and expectations, and who act on opportunities and constraints (Giddens 1984; Heinz 1996, 1999; Mannheim 1970). As Elder (1974) emphasizes, conditions and outcomes at one point in time provide a basis for subsequent analyses across the life course. These analyses have direct implications for the formulation, enactment, and evaluation of policies and practices that provide opportunities for young adults regardless of the lottery of birth (Esping-Andersen 2009). The findings from this study will help us understand how cross-national, national, and provincial or state policies on education, work, families, and children work towards or against the promotion of individual and collective well-being.

Our Analytical Approach

The major challenge in this collaborative endeavour has been to capture the complexity of the life trajectories of the young adults in our projects in a comparative perspective. In particular, an examination of experiences and events at the micro and macro levels is critical to our understanding of how existing structures serve to shape life trajectories and, in turn, how individuals act in relation to existing structures. In tables A.1 through A.2 in appendix A, the data-collection points for both the survey questionnaire and the interviews are documented. The Canadian *Paths on Life's Way* data were collected at five-year intervals, whereas the Australian *Life Patterns* data were collected more frequently. The Canadian study began in 1989 when survey questionnaire

---

5 For other important longitudinal research in Canada see Anisef (2000), Krahn and Lowe (1999), and Looker (1993).

respondents were around nineteen years old and interviewees were eighteen. Questionnaire data were first collected from the Australian sample in 1991 when they were seventeen years old. Interviews were introduced into the Australian study in 1997 when interviewees were around twenty-seven years old.

The analyses included in this book take many forms. Often we were able to match time points and questions exactly. For example, for both studies we asked identical questions of those who were ten years out of high school regarding physical and mental well-being. Sometimes we asked the same or similar questions, but the time points do not line up directly; in these instances we use the time points that most closely correspond with each other. Yet in other instances the questions in our respective surveys and interview data are complementary rather than identical, or closely similar in content, time points, or both. Important stories need to be and can be told from these data; by braiding complementary information gathered from the two data sets we endeavour to use the data to provide a comprehensive portrait of our respondents' lives. In this study we have not focused on tests of significance; rather, we are interested in examining shifts patterns over time.

The interview data also take several forms. In the Canadian study, questionnaire respondents and interview respondents comprise two separate and distinct groups. In the Australian study, the interviewees are a subset of the questionnaire respondents. We employ all of the interview data over time; that is, we do not back-censor the comments of those who did not remain in the study over fifteen years, as their comments remain relevant at a given point in time. In addition, in both the Canadian and Australian studies, we employ the responses to the open-ended questions that were asked as final questions on each questionnaire. Interview data are interwoven into our analyses. Where possible, we provide a quantitative indication of the magnitude of similar responses in order to showcase the voices of our respondents as representative of the sentiments of the young Canadians and Australians in this study. Lone voices are identified as such. To reduce confusion, throughout the analyses we refer to our respondents as simply Canadian or Australian.

Representativeness of the Samples

A defining feature of the two studies is that they both draw on samples of young people from one state (Victoria) or province (British

Columbia) of countries that are governed through federal systems of politics. Similarities in the nature of the political, social, economic, and geographical features of these two areas make our comparative analysis meaningful. Canada and Australia have many characteristics in common. Both countries are settler dominions and are similar in their traditions and formal educational and political systems. The state of Victoria and the province of British Columbia are part of the Pacific Rim and are multi-ethnic societies with influences predominantly from Britain, continental Europe, and Asia. Both have undergone a transformation from economies that relied almost exclusively on primary industries (and manufacturing) to post-industrial, service economies. There are also several important differences in the structure of the educational systems and the labour markets in each state or province, which make the comparison significant.

Moreover, the educational systems in each country are more or less consistent from province to province or state to state.[6] In Canada and Australia, typically students begin formal schooling at the age of five in kindergarten and progress through to Grade or Year 12. The completion of Grade or Year 12 signals the end of formal schooling. As we explain in chapter 5, entry into post-secondary education is competitive, with course work and academic achievement serving as the primary criteria for admission into universities and non-university institutions.

Other data sets, such as the Youth in Transitions Study (YITS) in Canada, the National Educational Longitudinal Study (NELS) in the United States, or OECD data (for example, 'Education at a Glance'), do exist. Although all these data sets have breadth in a few dimensions, none has the quantitative and qualitative depth that our data offer in the areas of education, work, family and relationships, and health and well-being. With our data we can answer the what, how, and why questions over time and provide insights that other data sets simply cannot provide. Indeed, we see this capacity to cover a breadth of policy issues to be a strength of this study. We encourage researchers and policymakers to assess the extent to which our findings, interpretations, conclusions, and implications are transferable to other settings.

The young people who participated in our studies are Australians and Canadians, and there are nationally relevant implications that

---

6 Quebec is an exception in Canada, where formal schooling ends after Grade 11, and all post-secondary students must begin their studies at collèges d'enseignement général et professionnel (CEGEPs).

can be derived from our analysis. First, the study shows the long-term impact of education and labour-market policies on the lives of young adults. Second, the study shows the failure of policies in the 1990s to significantly address the patterns of inequality based on rurality and socio-economic status. Third, the analysis shows how policy areas are linked and how even relatively subtle differences in policy approaches in one (for example, labour-market policy) can have significant long-term outcomes for individuals' lives across health, family formation, and education. These findings are relevant, not only to Australia and Canada but also to other countries.

At the outset of both the *Paths of Life's Way* and the *Life Patterns* studies, the focus was on gendered, classed, and geographical influences on young people's negotiations of education, work, and life. Although both studies include a proportion of young people from different ethnic backgrounds, of those who are indigenous (respondents self-identified with over one hundred different racial or ethnic groups in the Canadian sample alone), and of those who are same-sex attracted, the sample size of these groups in our studies is too small to enable a valid analysis because the number of cells would be so great as to render the results uninterpretable. A different sampling method and different conceptual frame, one that according to Sen (2008, 6) embraces 'the multiple identities that human beings have,' would be required to construct a comparative study of young people from these groups.

Missing data, as a result of both sample attrition and non-response to questionnaire items, have the potential to undermine the value of longitudinal data sets. Three types of missing data afflict our projects: (1) mailing lists that become outdated over time, resulting in the inability to reach all respondents for the next phase of the study; (2) individuals who receive survey questionnaires or requests to participate in further interviews and choose not to participate (sample attrition); and (3) non-response to certain items on questionnaires. The first and second of these is a problem of *structurally* missing data, and the third falls into the category of *accidental* missingness.

Appendix A contains two tables (tables A.3 and A.4) of response rates over time for the Canadian and Australian sample in relation to post-secondary status during the first year out of high school, father's occupational status, mother's educational level, and geographic region. These tables demonstrate that the proportion of those who were post-secondary participants within one year of high school completion increased over time, and those who were initial non-participants declined over time. In both samples, over time the bias favours women. Attrition by men in the Australian study has been higher than in the Canadian study. Despite problems with attrition, for the most part both studies have retained the essence of the original sample, with similar proportions of respondents from the different groups continuing to participate. The bias in response rates in the *Paths on Life's Way* study are similar to those of the *Life Patterns* project, with bias somewhat more pronounced in the Australian study. However, both samples are remarkably stable in terms of parental socio-economic status (as measured by father's occupation and mother's education) and geographic region. However, owing to the existing bias, our findings can be interpreted as the best-case scenario in both countries.

In the analyses in this book we use survey data of the 733 individuals from the Canadian study who responded to all phases of the project. To ensure that the sample size for the Australian study is large enough to conduct comparable analyses, for the most part we use data generated from all waves, up to and including 2004 ($N = 625$). Four tables have been generated using the 2006 data ($N = 334$). As table A.4 in appendix A indicates, there is little difference in the nature of the sample in 2004 and in 2006. However, because of the reduced sample size, these tables need to be interpreted with caution.

Overview of the Chapters

In this introductory chapter we have provided a brief overview of the main issues addressed in the book and have explained briefly the approach we have undertaken. We have introduced the two empirical studies that form the basis of the book and have identified the key issues and themes of social change, generation, gender, and social class. This chapter also introduces the conceptual basis for the book through which we will examine the lives of the young people, from the first years after leaving secondary school through to their early thirties.

In chapter 2 we scrutinize the strengths and limitations of the current theoretical and conceptual frameworks that are used to understand young people, social change, and generational change. These theories and concepts include cultural and social reproduction; individualization theory; acceleration of time; and issues of micro and macro analyses of events and experiences. Also, we examine the ways in which both theorists and the popular media portray and distort this generation in stereotypical ways, for example by drawing on the idea of failed transitions. In doing so, we set the stage for our comparative analyses. We explore the meaning of *agency* for these two groups and the extent to which structures, social class, and gender can affect the life chances of Canadian and Australian young adults. The introduction to theoretical perspectives on structural changes and educational and labour-force policies provides a transition to chapter 3.

The purpose of chapter 3 is to provide an overview of the policies that have framed the lives of this generation. We emphasize the significance of education and labour policies (and the lack of youth-specific policies that address, for example, health and well-being) and social and economic conditions on the lives of young people in both countries. We describe the structural changes to education that have resulted from government policies in both countries. While the shifts in post-secondary education in both countries are similar, there are noticeable differences between Canadian and Australian youth in the extent of their engagement in the labour market while they are studying and in their strategies for ensuring employment security. We develop the argument that this generation is distinctive partly because, through these specific conditions and policies, young adulthood has become defined in very particular ways.

Our comparative analysis of young people's lives begins in chapter 4. Through the voices of our participants we capture the hopes and dreams of Canadian and Australian young adults in relation to social, economic, and cultural opportunities and constraints, and we document the extent to which their stories differ by country – and within each country. In turn, through the use of questionnaire data we illuminate how these young people have acted on opportunities and confronted barriers, and we describe whether and how, over time, they were able to seize the former and overcome the latter. In this chapter we demonstrate that in neither country did these young people set out to establish new approaches or attitudes. Their hopes and dreams were remarkably modest and align with the previous generation.

In chapter 5 we focus on the educational experiences of the young people and their reflections on those experiences. We compare and contrast details of the secondary and post-secondary systems of British Columbia and Victoria in relation to their respective countries. Within the changing policy and economic contexts we trace the educational trajectories of these young people. We highlight how individuals act on structures and opportunities and also how structures, such as class-based inequalities, affect the choices that young people can make. We discuss the significance of the effect of family on educational choices and outcomes. We document which groups earned certain credentials and the extent to which post-secondary participation and completion remain gendered and class based. We draw conclusions about the sorts of institutional structures, policies, and practices that would promote access to and completion of post-secondary studies.

The focus of chapter 6 is to highlight our participants' experiences of and attitudes about work. We describe the ways in which young Canadians and Australians have struggled to establish a livelihood within labour markets that are increasingly uncertain and insecure. We ask whether the 'promise' of educational investment has paid off for all our participants. In this chapter we demonstrate how some groups (for example, women from higher socio-economic backgrounds) are able to draw very effectively on their available resources to maximize their educational investments through the labour market. We also show how other groups (for example, men from lower socio-economic backgrounds) do less well in achieving their employment goals. However, as we see in chapter 7, both labour-market successes and failures come with additional costs.

Chapter 7 focuses on the impact of social change on personal relationships. We focus on the differences and similarities in the patterns of living arrangements and household formation of Canadian and Australian young adults. We draw attention to the unique relationship that individuals from this generation have with their parents, by underscoring the ways in which these young people relate to and are supported by their parents. We examine marriage and childbearing patterns, and document our respondents' views about relationships and living arrangements. Our discussion takes into account the ways in which gender and social-class differences emerge in relation to household arrangements, relationships, and childbearing patterns.

Chapter 8 focuses on the health and well-being of our participants and draws out the implications for understanding this generation. We demonstrate empirically that being well has taken on new meanings for this generation. It has become an individual choice, something that they are responsible for and yet something that is difficult to achieve in their busy lives as they juggle multiple responsibilities across the many life spheres of employment, study, and personal relationships. We explore the participants' own assessments of and reflections on both social and generational change, and the implications for health and well-being. Drawing on the experiences of our participants and on the wider literature, we highlight the social and health implications of educational expectations and of a labour market in which individuals work long hours either in a full-time job or in several part-time jobs and in which uncertainty is prevalent.

The comparison of the two studies provides a unique insight into the making of a generation. In chapter 9 we identify the key insights of our research for the development of (a) education, labour, and social policies and (b) conceptual frameworks. In terms of policy developments, the chapter identifies several key tensions and areas of mismatch. While we can identify different policy directions that have been taken in Canada and Australia, nonetheless, the overall impact on the lives of young adults is remarkably similar. In particular, we highlight the need for a closer examination of the ways in which education contributes to unequal outcomes for this generation. In both countries education is a demonstrably more effective tool for securing the life chances of young people from socio-economic backgrounds that are high than from those that are low. Turning to labour policies, this chapter draws on the lives of our participants in order to ask to what extent current policies in both countries provide strains on the health and well-being of young adults. We explore the implications of their experiences for employment policies and for new commitments to family care. We link the discussion of policy implications with a reflection on the usefulness of current conceptual and theoretical frameworks for understanding this generation. We challenge the usefulness of popular stereotypes of this generation, many of which are either negative or imply that the generation has failed the transition process to adulthood. The research provides a basis for the systematic review of current theories of generational and social change, to produce a new conceptualization of youth, generation, and social change.

2 Concepts and Theories: Understanding Generation and Change

This chapter provides an overview of the key concepts and debates that inform our comparative analysis of the lives of young Canadians and Australians during the 1990s. In making sense of their experiences and perspectives, the pathways they have navigated, and the patterns of life they have established, we draw on conceptual ideas from the fields of higher education and youth studies. The field of higher education (including educational policy) provides insights into, among other things, the ways in which structural processes shape outcomes and produce patterns. The field of youth studies provides a perspective on the ways in which individuals negotiate their outcomes and emphasizes the importance of understanding subjectivities. Our comparative analysis of young people's lives highlights the partial nature of conceptual frameworks, the need to employ a critical lens for all theoretical frameworks, and the potential that using concepts from different theoretical traditions offers for advances in understanding young people's lives. We agree with Ball (2006) that conceptual frameworks are useful because they provide tools for practising social science research. In undertaking our analysis of the lives of young Canadians and Australians during the 1990s, we have tried to avoid closure and 'making the social more real, more orderly, more predictable than it is' (Ball 2006, 4) through the imposition of theoretical schemas, but rather to build some useful knowledge. Also, we heed Esping-Andersen's call (2009) for a more holistic approach to analysis.

In answering the questions posed in chapter 1, we have drawn on conceptual frameworks that highlight structural processes and enable us to analyse change and continuity and to make sense of attitudes and perspectives. The following chapter (chapter 3) is a companion to this chapter, in which we provide an in-depth discussion of education and employment policies, recognizing that theory and policy are interrelated fields. For example, much of our work relates to questions about youth and young adulthood as a time of *transition*, which carries multiple meanings. There is the more traditional understanding of youth transition as a stage of life (between childhood and adulthood), and this approach is evident in much of the literature about young people's lives – and often in the assumptions underlying policy. It is less common to acknowledge that *youth* as a social category is constructed through government policies as a tool for broader economic and social change. In the 1990s, for example, as we explain in chapter 3, young people were positioned explicitly by government policies as a key resource for bringing about social and economic transition in Canada and Australia through their participation in the expansion of higher education. This means that young people were at the forefront of social change while they were going through personal transitions. We argue that it is important to recognize *both* biographical and societal dimensions of change and their interactions with each other, in understanding the experiences of a generation (White and Wyn 2007).

To put this in another way, we are simultaneously researching two kinds of temporality. The first temporal element is sociological: we are researching a period of life that is commonly conceptualized as the transition from youth to adulthood. The terms *youth* and *young adulthood* have an imprecise meaning because they involve the social construction of age, but the period is almost universally defined as a transitional phase of life, the last stage before the point of arrival at adulthood – which, curiously, is almost never defined as involving a temporal dimension (Cohen 1997). The second temporal element is historical: we are researching a historical period (late modernity), but more specifically the 1990s and early 2000s, in Canada and Australia, which involved distinctive and specific conditions and framed the lives of our young people. The young Canadians and Australians who participated in our studies were inevitably affected by the conditions surrounding them, including changes in the nature of labour markets and workplace relations; the nature of educational systems; and the impact of social policies, including social security and welfare. By focusing on social change as well as youth transitions, we are able to see the impact of globalizing processes on young people in different countries, as well as the effects of local conditions.

Social change plays a central role in our analysis. In this chapter we explore current debates on social change and the impact of changed political, economic, and social conditions on the experience and meaning of youth, as well as the ways in which material and cultural resources are accessed to create new patterns of inequality. Each of these areas provides important insights for higher education, employment, and labour-market policy. Our analysis of the nature of social change and its impact on our young participants has been influenced by the work of Ulrich Beck, Elisabeth Beck-Gernsheim, Gøsta Esping-Andersen, Zygmunt Bauman, and Christoph Lau (Bauman 2000, 2001; Beck and Beck-Gernsheim 2002; Beck and Lau 2005; Esping-Andersen 1990, 1999, 2009), whose writings focus on the implications of global shifts in social and economic processes for personal and social life. In various ways these writers have provided conceptual tools that assist our analysis of the change processes that have affected the lives of the young people in this study. Although there is agreement that there has been significant social change, researchers disagree on the extent to which this change represents a break with the past or involves a reconfiguration of structural patterns of inequality. These ideas have been especially significant within the youth studies literature (Furlong and Cartmel 2007; Henderson et al. 2007; Leccardi and Ruspini 2006; White and Wyn 2007), particularly through the concepts of individualization and risk society; reflexive biographies and the production of 'self'; and the concepts of acceleration and temporality (Rosa 2003, 2005). Esping-Andersen's writings (1990, 1999, 2009) remind us to pay attention to the structure and policies of the welfare-regime framework of countries when considering the changing nature of work for young women and men.

We also find Pierre Bourdieu's ideas (1979, 1987) especially useful in enabling us to understand the ways in which structural inequalities retain their potency, even within a context of change. We draw on Bourdieu's work to highlight processes of class and gender divisions in late modernity. The concepts of *cultural capital* and of *habitus* are useful tools for us to understand the ways in which individuals are located within (changing) social spaces and how these social spaces are constituted by individuals as well as by social processes. This is especially important for our work because, in analysing young Canadians and Australians, we need to be able to understand the impact of local and historical factors on their lives. Bourdieu's ideas also assist us in addressing the apparent 'invisibility' of classed and gendered processes to the young people in our studies. Hence, subjectivities and identities play a significant role within this framework of analysis as well, providing a link with theoretical positions that focus on social change. Throughout this book we use parental education as an indication of the transmission of cultural capital from parents to their children.

A focus on change alone may obscure important continuities and especially the extent to which traditional patterns of advantage and disadvantage continue to mark young people's lives. For example, some studies have found diverse patterns of consumption and leisure among young people that appear to have little correlation with class background (West 1997), which suggests that class divisions are a thing of the past. However, a focus on educational and labour-market outcomes reveals that both class and gender remain significant in structuring young people's life chances (Furlong and Cartmel 2007; Teese and Polesel 2003). We therefore need conceptual tools that enable us to analyse how social class works in young people's lives and how this process intersects with gender and other social divisions.

The conceptual themes discussed in this chapter are presented through a discussion of four key areas: youth and social change; generation; social class; and gender. We show how, within these broad areas, different theoretical approaches allow us to analyse particular dimensions of young people's lives. At the same time, there are limits within each position, and there are ongoing debates about how to overcome these limitations.

Youth and Social Change

Economic changes experienced during the early 1990s in Canada, Australia, and many Western societies had an immediate effect on young people. Bourne and Damaris (2001) draw attention to key 'transformations' that have had a significant impact on Canadian life in this century: demographics, changes in family structure, immigration, changes in the relationship between households, labour markets, and the sphere of civil society. These structural and economic changes have also been felt in Australia, especially in relation to youth labour markets, as economies changed and workplaces began to require more skilled labour, and older jobs (for example, in manufacturing) began to disappear (Bynner 2005; Te Riele and Wyn 2005).

Our thinking about change is also influenced by Esping-Andersen's argument (2009, 1–2) that the period of the late 1980s and 1990s brought in a 'new social order' involving 'major transformations' for many Western countries. His analysis of the implications of these changes lead him to argue, highlighting the shift in women's roles, that social scientists and policymakers have yet to fully understand the social and policy implications of the 'incomplete revolution' that has occurred. This means that considerable change was occurring across many dimensions of life in Canada and Australia when our participants were aged eighteen to twenty-five years. Their lives are often contrasted to those of the previous generation, called baby boomers who were born between 1945 and 1965 (Bourne and Damaris 2001) and whose patterns of life, supported by vastly different social and economic conditions, stand in stark contrast to the generation of our participants (Wyn and Woodman 2006). At the time that the latter were completing secondary education and taking the next steps into work, study, or both, new terms were being invented to describe their generation, including *baby busters* and *Generation X*. The term *Generation X* has survived and is now commonly used to describe people who were born between 1961 and 1981. Our work enables us to go beyond the generalizations and stereotypes of these sweeping generational labels; therefore, we do not use these terms in our analysis. However, it is important to acknowledge the global patterns of change that underpinned the need to give them a distinctive name.

According to the Australian Bureau of Statistics (2005), there was an unprecedented increase in the rate of participation in post-compulsory education in Australia during the early 1990s. In 1976 only 12 per cent of twenty-year-olds were participating in some form of education. By 2001, 25 per cent of all young Australians in their twenties were engaged in education. Over this time, post-secondary education became a normative experience, an expected part of growing up. Employment patterns for young people shifted from full-time to part-time and became increasingly based on casual contracts in which non-standard working hours were common. This time period also saw a significant increase in the proportions of women in the workforce. In 1976, 92 per cent of young men and 54 per cent of young women aged twenty were employed, with more than half working full time. In 2001, 87 per cent of young men and 75 per cent of young women were working – but they were overwhelmingly (86 per cent) in part-time jobs. In addition, there were changes in marriage and fertility patterns. There was a significant shift in household patterns, with a decrease in couples living in a household with their children and an increase in single-person households and lone-parent households. Young people tended to reside longer in their parents' household, and there was a slight trend towards group households. Women were increasingly having their first child when they were over the age of thirty, and both men and women were marrying later than they were in 1976. In terms of participation in secondary education, the gender gap has closed, compared to the previous generation. By the mid 2000s, men and women in their early twenties were equally likely to be engaged in education and work. The young people in our longitudinal cohorts were in the vanguard of change between two generations, pioneering the shifts in patterns of life.

The Canadian participants were similarly positioned as a generation that saw significant social change. In 1960 just under 9 per cent of all Canadian households were non-nuclear family households, but by 1998 they were 25 per cent of all households (Bourne and Damaris 2001). Common-law marriages, lone-parent families, smaller households, and people living alone have been on the rise in Canada since the 1960s, and rates of marriage have been on the decline. The proportion of common-law families more than doubled, from 6 per cent in 1981 to 14 per cent in 2001 (Statistics Canada 2006a). Change in the gender composition of the workforce, like their Australian counterparts, was a significant feature. Between 1976 and 2006 women's employment increased from 42 per cent to 58 per cent. As in Australia, there was also a shift in the proportions of men employed. In Canada, between 1976 and 2006 the proportion of men employed dropped from 73 per cent to 68 per cent (Statistics Canada 2006c).

In chapter 6 we provide an in-depth analysis of these young people's experiences of work and how young people have negotiated new work conditions, especially in the Australian context. We show how changing labour markets have had a direct impact on their lives and how differences between Australian and Canadian labour markets have resulted in different experiences and approaches by young people. In Australia during the late 1970s, jobs shifted from manufacturing and primary production to service. This resulted in the creation of new highly skilled jobs in some industries that required higher levels of education, but even low skilled jobs came to require educational qualifications (Wooden and VandenHeuvel 1999). Changes to industrial relations meant that most sectors required part-time workers on short-term contracts (thereby opening up many opportunities for school-aged workers).

In Canada, non-standard work has 'proliferated since the 1980s' (Vosko 2003, 2), as employers throughout the 1990s cut back on 'core permanent workers and increased the periphery of flexible workers' (Lewchuk, et al. 2003, 25). Although there were important differences between the workplace regulations for each country during the 1990s and 2000s, both countries were experiencing significant changes in the nature of work (towards higher-skilled jobs) and in the conditions of work. By the mid 2000s in both Canada and Australia, concerns about work-life balance had begun to emerge (Todd 2004). These changes in labour markets illustrate one dimension of a complex process of social and economic change.

Youth researchers also identify many other areas of change, including patterns of educational-participation leisure (Gayo-Cal 2006) and consumption (Frost 2003). This evidence has resulted in widespread agreement that the last quarter of the twentieth century witnessed social changes of significant dimensions with profound implications for young people's lives. For example, Furlong and Cartmel (2007, 138) conclude that 'the experiences of young people growing up in the contemporary world are quite different from those encountered by previous generations,' and Bynner (2001, 6) argues that '"a radical transformation" has taken place in the context of youth transitions.' Their conclusions are supported by Leccardi and Ruspini (2006), who discuss the impact of these changes on young people in Eastern Europe, Italy, the Netherlands, Finland, Georgia, the United States, the United Kingdom, Germany, and New Zealand. They argue that as a result of social and economic change there is evidence of the emergence of a 'new youth.' Other research on young people's transition patterns in Australia, New Zealand, the South Pacific, England, the Netherlands, and France (Bagnall 2005, 7) comes to the conclusion that 'social change is occurring at such a rate that traditional forms of transition into adulthood have become increasingly undermined.'

Each of the edited collections and studies referred to above emphasizes social change in order to provide a framework for understanding how young people in contemporary times have forged meanings (and often also new patterns of life) that are different from those of the previous generation; in other words, theories of social change have been used largely to provide an understanding of shifts in patterns, subjectivities, and identities. None suggests that continuities with the past across various dimensions have vanished; rather, the focus on social change has been used to question and interrogate assumptions about the nature of youth, adulthood, transitions, and generations.

The focus on social change has also fostered debate within youth studies about the extent to which youth is a universal stage of life, a biological given, or whether it is a social construct (like adulthood) that gains its parameters and meaning from social conditions and definitions. According to some interpretations, both youth and adulthood are changing (Mizen 2004). This signifies that the meanings that young people give to education, work, and relationships will have enduring effects. Even if their priorities change as they get older, the distinctive experiences of their young adulthood will provide a unique framework for viewing their futures. An example is the heightened significance that 'achieving a balance in life' has come to hold for this generation, as we illustrate in the chapters that follow (Beutell and Wittig-Berman 2008; Dwyer, Smith, et al. 2005).

We have found the concepts of individualization and risk society useful for understanding the impact of social change on young people's lives and on the very concept of youth itself. We explore these concepts in the next section.

The New Modernity, Individualization, and the Risk Society

Many of the dimensions of young people's lives that we discuss in this book (education, family, work, health, and well-being) have demonstrably undergone changes over the last twenty-five years. These shifts are seen as indicators of a shift in modernity, in the conditions under which society functions. Beck and Lau (2005, 525) argue that 'all around the word, society is undergoing radical change – radical in the sense that it poses a challenge to Enlightenment-based modernity and opens up a space in which people choose new and unexpected forms of the social and the political.' They use the term *first modernity* to refer to nation-state societies that existed in a territorial sense and exercised control over their dominions. The shift to second modernity has involved both the fragmentation of collective ways of life based on the nation state and, through globalizing processes, the undermining of the possibilities for nation states to control social conditions (full employment, for example). The use of the terms *first modernity* and *second modernity* indicate that, while there has been a radical change, there has not been a clear break with modernity. With the demise of older traditions and networks, they argue, people now need to negotiate new meanings and social relationships.

While Beck and others do not focus specifically on young people as such (because they argue that these conditions affect all age groups), others have found it useful to apply their ideas about the social implications of change to young people's lives. For example, as the sources of collective identity that were characteristic of industrial societies have begun to lose their relevance, and with the fragmentation of traditional structures (including nation states, families, and trade unions), young people have been presented with new challenges in identity formation. Identity has become a task rather than a given: 'Needing to *become* what one *is* is the hallmark of modern living' (Beck and Beck-Gernsheim 2002, xv).

The decline in control over social processes by nation states has meant that individuals have come to bear increasing responsibility for their lives. The capacity to be proactive in uncertain times relies in part on the ability to be reflexive – that is, to see one's own life and biography as something that does not just unfold but is actively constructed through one's own efforts. This active construction of one's biography is called the project of the self (Beck and Beck-Gernsheim 2002) and involves an active process of personal management, even in circumstances where, objectively, individuals would have little control.

The concept of *individualization* has been widely used to describe this process. A key element involves the development of dispositions that involve acceptance of responsibility by individuals for their lives (Kelly 2006; McLeod and Yates 2006). Responsibility for one's own life with minimal state support is a defining feature of liberal welfare regimes (Esping-Andersen 1990, 1999, 2009), to which Canada and Australia belong. Hence, young people are seen to be responsible for bearing risks that are actually related to how our society functions. As Beck and Beck-Gernsheim (2002, 39) argue, social inequalities in late modernity have become redefined in terms of 'an individualization of social risks.' They explain that, as a consequence, social problems become perceived through a psychological, and therefore individualizing, lens (for example, as personal inadequacies or neuroses). Beck and Beck-Gernsheim argue that this 'do-it-yourself biography' is also a 'risk biography' (2002, 3); that is, in a society where individuals must make choices against a backdrop of uncertainty and impermanence, it is easy to make the 'wrong' choices. Nonetheless, it is seen both as the right and responsibility of the individual to make choices and as the failure of the individual if the choice is not a good one. Individualization, then, is a process that makes risky social processes and structures invisible to individuals and vests them with the responsibility for bearing these risks.

These ideas have coincided with an upsurge of interest in the ways in which young people undertake identity work. Various authors, especially those researching school-aged youth (for example, McLeod and Yates, 2006), have drawn on Giddens' (1991) idea of autobiographical thinking, that is, the capacity to narrate and create one's self-history as a central aspect of identity-making, and understand reflexivity as a characteristic of contemporary identities. Drawing on the work of Beck and Giddens, and also to some extent on Foucault (1988), many researchers have argued that it is important to understand the relationship between social conditions and the formation of subjectivities – or the ways in which our society frames the possibilities for being and becoming.

The processes of individualization are supported by government policies. In chapter 3 we show how Canadian and Australian governments encouraged young people (and their families) to make a personal investment in their education so that they could reap the personal benefits. In other words, education was positioned as a personal benefit, not a public good, even though increasing the rates of participation in post-secondary education was a major element in the strategies of both governments to improve the global competitiveness of their economies. Mizen (2004) traces the shift in the United Kingdom from Keynesian policies of the 1970s that involved support for a welfare state, a commitment to full employment, the expansion of secondary schooling, and the inclusion of youth into civic life, to the monetarist policies of the 1990s. With economic goals as the primary focus, universal state support for young people was gradually eroded, to be replaced by categories of deserving youth and undeserving youth and an emphasis on instrumental, vocationally oriented education (Mizen 2004, 14–16). In Australia too, monetarist policies have narrowed the fiscal responsibility of the state for young people while at the same time hugely expanding the reach of monitoring, surveillance, and control over both young people's lives and the institutions in which they spend their time. In Canada, as federal and provincial funding for post-secondary education has declined, tuition rates across the country have risen dramatically.

These concepts provide a framework for understanding social processes, and patterns across groups, as well as individual actions. Our comparative analysis shows that the positive possibilities of individualization processes (for example, being mobile and flexible as a worker) have been evident for some groups of young people, but, for others, these conditions have been burdensome as they have borne the risks of changing times.

The concepts of risk society and individualization are not concepts that can be mapped onto individual young people, just as class cannot be read from patterns of success and failure at school. As McLeod and Yates (2006, 214) caution, the effects of the processes of individualization, described in broad terms as *choice biographies* and *processes of reflexivity*, are only shorthand descriptions of complex processes. To attempt to link these ideas empirically with individual young people's pathways is to 'risk reifying biographies as categories.' We are aware that attempts to do so tend to oversimplify the complex, and we have kept this in mind as we have attempted to do justice to the realities of young people's lives and to their sense of making active choices.

Lehmann's comparative study (2005) of Canadian and German youth highlights the concept of agency as a key element of individualization. In analysing their transitions through school and their plans for work, he argues that 'although their decisions were not entirely structurally determined or void of agency, both the academic-track students and youth apprentices' (Lehmann 2005, 394) formed predictable 'dispositions' based on the class backgrounds of their parents. Yet, it raises a further question about the characterization of transitions – as actual processes over time or as plans and aspirations. The temporal element is important, because one of the elements of risk society is the fracturing of traditional processes, including youth transitions. It has become commonplace across many Western countries to find that young people take a long time to find the right pathway for them – well into their late twenties and possibly later (Furlong and Cartmel 2007; Leccardi and Ruspini 2006). Even where young people initially make decisions that reflect the limits and constraints (or opportunities) of their parents' world, they do not necessarily find that these decisions are the right ones for them. The trend towards 'extended transitions' has partly been fostered through the struggle that many young people have when they are forced to reassess the goals that they had in the first year after leaving school. Hence, reading the aspirations of school-aged youth onto their future lives is itself risky.

The long-term view that we are able to provide through the analysis of these two studies of young people over a period of fifteen years provides a valuable and relatively rare point of reference for assessing the relative value of contemporary theories of social change.

Transitions

The concept of youth transition is widely used in youth and educational research. In Australia the concept of youth transitions gained prominence during the early eighties when the youth labour market (that is, full-time jobs for fifteen- to nineteen-year-olds) began to collapse, and groups who had previously not considered post-compulsory education to be an option remained at school (Wooden 1998). In Canada the deterioration in labour-market conditions for some sectors of the young population also led to changes in patterns of school retention, but the evidence shows that this was related more to changes in perceptions about the importance of post-secondary education than to conditions in the labour market (Beaudry, Lemieux, and Parent 2000). However, in both countries by the early 1990s, as young people responded to changing social conditions, new patterns of education and employment emerged, provoking a widespread interest in 'transition' (Krahn 1996; Wooden and VandenHeuvel 1999).

The concept of transition has been especially prominent in policy-related discourses about young people (Dusseldorp Skills Forum 2006; McLaughlin 1999). In Australia the policy focus on transition through education and labour markets is part of a wider approach that defines youth primarily as a human resource for economic development, which has resulted in heightening inequality among groups of young people. In Canada, although the rhetoric of flexible workers was not as pronounced, the policy directions were clearly focused on ensuring the smooth transition of young Canadians through education and into employment to contribute to Canada's economic growth (Economic Council of Canada 1990).

Yet, perhaps because the term *transition* is so ubiquitous within the youth and education policy literatures, it has become taken for granted. There are three main ways in which this term is used: transition as development, transition as linear pathways, and transition as the norm.

First, young people's transitions are often assumed to be related to a developmental process because the term *transition* tends to draw on psychosocial (human emotional development) or biomedical (brain development) theories. It either ignores or underestimates the significance of social meanings and experiences of age. As Cohen and Ainley (2000) have argued, a focus on transition has become narrowly defined as (vocational) maturity and (nuclear) family formation. This is illustrated by Bagnall (2005), who draws on a descriptive schema of four 'thresholds' that define and pattern the progress of transition into adulthood: completing education, entry into employment, leaving home, and forming a couple. The problem with this kind of schema is that it inevitably involves the definition of 'standard' points of progression from youth into adulthood and leaves unexamined the question of what adulthood actually means.

Bagnall's concept of transitions tends to overlook the blurring of the boundaries between youth and adult, and student and worker, as young people engage in adult practices incrementally and early, across many dimensions of their lives. In addition, it ignores the importance of newer dimensions of life that are important to youth, especially leisure and consumption. In a critique of this approach, Dwyer and Wyn (2001) have argued that new patterns of transition are foreshadowing the emergence of a 'new adulthood' – one in which uncertainty, unpredictability, and flexibility are common features.

Second, transitions are also often assumed to involve linear pathways, partly because the term implies progress from one clearly defined status to another. Although gaining a secure job is a priority that is frequently expressed by young people, policy approaches that focus only on the links between study and work tend to overemphasize the linearity of this process and its direction. The assumption of linear movement that underpins the metaphor of transition masks the reality of more complex and often chaotic processes in young people's lives. Linearity can often only be sustained if the time frame of analysis is short (for example, 'the' transition from school to work). A longer longitudinal time frame (as suggested above) is more likely to reveal complexity in pathways.

Third, particular transition patterns are seen to be normative. The concept of transition is often used in a way that rests on an implicit assumption that the patterns of one generational group, the baby boomers, represent the standard (Wyn and Woodman 2006) against which subsequent generations are found wanting. The problem with using the baby boomer generation as a standard biography is that the social and political conditions that enabled their distinctive patterns of transition were short lived and no longer exist (Pomerantz 1999). Inevitably – and, in our opinion, erroneously – the transitions of the next generation are seen as faulty or lacking, with transition patterns that are 'on hold' (Côté and Allahar 1994), 'extended' (Jones and Wallace 1992), 'emerging' (Arnett 2005), and 'lost' (Howe and Strauss 2000).

Although the use of transitions as a framework for understanding young people's lives, especially in terms of education and employment pathways, acknowledges social change, this dimension tends to remain at a descriptive level of analysis, which reduces its capacity to analyse how social change has affected not only life patterns but the very meaning of youth – and of adulthood. Even the excellent defence of transitions as a framework for understanding youth by Bynner (2005) ends up highlighting the fragmentation of timelines and the incomparability of 'thresholds,' which, rather than supporting the idea of youth as a transitional part of the life cycle, should lead us to question what youth and young adulthood mean. We agree with Bynner that youth and young adulthood need to be understood in socio-historical terms, but we would take this further, to argue that transitions alone do not provide such understanding.

It is telling that the concept of transitions has not played a significant role in our longitudinal analysis. Instead, we have found more useful the concept of *social generation*, which strengthens and captures a broader and socially contextualized meaning of life trajectory and through which insights from different theoretical approaches can be applied.

The Idea of a Generation

Generational stereotypes have come into common usage in the popular media and in some academic writing. In the main, *generation* has become a stereotype, a highly simplified description of and shorthand for population groups in Western countries. In the 1990s, just as the concerns about transition into adulthood had begun to emerge in the more academic literature, the labels *Generation X, Generation Y, Generation Z, Generation Me, Millennials, baby boomers, baby busters,* and many others came into usage (Coupland 1991; Foot 1996; Sheahan 2005; Twenge 2006). It is widely acknowledged that these terms have largely derived from market research and human resources management sources (see, for example, Howe and Strauss 2000; Jurkiewicz 2000). However, they refuse to go away. There is obviously something compelling in their assertion that there are differences between generations based on the context in which they were born and have grown up and that these differences are not simply age effects. They go beyond simple age-based generational cohorts (that is, biological cohorts). Indeed, there is a surprising convergence of thinking about the time period that each of these cohorts represents, based on a consensus about social conditions and their impact on the possibilities for and the constraints on individuals who are born into and forge their lives through the time period.

Generations and Labels

The line between generations is difficult to draw with precision. However, there is considerable evidence across a number of indicators to suggest that in Western countries a significant shift in life patterns has occurred between the baby boomer generation (those born between 1946 and 1965) and the generation born after 1970, which at one stage was called the baby buster generation and which has come to be widely known as Generation X. Table 1 provides a summary of current thinking, based on a wide range of commentators, including the Australian Bureau of Statistics (2009), Howe and Strauss (2000), Jurkiewicz (2000), Ortner (1998), and Williams et al. (1997).

From a sociological point of view, social generation provides a useful frame within which to recognize age as a sociological variable, the meaning of which is given through social, economic, and political relations (Allen 1968; Finch 1986; Mizen 2004; Pilcher 1994; Wyn and White 1997). Mannheim (1970) argued that people who belong to a common period of history, or whose lives are forged through common conditions, form a 'generational consciousness.' His study made the distinction between social generation and age cohorts, arguing that individuals are constituted historically, but they also contribute to the way in which history plays out. A concept of social generation is of value because it overcomes the reliance on age alone as *the* defining feature of youth (Cohen 1997) and embeds youth and young adulthood within historical and local conditions. Perhaps most important,

Table 1
Terms for generations

Popular term	Born
Early baby boomers	1946–1954
Late baby boomers	1955–1965
Generation X	1966–1976
Generation Y (early)	1977–1990
Generation Y (late)	1991

this concept also has value because, through its identification of both distinctive patterns of life and subjectivities, it focuses on the meaning of change to young people, expressed in their priorities, decisions, and attitudes, as well as their behaviours.

A number of researchers have employed the concept of social generation as a tool for analysing the links between distinctive transition patterns and historical and local conditions. Edmunds and Turner (2005, 7), for example, argue that social generations develop a 'cultural identity' that they form as a result of 'their particular location in the development of a society or culture.' We agree with other researchers (for example, Jones 1995; Nayak 2003; Pomerantz 1999) that while the idea of social generations is useful, it is important to exercise caution in applying the idea of a single 'cultural identity' across classes, genders, cultural groups, and spatial and national boundaries. We especially agree with the need to link social generational patterns and subjectivities with local conditions. Social generation provides a framework for researchers who seek to understand the active role that young people play in constructing the kinds of reflexive subjectivities that will enable them to navigate their way through life. The concept of social generation gives significance to the meanings that young people themselves attribute to their lives. However, by identifying patterns of behaviour and subjectivity that appear to be in the vanguard of a social generation and that may define it, we are also able to show how groups have differential access to the material and cultural resources that make this possible, and hence the groups become marginal. We therefore find the notion of social generation useful as a tool for highlighting distinctive attitudes and life patterns within a particular socio-historical context, but we do not see these patterns as evenly experienced.

Subjectivities

The concept of *subjectivity* and its related concept of identity are crucial to a social generational approach, because subjectivities provide expression of the different possible subject positions within each social generation. It is a concept that runs through a number of theoretical frameworks (for example, Beck and Lau 2005; Bourdieu 1976). Subjectivity refers to the social, economic, and political frameworks, constraints, and limits within which identities are formed. Young people's social identities are shaped within the specific social contexts of their lives, so that only a limited number of subject positions (subjectivities) are possible (B. Davies

2004). In other words, identities are produced by young people, but this production is mediated through the experiences they have in schools, their family relationships, workplaces, consumption, and leisure. Young people's subjectivities and the ways in which their possibilities for being are framed provide another very important source of information for understanding what has changed and how new meanings of older patterns are formed. The focus on subjectivities also enables researchers to understand how new meanings of career, employment, and family are emerging (Wyn and Woodman 2006) and how they are emerging for different groups of young people.

The Australian literature identifies the proactive, reflexive, and pragmatic identity characteristics of Generation X. Kelly (2006), for example, argues that contemporary conditions favour and in one sense require the performance of an 'entrepreneurial Self.' This self, his study contends, is one that requires young people to demonstrate considerable autonomy in making decisions and to take responsibility for their mistakes. Similarly, Harris (2004) describes the phenomenon of the 'can-do' girls, young women who believe that they can achieve anything, and McLeod and Yates (2006) describe the emergence of distinctive subjectivities that enable young people to 'self monitor' and adjust their goals and performances. However, Currie, Kelly, and Pomerantz (2009, 202) point out that the term 'can-do' usually applies to 'expectations for white, middle-class girls.' The North American literature has emphasized different characteristics of Generation X, linking this generation with terms such as *arrogant* and *slackers* (Hays 1999; Heiman 2001). However, the literature overall reveals very mixed messages, and some North American literature also refers to Generation X as valuing 'a sense of belonging/teamwork, ability to learn new things, autonomy and entrepreneurship' (Jurkiewicz 2000). The very small amount of literature actually produced by members of Generation X points out that it is mistaken to characterize the diversity of any generation so narrowly, and some find strong points of commonality across the generations (for example, Mensik 2007; Pomerantz 1999).

We are interested in the idea of generation because it provides a tool for linking young people's lives to their social and historical conditions. This is especially important in the project of analysing young people's lives across time and national boundaries. There are two key dimensions that exert a powerful influence on young people's experiences – class and gender – and we discuss these briefly in the following sections.

Social Class

Most understandings of social class derive from two distinct approaches: *categorical* (descriptions of static hierarchies or tiers of classed positions) and *relational* (class as a social process, constituted through relations of production and consumption and involving the control and use of resources as a form of capital). These approaches are not necessarily mutually exclusive, because at times a categorical approach can be used to illustrate inequalities in resources and outcomes. Both approaches acknowledge that class, whether it comprises the patterns produced by relations of production or the dynamics of these relations themselves, is not static. As the economic bases of modern societies change, so do the dynamics that drive social class. The social changes associated with the shift to second modernity (Beck and Lau 2005) have implications that we believe have a particular impact on young people's experiences of class in two ways: (a) the fragmentation of collective experiences and understandings (Furlong and Cartmel 2007), and (b) the emergence of culture as a commodity in capitalist economies (Skeggs 2005).

Indeed, as young people are forced to make more choices and their pathways become complex, the traditional social divisions become at one level more obscure and at another level reinforced. This paradox is illustrated by the way in which the significance of leisure and consumption in young people's lives creates a sense of diversity and individual choice that blurs class difference (Furlong and Cartmel 2007). Yet, class forms the parameters of the 'choices' that young people make.

As Ball, Davies, et al. (2002) identify, choice is, sociologically speaking, a problematic concept because it implies agency and freedom from constraint. Their study employs Bourdieu's concepts of classification and judgment to show how young people's higher education choices in the United Kingdom are understandable in terms of the embodiment of class practices. They show how embedded perceptions and expectations make certain choices 'obvious' and others unthinkable according to where a person stands in the overall landscape of choice. They also demonstrate how different kinds of practical knowledge are being utilized by students, based on their location and experiences, that ultimately reflect a classed position. These findings concur with earlier work on the Canadian data by Andres (1993), which employed Bourdieu's theory that confirmed the relationships among cultural and social capital, habitus, and educational choices.

Sociological research on young people and education often reveals a sense of class struggle: the awareness by some of the need to position themselves in uncertain times and the struggle by others to reach generational goals. Bourdieu (1988, 163) points out that 'for the privileged classes, the gap between expectations and opportunities and the concurrent threat of "downclassing" is "particularly intolerable."' This is especially evident in the conscious and unconscious strategies used by middle-class families to maintain advantage in an uncertain and changing world, and it is especially relevant to the aspirations of some of the young people and their families in our comparative research.

We argue that this class struggle is occurring in a context where the experience and meaning of social class is changing, and many young people are more aware of their own efforts and the risks they must bear than they are of the class-based patterns that structure their lives. While young people may not be aware of the operation of classed processes, there is emerging evidence that many young people and their families are aware of the uneven distribution of resources (Ball 2003; Teese 2000). Recent educational research on young people in the 'middle' class documents the ways in which class is perpetuated through the efforts of families, schools, and young people themselves to forge identities that will be marketable.

Like Ball (2003), McLeod and Yates (2006) have studied the practices of young people and their families in order to reveal how individuals form themselves and how social inequalities are created. This research describes the construction of middle-class identities that would position young people favourably within new economies and labour markets, not just with the right educational credentials but also with the capacity to deliver the right kinds of cultural performances. Skeggs (2005) has argued that culture itself has become a commodity under late capitalism; the study describes how culture is deployed as an economic resource, and how this is shaping our ideas of what class is, through the identification of (class) attributes that are deemed to be morally worthy and unworthy. When class is also cultural property, we learn how our cultural practices do or do not have a worth and value for others. The research on young people and middle-class families shows that culture and identity formation are sites of class struggle in contemporary society (Ball 2003; McLeod and Yates 2006). Hence, as Furlong and Cartmel (2007, 5) argue, 'life chances remain highly structured,' and as Esping-Andersen (2009, 59) asserts, 'ours is an epoch of rising inequalities.'

What has changed is the nature of the effort required by young people and their families to ensure security and privilege.

Gender

Our discussion of the paradoxes that confront us in analysing social class in a context of social change has described many of the issues that also confront us with a discussion of gender. The two dimensions are inextricably intertwined. Rather than repeat the discussion (which is presented in many other places, for example Andres and Adamuti-Trache 2008, Kenway and Bullen 2004, McLeod and Yates 2006), we will only briefly comment on these issues before taking the opportunity to show how research that draws on ideas from Bourdieu and Foucault has inspired new approaches to the issues.

Social change and the fragmentation of institutional and traditional forms and pathways have also created new forms of gender division and fostered intense debate about what has changed. During the 1990s, when the research that informed this book was getting under way, it became evident that young women's participation in education was increasing and that some groups of young women were using education effectively (Teese 2000). By the late 1990s and early 2000s, these shifting gender patterns became associated with new debates about disadvantage and gender, in which some argued that boys had become the new disadvantaged. This claim has been answered by research which shows that there has in fact been very little change in the broad gendered patterns of outcomes. In Australia in the 1970s, as now, young men from low socio-economic backgrounds did least well at school, and young women from low socio-economic backgrounds were the most disadvantaged in the labour market (Yates 1993). Although there has been an improvement in the educational achievements of young women from high socio-economic backgrounds, nonetheless gendered patterns within universities and workplaces have remained largely intact, with women continuing to be represented in a narrow band of occupations compared to their male counterparts, and with women earning a lower wage than do men (White and Wyn 2007). Indeed, this has also been the pattern in the Canadian context (Andres and Adamuti-Trache 2007; Bourne and Damaris 2001).

It is important not to underestimate the importance of these shifts in gender patterns. The dramatic uptake of higher education by young women from the higher socio-economic backgrounds is a process that has been noted in other Western countries. In an analysis that concurs with our findings, Esping-Andersen (2009) argues that this group of the population, across most Western countries, is caught in an 'incomplete revolution.' New patterns of employment for these women have not been matched by new labour-market and family policies. The result is a stalling of change in the domestic sphere as women continue to hold the major responsibility for children and domestic labour. Evidence reveals a critically low level of fertility for this group.

The challenge presented by the claims that boys had become the new disadvantaged has spurred a renewed interest in the complex processes whereby gender (and class) patterns are produced and reproduced. Much of this work has taken advantage of the conceptual tools provided by Bourdieu (1986; 2000) and Bourdieu and Passeron (1979; 1977). For example, Kenway and Bullen (2004, 143) have challenged the way in which young women from poor backgrounds are routinely denigrated through representations in both the popular media and academia as unworthy and in which academic and employment failure is seen as 'cultural and moral rather than economic.' Kenway and Bullen's study shows how even the structurally based underclass approach reverts to understandings about cultural practices. Kenway and Bullen employ a Bourdieuian theory of subcultural capitals to conceptualize the 'interaction between material structures and individual agency, between class and gender, between culture and subculture' (2004, 149). This produces a framework within which the actions of poor and marginalized young women can be seen as strategies involving the use of capitals that are available to them. Kenway and Bullen's study argues that there is a lack of fit between their gendered habitus and the world with which they must engage.

This lack of fit can be compared with the highly honed reflexivities of the middle-class girls in McLeod and Yates's research (2006). It makes extensive use of Bourdieu's concepts of cultural capital as 'the knowledge and attributes that the middle class ... have that enables them to work the system to their advantage,' in order to show how these young women were learning to work with new economies and to present the self in new ways (McLeod and Yates 2006, 163). Their research explores questions of class subjectivities involving both self-conscious orientations and the less conscious dispositions acquired in family settings. McLeod and Yates argue that young women, and especially those from middle-class backgrounds, have responded to the need to be flexible and adaptive to new conditions; in general, the young men appeared to be less confident than the women were about their futures as they left secondary school. McLeod and Yates (2006, 206) conclude: 'This is not to suggest that there has been a reversal or inversion of the gender binaries, but rather to point to some emergent themes in the changing forms of masculinity and femininity as we see these young men encounter dilemmas that have been typically aligned with femininity, and these young women work hard toward an autonomous future.'

Our work is also influenced by the desire to see how both class and gender frame the nature of the options that are open to young people and the resources that they use to make decisions about these options.

Conclusion

In answering the questions posed in the introduction to this chapter, we reiterate that our project has been to engage in good social science research, through which we aim to contribute useful knowledge about the relationship between individual lives, projects, and outcomes, and the social conditions and processes for young people in the 1990s. We ask how economic and social conditions and global processes affected the lives of this generation, and in answering this question we draw on theories of social change and research on higher education and labour markets. Our analysis makes a significant contribution to the question of whether the generation born in the early 1970s has taken distinctive pathways and formed new attitudes and priorities. The strength of our longitudinal analysis, which extends over fifteen years of their lives, enables us to examine the degree to which these attitudes and priorities have been enduring, and the depth of our analysis enables us to go beyond the stereotypes to look at differences that exist within the generation. Concepts of class, gender, and social change have provided essential tools for making sense of the complex processes of the gender and class patterns that not only shift but also stay the same.

We ask what the implications of our analysis are for of education, employment, and labour policy. Our analysis shows that policies have both intended and unintended consequences, and drawing on theories of social change, we note that the very concept of engineering outcomes through policies, in a time when social structures are less and less predictable, creates challenges for the idea of policy.

Finally, our analysis focuses on the comparison of the Canadians and Australians in our respective studies. Conceptually this has been relatively easy because of broad similarities in the economic and social processes that define both countries. However, in this social science research project the comparison has perhaps been more difficult than we had anticipated because it has exposed realities that do not fit with theory and has revealed a world that is 'complicated, confused, impure, and uncertain' (Bourdieu, Chamboredon, and Passeron 1991). We are able to point to strong patterns that bear theorizing, but the depth of our analysis also exposes the finer grain of complexity and unexpected outcomes.

The concepts and theoretical frameworks discussed provide us with the tools to highlight young people's active roles in making meaning and shaping change; the diversity and extent of local cultures and individual meanings; and both change and continuity in the way in which life patterns are shaped and paths are taken on life's way. In the following chapters we make use of the concepts that we have introduced here to shape our own stories about the lives of the young people in Canada and Australia, and it is our hope that the reader will appreciate the use of conceptual signposts that link our work to ideas and theories about higher education, youth, social change, and social division.

3 Shaping Generational Change through Policy

In the 1980s the educational and labour-market policy literature in the Western world was rife with warnings and dire predictions regarding the educational practices and related occupational fates of current and future generations of young adults. It was widely acknowledged that advanced industrial countries were undergoing a radical transformation from an industrial society to a society characterized by economic globalization, that the labour force was shifting from the goods-producing sector to the service sector, and that there was a rapid diffusion of technology into the workplace. The impact of these interrelated factors on the transformation of the labour market was seen as equivalent in magnitude to the earlier shift from the agrarian to the industrial eras (Economic Council of Canada 1990; Radwanski 1987). The young people in our respective studies were about to enter a world that would be fundamentally different from that experienced by previous generations. In Canada and Australia, as in most developed countries, the government responded to these changes and their anticipated effects through a raft of new policies in which education was central. Education was seen as the key to creating a workforce with the skills and capabilities to support the transformation from an industrial to a post-industrial mode and to compete in emerging global markets.

In this chapter we provide an overview of the education policies that have framed the lives of this generation. We emphasize the significance of social and economic conditions to the lives of young people in both countries, and we describe the structural changes to education that have resulted from these government policies. The conditions include the enormous expansion of post-secondary education, which makes this the new mass education sector, and changes in the labour markets in both countries. Although shifts in post-secondary education in both countries are similar, there are noticeable differences between the Canadian and the Australian youth in their engagement in post-secondary education and the labour market. Policy frameworks have driven three significant expectations: young people would invest in some form of post-secondary education, (b) this education would give them the skills and knowledge to be successful within new labour markets, and (c) they and their parents would bear the cost of post-secondary education and the risks of increasing uncertainty in labour markets. This last expectation was justified through the assumption that individuals would also reap the financial and social benefits of post-secondary education. We develop the argument that this genera-tion *is* distinctive partly because, through these specific conditions and policies, youth has become defined almost exclusively in terms of the transition from education to employment. Indeed, youth policies have aligned with education policy to substantially shape what it means to be young (Wyn 2009).

In broad terms, our discussion identifies the crucial shift from the economic policies that formed the backdrop for the previous genera-tion's lives (for example, a commitment to the welfare state and to full employment, a comprehensive system of student financial aid that included both loans and grants, and relatively low levels of tuition fees) to the monetarist policies that have shaped the lives of our study's generation. In varying degrees in Canada and Australia, policies have shifted towards less public funding for education, more exclusionary welfare support, and an emphasis on vocationalism within education. In both countries young people tend to be seen as being valuable in the future, but they are expected to develop their abilities and talents with limited state support. It is also important to note that the shift to monetarist policies involved a fragmentation of policy spheres that distanced educational and labour-market policies from health and family policy spheres.

The Knowledge Society Discourse

By the 1980s in both Canada and Australia a knowledge society dis-course had dominated educational and labour-market policy dis-cussions although its implications for the design of post-secondary education in each country were different. In general, the argument was advanced as follows: for members of previous generations, virtually anyone who was willing to work, including those with low levels of education or limited skills, was able to obtain steady, reasonably well-paid employment. At one time it was possible for bright, highly motivated people with little in the way of educational credentials to be upwardly mobile in their chosen occupations. However, the emergence of a knowledge-based economy demanded the related emergence of a knowledge society in which employment would become increasingly tied to educational qualifications, and jobs would require higher levels of learning (Coleman and Husén 1985).

Creating New Inequalities

The knowledge society discourse framed learning within a market economy where education was seen as a commodity that individuals purchased. Indeed, during the 1990s and early 2000s, both Canada and Australia were considered to be archetypical examples of liberal welfare states in which citizenship was defined in relation to the obligation to work and in which the state increasingly limited its responsibility to provide income support for those could not work (Esping-Andersen 1990). This discourse also involved a shift from the idea that technological change offered the promise of progress to the idea that technological acceleration was seen as inherently necessary and as an 'unavoidable adjustment' (Rosa 2003, 18) to a highly competitive world. For example, Watts (1987) argued that the reliance on the 'brawn of industrial workers and machines' that was associated with the processing of raw materials would be replaced with 'the brain of technology' that would be associated with processing knowledge.

It was acknowledged that there would be casualties along the way. Technological change was anticipated to move at a pace that would ridicule any attempts to either predict it or adapt a school system to it (Psacharopoulos 1986). These inevitable changes were widely predicted to have grim consequences for poorly prepared youth in developed countries, in that educational attainment would supersede willingness to work, as the principal job entry-level credential (Coleman and Husén 1985). It was expected that those with limited education and few skills would be severely limited in their choices of employment and advancement and that, as a result, the 'career ladder' for the undereducated and underskilled would be 'truncated' (Radwanski 1987, 15). The policies adopted by both Canada and Australia tended to involve means-testing approaches to social assistance, and both countries embraced modest levels of universal transfers and social insurance. In Australia this represented a shift from the Keynesian-based approach of the 1950s to the 1970s, in which the government accepted a high level of responsibility for social inclusion through policies that expanded free and secular secondary education, to monetarist policies that emphasized instead the role of market forces, distancing the government from meeting popular aspirations and placing responsibility onto individuals. Although Canadian policies did not embrace the role of market forces as enthusiastically as the Australian policies, the expansion of post-secondary education nonetheless reflected the same adherence to individual responsibility for investing in learning.

Ten years later this refrain was taken up by global economic think tanks, including UNESCO and the OECD. The latter's documents actively promoted the idea of a 'knowledge-based economy,' and the former's policies warned that individuals who were not lifelong learners would suffer economic and social exclusion, as would nations that were not primarily learning societies (Delors 1996). These organizations also linked lifelong learning to the growth of knowledge-based industries that would require educated workers who would engage in reskilling throughout their working lives (OECD 1996). Education was positioned as a fundamental tool for economic advancement and security. International studies such as PISA were set up with the specific goal of measuring the educational levels of young people in OECD countries, with a focus on the types of knowledge that aligned with the needs of knowledge economies (OECD 2001).

Aligning Education to Economic Needs

While policies in both Canada and Australia supported the close alignment of education and labour markets, they were based on different interpretations of the way in which this relationship should unfold. In Canada the need for educated, skilled, lifelong learners focused on the production of young people with the capacity to be flexible workers and to build on the social capital they had acquired through a generalist education. In Australia the creation of a flexible labour force was based on a vocationalist approach to post-secondary education, with an emphasis on specific work-related skills that would result in an efficient use of human capital; it was acknowledged, however, that these skills would need to be 'updated' from time to time.

Although Canadian post-secondary education policy in the 1980s also drew on the available evidence of rapid social change, it took a different approach, arguing that job-specific training and specialization in high-tech skills alone would risk obsolescence (Watts 1987, 9). This approach suggested that a general education, not a vocationally oriented education, would equip young people to meet the demands of Canada's new economy most effectively. A general education would produce individuals who would be adaptable to changing opportunities, motivated to continually seek new knowledge, and capable of critical thinking and decision making (Bowen 1977; British Columbia 1988c; Canada 1988; British Columbia 1988b; Science Council of Canada 1988; Watts 1987).

Despite these differences in orientation, the dominant policy discourses of the mid 1980s in each country converged around the serious implications of low educational levels. In the Canadian context those who left school with the 'mandatory minimum' but without the requisite abilities and skills to cope with the demands of the modern workplace, would become, as Coleman and Husén (1985) predicted for the Western world, a 'new underclass.' In Australia, Wooden (1998) warned of the risks facing young people whose educational credentials did not enable them to escape the part-time, casualized labour market. For this group there was little chance of becoming meaningfully employed, and subsequent developments have reinforced predictions of the entrenchment of new social divisions. Those who were educated, qualified, and skilled have been able to become what Bauman (2001) described as a class of 'flexible' workers with opportunities, choices, and the capacity to reinvent themselves. However, for those who were immobile and/or with little or no ability to reinvent themselves, 'flexibility' would lead to precariousness and misery. By the early 2000s the transformation of the workforce had resulted in the structural exclusion of some groups of workers who were unable to 'keep up with the flexibility and speed required in modern Western economies' and suffered 'deceleration in the form of long-term unemployment' (Rosa 2003, 15).

The Economic Council of Canada (1990) predicted that as global competition accelerated, high-cost countries such as Canada would be increasingly compelled to rely on the excellence of their workforces to provide a comparative advantage in the global marketplace. Similarly, the Australian government of the day claimed that 'our industry is increasingly faced with rapidly changing international markets in which success depends upon, among other things, conceptual, creative, and technical skills of the labour force, the ability to innovate and be entrepreneurial' (Commonwealth of Australia 1988). As the volume of international trade continued to increase, the demand for domestic low-skilled, entry-level labour continued to decline in developed countries. Goods and services requiring less skilled labour began to be produced in countries with the lowest production costs and then readily transported to markets located anywhere in the world. Young people in the mid 1990s began to compete not only with adult workers in their own society but also with workers from other countries who were paid at much lower levels (Coleman and Husén 1985). The Canadian government asserted that 'of all the jobs forecast to be created between 1989 and 2000, two thirds (62.9 per cent) will require at least 12 years of education and training; 40 per cent will require more than 16 years of training' (*Learning well . . . living well* 1991, 5). However, 'in 1986, nearly half (46.7 per cent) of all workers beyond school age possessed less than secondary school education' (*Learning well . . . living well* 1991, 5).

Increases in Educational Participation

For the most part, these predictions have been realized. Today, in both Canada and Australia, increases in the population as well as increasing demand have led to higher enrolments at the post-secondary and tertiary levels. In both countries, participation in post-secondary education is a normative activity for young adults. In Canada the proportion of the population aged twenty-five to sixty-four with post-secondary credentials increased from 28 per cent in 1991 to 45 per cent in 2004. The comparable figures for Australia are 22 per cent and 31 per cent, respectively (Canadian Council on Learning 2007). According to the OECD (2007, 269), 'today, 53 per cent of young people in OECD countries will enter tertiary-type A programmes during their lifetimes.' The comparable proportion of those who will enter tertiary-type B programs is 16 per cent.[1] The OECD reports that in Canada a seventeen-year-old can expect to participate in 2.9 years of tertiary-level education. For Australia this figure is 3.6. In both Canada and Australia 35 per cent and 37 per

---

1 *Tertiary-type A programs* are defined as 'largely theory-based and are designed to provide sufficient qualifications for entry into advanced research programmes and professions with high skill requirements' (OECD 2006, 15). *Tertiary-type B programs* are 'typically shorter than those of tertiary-type A and focus on practical, technical or occupational skills for direct entry in the labour market' (OECD 2006, 15).

cent, respectively, of nineteen-year-olds and 37 per cent of twenty-year-olds are enrolled in higher and tertiary education. Some researchers point out that the educational system has expanded from K–12 (kindergarten to Grade 12) to K–16 (kindergarten to Year 16), hence moving from 'mass' to 'universal' post-secondary participation (S. Davies 2005; Sweet and Anisef 2005). However, the proportion of the population with post-secondary credentials is considerably higher in Canada (45 per cent) than in Australia (31 per cent) (OECD 2007).

These developments had a powerful effect on young people's lives, as we discuss in the next section where we review country-specific policies and frameworks in relation to education, labour-force participation, and issues of equity.

Canada

'There is no such thing as an over-educated person.'

(Watts 1987, 4)

This statement captured the sentiment in Canada of the importance of education for both individuals and society. In the late 1980s and early 1990s the Canadian education and labour-market policy context was shaped by several key documents. In one such document, entitled *Good Jobs, Bad Jobs,* the Economic Council of Canada (1990, 18) summarized the nature and impact of various factors on the labour force: 'The growth of services, along with the information explosion and the internationalization of business activity, is fuelling the demand for an increasingly well-educated and skilled work force. Canada's future economic welfare will be dictated in no small measure by its capacity to develop human resources. The "education and training" imperative will also be compelling for individuals, since employment experiences will be less and less favourable for those who have skill deficiencies.' In other words, effective competition in an internationalized economy would require knowledge-intensive service and manufacturing activities that employed an expert and flexible workforce. According to the Economic Council of Canada, all recent employment growth had occurred in one of two quite distinct 'growth poles' – either highly skilled, well-compensated, and secure jobs or non-standard, unstable, and relatively poorly paid jobs – hence the 'good jobs, bad jobs' label.

Although it was acknowledged that *skill* was a difficult concept to measure, the Economic Council of Canada asserted that the nature and level of skills required in the labour market were being transformed by a combination of three factors: growth of the service sector, technological innovation, and changes in the way work was being organized. Because of this transformation, employers would be seeking individuals with qualities that included 'basic academic competence, creativity and initiative, analytical and problem-solving abilities, adaptability, and communication and interpersonal skills' (Economic Council of Canada 1990, 13).

These changing views about the relationship between education and the labour market coincided with changes to the Canadian post-secondary education system, which, from the 1960s onward, experienced extraordinary expansion. During this period strong links were established between higher educational levels and economic growth. As a result, 'democratization of access [to post-secondary education] was a necessary condition for greater social and political equality' (Fortin 1987, 1). Education became a top priority of both the federal and provincial governments of Canada. Eventually, public sentiment followed the lead of government, and Canadian society embraced the importance of the need for higher levels of education and support of 'extensive spending in the educational sector' (Fortin 1987, 1). As Pike (1986) pointed out, human capital theory, 'which both encouraged investment in education and an emphasis upon moves to eliminate barriers to educational achievement, ... created ... an almost irresistible set of arguments in favour of educational expansion and reform' (Pike 1986, 11).

Although economic imperatives were clearly driving the expansion of the post-secondary education system, other factors were also at play. As Watts (1987) maintained, 'if our human resources are not to be underdeveloped, policies related to post-secondary [education] must ensure that all students who have the requisite capability also have the opportunity to develop their intellectual, aesthetic, ethical and practical capacities through higher education ... Moreover, in a rapidly evolving learning society, what Canada requires is an educated populace of individuals motivated to seek new knowledge through their lives' (Watts 1987, 4).

Despite the prevailing arguments for a skilled workforce, some cautioned that nurturing the development of a knowledge-based society required more than a narrow vocationalism. According to Watts (1987, 5), 'the genuine vocational need that must be met is for creative and intellectually rigorous entrepreneurial individuals who are broadly informed and outward-looking.' He argued that efforts towards designing vocational education with lifelong learning as its foundation would help to facilitate shifts in employment over workers' lifetimes.

In addition, institutions of higher education in Canada were recognized as playing a key role in supporting social and cultural development and 'improving the moral fibre of society' (Watts 1987, 10) by reducing racism, strengthening multiculturalism, promoting social welfare, and 'heighten[ing] our concern for democratic freedoms, for the rights of others, and for ethical values in private and public behaviour' (Watts 1987, 10). Such developments would be fostered in terms of enhancing social mobility, 'but also by serving as exemplars for desirable national policies such as providing equal opportunities for women and for racial minorities, eliminating racism and sexism from courses, and nurturing social values' (Watts 1987, 6).

Over the three decades since the 1950s, significant improvement had occurred in most forms of post-secondary participation, including the transition from high school to post-secondary education. In terms of overall expansion, Canada was considered to be among the educational leaders (OECD 1976). The number of places available in existing universities increased, new universities were established, and a community college system was developed in each province. By the mid to late 1980s Canada had approximately 65 universities, 123 public community colleges, 53 public post-secondary institutions, and an assortment of private post-secondary institutions (Dennison and Gallagher 1986; Canada 1990). The 'if you build it, they will come' approach paid off (Krahn and Hudson 2006, 60). Full-time enrolment in post-secondary institutions increased from 91,000 in 1951–52 to 817,000 in 1988–89 (Canada 1990). Transition rates from Grade 12 directly to post-secondary education increased from 45 per cent in 1979–80 to 53 per cent in 1985–86.

Concurrently, the early school leaving rate from high school had declined from 54 per cent in 1951 (Lennards 1980) to 21 per cent in 1991 (Anisef and Andres 1996), and high school graduation rates of the eighteen-year-old population increased from 63 per cent to 68 per cent (Canada 1987). Full-time post-secondary enrolment among the eighteen to twenty-four age group in 1986–87 totalled 26 per cent (Statistics Canada 1989a, 1989b). The message from government, communities, and families was clear: the acquisition of higher levels of education was good; the more educational attainment the better. It was into this educational environment that the British Columbia class of '88 graduated from high school.

Graduates from the British Columbia secondary system were fortunate and privileged to have a dynamic provincial post-secondary system at their disposal. Described as a 'diversified and well-developed structure for advanced education and job training' (British Columbia 1988b, 3), by 1998 the BC post-secondary system, whose expansion had begun in the 1960s (MacDonald 1962), included three public universities, one private university, fifteen community colleges, four public institutes, an open-learning university, and an open-learning college, as well as many private colleges and trade schools. At about the same time as the *Paths on Life's Way* participants graduated from high school, a new university in northern British Columbia was scheduled to open and four university colleges within the existing community college system were created, which further increased the availability of university-degree programs. Approximately 116,500 full-time and part-time students participated annually in non-vocational education,[2] and over 12,000 students were enrolled in full-time vocational programs (Canada 1990; British Columbia 1988a). The transition rate[3] for British Columbia students moving directly from high school to college or university had increased to 45 per cent in 1985–86 from 35 per cent in 1978–79 (Canada 1987).

Despite these sanguine numbers for Canada as a whole and British Columbia in particular, high post-secondary participation rates did not solve all social problems facing young adults. The scope and pace of change caused by global competition had resulted in the restructuring of the Canadian labour market, both in the private and the public sectors (Marquardt 1996, 2). As a result, several concomitant forces affected young adults, including a decline in the industries that had traditionally provided entry-level jobs for a large proportion of young people, and the expansion of the service sector and its 'good and bad jobs.' Using data from Statistics Canada, Marquardt demonstrated that the absolute number of jobs in goods-producing industries for the fifteen to twenty-four age group declined by almost 50 per cent. However, the absolute number of jobs in the service-producing industries also declined by 9 per cent in the same period for the same age group. Increases occurred in only some service-producing subsectors, including retail trade (5 per cent) and

---

2 This figure includes university-transfer, career or technical, general-studies, and college-preparatory programs. Of the 1988–89 full-time students in British Columbia 38,580 attended university and 25,488 were at community colleges. Part-time participants included 17,997 at university and 34,658 at community colleges (Canada 1990).
3 The *transition rate* is defined as the percentage of high school graduates proceeding directly to either college or university following high school graduation (Canada 1987).

community, business, and personal services (2 per cent, with the largest increase being in the subcategory of accommodation and food).

Between 1981 and 1992 the absolute and relative earnings of young adults declined across all groups regardless of educational level and sector of employment, while the number of standard hours worked increased for those in high-wage categories and declined for those in low-wage categories (Marquardt 1996). According to Crompton (1995), between 1979 and 1984, declines in real earnings were greatest for male university graduates, at 18 per cent. As a result, the wage levels for young workers may have been depressed. Hence, the projected benefits expected to accrue from increased educational attainment were not being realized.

Unemployment and underemployment also emerged as issues in the 1980s and the first half of the 1990s. The unemployment rate for Canadians and British Columbians aged fifteen to twenty-four was the worst of three age groups (the other two groups being aged twenty-five to forty-four and forty-five to sixty-four), and those at all levels of educational attainment experienced increased rates of unemployment throughout the early 1990s. A few studies sought to measure underemployment by employing General Educational Development (GED), a measure provided in the *Canadian Classification and Dictionary of Occupations* that assesses the educational requirements of a given job. Employing this measure, Anisef (1980) determined that 42 per cent of male university graduates and 56 per cent of female university graduates held jobs that did not require a university degree, and 77 per cent of males and 57 per cent of females with non-university credentials held jobs requiring high school graduation or less. In other words, both of these groups were underemployed.

Similarly, in a study of 1985 university graduates, and employing the GED measure, Redpath (1994) demonstrated that two years following graduation, 35 per cent were mismatched in that they were working in jobs that did not require a university education. The proportion of mismatch ranged from 10 per cent among education graduates to 69 per cent among arts graduates. However, 33 per cent of business graduates and 45 per cent of science graduates also experienced a mismatch between their education and jobs. When jobs were examined by occupational category, over 50 per cent of mismatched jobs were in clerical, sales, and services occupations, with more women in low-paying clerical jobs and more men in higher-paying sales jobs. Redpath concluded that the mismatch between education and jobs as well as the skills shortage should be understood in a broader context, which we have been discussing here. It includes the shift in skill requirements, the rise in educational participation, as well as the nature of employers' hiring criteria across different occupations. Her study concluded that the structure of labour-market opportunities required more attention to identify both the opportunities and the barriers to utilizing the skills of graduates. Most significantly, it pointed out that employers need to accept some responsibility for specifying the type of curricular content that would be relevant in the workplace, and they need to make an effort at considering what skills and knowledge from various disciplines can be transferred to the workplace. This statement is reinforced by the finding recently reported by the Canadian Council on Learning (2007) that 25 per cent of those with university degrees in Canada have lower earnings than the average high school graduate.

The very structure of the Canadian K–12 and post-secondary systems and their relationships with the labour market were also problematic for young people in transition. In contrast to the institutional models with strong links between secondary schools, employers and firms, unions, and government that were adopted by some European and Japanese systems, Canada embraced a market model where individuals were increasingly expected to invest their own capital – in terms of time and money – on post-secondary credentials earned through study, with the hope of making the right choices for future employment (Ashton and Lowe 1991). In the 1980s several reports and commissions advocated a more direct user-pay orientation for financing post-secondary education (see Canada 1983; Nova Scotia 1985; Ontario 1984).

This major shift in ideology from a social to a private rate-of-return approach redirected the responsibility for deciding on educational paths, devising strategies for labour-market entry, and arranging for ongoing skills training to individual students and their families (Andres and Adamuti-Trache 2009; Marquardt 1996; Pike 1986). In Canada in 1990 the median domestic undergraduate-tuition fees were $1545, ranging from a low of $904 in Quebec and a high of $1941 in Nova Scotia. In BC this figure was near the higher extreme, at $1808. Within five years, tuition rates in BC had escalated by 25 per cent, to $2563 (Statistics Canada 2005, 2006b, 2007). Between 1996–97 and 2002–03, in an attempt to bolster post-secondary participation rates, a tuition fee freeze was instituted; however, once this policy was abandoned, tuition fee rates continued to rise steadily.

During the same time period, although university enrolment increased by 44 per cent, funding support for BC students decreased by over 17 per cent (unweighted), or almost $2000 per student (Malcolmson and Lee 2004, 10). As Malcolmson and Lee's study points out, the benefits of enormous expansion throughout the 1990s were mitigated by inadequate funding of the additional seats. It concludes that provincial policies might have the effect of reducing one barrier to accessing post-secondary education while at the same time increasing another barrier in the form of the financial cost of attendance. In contrast, as we describe below, in 1974 the Australian government had abolished tuition for higher education. Arguing against increasing tuition rates, through the use of the Australian example, Pike (1986, 21) asserted that Canada should take heed that 'it is one thing to suggest that the lowering of economic barriers may not result in the greater democratization of university education but quite another to suggest that this constitutes proof that *raising* [emphasis in original] economic barriers does not harm accessibility.' As we shall see, in 1988 while Canada was promoting a user-pay approach, Australia reversed its no-tuition-fee policy, and ironically, both countries did so under umbrella policies that espoused the rhetoric of enhancing equity of access to post-secondary education.

Echoing Redpath's finding that there was a mismatch between the skills required in the labour market and the qualifications acquired by graduates, Bills (1988) pointed out that employers depended on the post-secondary education system to provide broad, portable skills, but little in the way of formal training, and they used post-secondary qualifications as a screening mechanism. During this time young people were forced to make decisions about the educational credentials that they hoped would enable them to achieve their work goals, based on imperfect information. Indeed, as new types of work were emerging and employers were asking for higher levels of educational credentials, it was a period of difficulty for even the well-informed to predict the most effective education-work pathways. This meant that it was not uncommon for young people to change track during their studies, to be unemployed, or to have a period of employment that was not related to their area of study, leading to the criticism of 'inefficient school-to-work paths' (Marquardt 1996, 11).

By the late 1990s the need for higher levels of education and hence longer times spent in post-secondary studies, together with increased tuition fees and a reduction in funding by federal and provincial governments for post-secondary education in Canada, were straining the budgets of even the middle classes. Marquardt (1996, 4) summarized the key issues faced by young people: 'increased participation by students in the labour market [while attending school], prolonged years of schooling, and a greater diversity in transition paths, that is, in ways of combining schooling and labour force participation.'

Australia

'During the 1980s and 1990s the pressure was to finish school to get jobs. Now this is not good enough.'

(Teese 2000, 53)

In Australia, expansion of the post-secondary education system was driven by and linked to labour-market policy and economic change. The scale of these changes in the 1980s is illustrated by considering the situation before the outbreak of the Second World War. In the 1930s the Australian post-secondary education system was comprised of six universities and two university colleges, with a total enrolment of 14,236. Of these students nearly 60 per cent were enrolled at two universities, the University of Sydney and the University of Melbourne. Seventy-two per cent were enrolled in degree programs, and of this group only eighty-one students were studying for 'higher degrees' (that is, at the master's and doctoral levels). In contrast, almost 30 per cent were enrolled in 'sub-degree or non-award courses' (that is, for certificates and non-matriculation). In 1939, only 30 per cent of the student population was female (Commonwealth of Australia 1993, 6). In 1942, through the Commonwealth Reconstruction Training Scheme, students were provided with financial assistance to encourage them to participate in post-secondary studies. Following the end of the war, this scheme provided financial support to thousands of returning veterans (Commonwealth of Australia 1993).

In the post-war years, the post-secondary education system continued to expand. By 1968, 100,000 students were enrolled in universities and 45,000 in colleges of advanced education. By 1978, the comparable enrolment figures were 159,500 in universities and 153,000 in Colleges of Advanced Education (CAEs), an increase of 59 per cent and 242 per cent respectively (Commonwealth of Australia 1993). Following this period of rapid expansion, conditions changed dramatically. A decline in enrolments across the complete range of post-secondary institutions was attributed to falling birth rates and an increase in the proportion of early school leavers, particularly males. Between 1976 and 1981 the transition rate from secondary school to the post-secondary education sector declined by almost 10 per cent (from 51 to 42 per cent) (Commonwealth of Australia 1993, 25).

These declines, which were accompanied by a downturn in economic growth and a decline in full-time employment by young adults, were of considerable concern to the government of the day. As a result the government placed 'particular emphasis on the role of technical and further education (TAFE) in better preparing young people for the workplace' (Commonwealth of Australia 1993, 25). The increased role of TAFE in post-secondary education provision was, however, to be achieved without increases in funding.

In 1983 a change in government – from the conservative Liberal Party to the Labour Party – led to a major shift in policy, towards a new emphasis on 'participation and equity in all sectors of post-compulsory education: schools, TAFE and higher education' (Commonwealth of Australia 1993, 25), with a particular emphasis on improving the educational qualifications of under-represented and disadvantaged groups. To accomplish this goal, between 1984 and 1988 over 13,000 new places in the post-secondary education system were created. However, this expansion was coupled with 'establish[ing] a closer relationship between labour market needs and educational outputs. For the 1985–87 triennium, growth was to be concentrated as much as possible in science, technology and management based courses and other courses that were of the greatest relevance to economic development' (Commonwealth of Australia 1993, 25)

According to the Department of Employment (Commonwealth of Australia 1993, 26), the goal of 'mak[ing] higher education institutions more responsive to the needs of industry . . . along with major structural change, [was] the distinctive characteristic of the period post-1987.' Similarly to Canada, the focus of government was on 'diversity,' 'quality,' and 'excellence' through a wide range of post-secondary offerings at a variety of institutions, but unlike in Canada, the policies focused on vocational education rather than on broad-based education.

Throughout the 1980s the Australian post-secondary education sector continued to grow. Between 1982 and 1992 total enrolments increased by 64 per cent, new entrants to the system increased by 68 per cent, and the number of graduates increased by 61 per cent. By 1992, 559,365 students were enrolled in the post-secondary sector, and in 1991 the sector graduated 107,561 students. In other words, Australia

was well on its way to achieving the goal of being among the leading
OECD countries in terms of post-secondary participation by the year
2000 (Commonwealth of Australia 1993, 48). The greatest increase
(42 per cent) in total student enrolments occurred between 1987 and
1992, the period during which the *Life Patterns* participants were making the transition from secondary school (Commonwealth of Australia
1993, 46). Leaving secondary school in 1991, they were part of the vanguard that changed the face of post-secondary education forever.

Taking an approach to education and labour-market policy development that was consistent with that of Canada, government policies
emphasized Australians' positions as workers in a global economy
who would be required to be 'multi-skilled, creative and adaptable'
(Commonwealth of Australia 1991, ix). However, unlike Canada, the
Department of Employment Education and Training strongly emphasized the convergence of general and vocational education, with the
goal of enhancing both individual and industry needs as it brought
about the transition from an elite to a mass system of post-secondary
education. According to the department, 'regular updating of skills and
knowledge became essential to maintaining and enhancing productivity in the workplace[;] the concepts of working and learning would con-
verge' (Commonwealth of Australia 1993, 24).

Major changes in the structural arrangements of the secondary,
higher, and tertiary systems had significant implications for the lives
and choices of *Life Patterns* participants. Their participation in secondary education opened up opportunities for them. Before 1980 the
majority of school leavers had left school before completing Year 12;
in fact, it was considered 'normal for young people to leave school
at about Year 10' when they were aged fifteen (Commonwealth of
Australia 1993, 199). However, as part of a planned government intervention to align Australia's workers with the needs of new economies,
more students began to stay in school. Government policies supported
this trend through targeted social policies involving financial support,
such as AUSTUDY allowances that were extended to secondary students to encourage them to continue with their education. Other factors that encouraged educational participation were a restricting youth
labour market that was especially unwelcoming to unskilled youth and
the shifting attitudes of students and their families towards supporting
high school completion. As a result, Year 12 completion rates increased
from 35 per cent in 1980 to 71 per cent by 1990. This significant spike in
school-completion rates created a demand for university places by 1991

that could not be met. The *Life Patterns* participants were among the young people who were faced with having to redirect their preferences for post-secondary education to the colleges or to TAFE.

In addition, the abandonment in 1988 of a binary model of post-secondary education and the subsequent adoption of the Unified National System (UNS) blurred the once deliberately separated boundaries between university and non-university sectors. During the 1980s the number of large Colleges of Advanced Education increased while smaller CAEs were amalgamated. By 1991 thirty-eight institutions were members of the UNS. In Victoria there were seventeen member institutions[4] (Commonwealth of Australia 1993, 30). It is important to note, however, that the new 'unified' national system did not include TAFE institutes. These remained as a separate system of vocational education institutes.

Changes in tuition fees, student financial aid, and related repayment schemes would also affect *Life Patterns* participants. In 1974, in an attempt to democratize post-secondary education, university tuition fees were abolished. However, in 1988, the government introduced the Higher Education Contribution Scheme (HECS). This 'user-pays,' income-contingent repayment scheme was presented as a more equitable arrangement for two reasons: (1) those who benefited from post-secondary education would bear some of the costs, and (2) disadvantaged groups would not be required to pay 'up-front fees or commercial loans' (Commonwealth of Australia 1993, 26) but could defer their fees, thereby incurring a debt to the government that would be repaid when they earned over a threshold amount. Those who paid upfront were offered a fee reduction, which provided a financial advantage to students and their families who were wealthier. Income support was also provided through the AUSTUDY scheme, which was introduced in 1987 to rationalize and streamline student assistance and to align it with other forms of income support for youth, integrating education and

---

4 These institutions were Australian Catholic University, La Trobe University, Monash University, Royal Melbourne Institute of Technology, Swinburne University of Technology, University of Melbourne, Victoria University of Technology, Ballarat University College, La Trobe University (Bendigo), Monash University (Churchill), University of Melbourne (Dookie), University of Melbourne (Glenormiston), Deakin University (Geelong), University of Melbourne (Horsham), La Trobe University (Wodonga), University of Melbourne (Warragul), and Deakin University (Warrnambool) (Commonwealth of Australia 1993, 31).

youth policies. The objective of AUSTUDY was to remove disincentives to study through a youth allowance structure across a range of income support schemes (Commonwealth of Australia 1993). Between 1987 and 1991, approximately 40 per cent of full-time tertiary students received AUSTUDY grants. Nonetheless, incurring a debt in order to become educated was a disincentive to already disadvantaged groups, especially those from rural areas where debt was not widely perceived as an acceptable strategy (James et al. 1999).

Equity and Educational Outcomes in Canada and Australia

In the 1980s both the Canadian and the Australian governments acknowledged that despite their having taken positive steps to improve their post-secondary education systems, the goals of advancing equality of educational opportunity for all who were qualified and who wanted to study had fallen short. In Canada, despite dramatic increases in post-secondary enrolments, numerous studies demonstrated that (1) children of upper-middle- and upper-class parents continued to be overrepresented in university education, (2) students attending non-university institutions (for example, community colleges) were more likely to come from less educated parental backgrounds, and (3) expansion of the post-secondary education system and concomitant growth in enrolment did little to reduce the class bias (Anisef 1985; Guppy 1984; Pike 1986; Porter and Jasmin 1987). Almost identical findings were cited by the Australian government;[5] however, rather than no or little change, one government document reported that 'there has been a very high and increasing level of socioeconomic imbalance over this period' (Commonwealth of Australia Department of Employment Education and Training and National Board of Employment Education and Training 1990, 15).

The following disadvantaged groups were identified in numerous Canadian reports written in the 1980s: native Indians, people from remote communities, the disabled, the socially and economically dis-

---

5 Neither the Canadian government nor the Australian government collects data on post-secondary participation and completion rates by social class background. Instead, as Commonwealth of Australia Department of Employment Education and Training and National Board of Employment Education and Training (1990) and Commonwealth of Australia Department of Employment Education and Training (1993) point out, they rely on academic research to provide this information.

advantaged, women, visible minorities, immigrants, mature and part-time students, minority official language group members (that is, francophones), and unemployment insurance recipients (see Andres 1992, page 37, for an extended discussion). A strikingly parallel list was generated by the Australian government. The Williams Committee of Inquiry into Education and Training (1979) found that Aboriginal people, migrants, the physically handicapped, and women were under-represented in post-secondary education (Clarke and Edwards 1980). This report noted that women constituted only a small percentage in the sciences, applied sciences, and technologies and recommended a raft of programs and initiatives specifically designed to increase access to university for women with children (Clarke and Edwards 1980).

In 1990 the Australian government set national equity objectives in its policy document *A Fair Chance for All* (Commonwealth of Australia Department of Employment Education and Training and National Board of Employment Education and Training 1990), targeting six groups that were identified as disadvantaged in gaining access to higher education: people from socio-economically disadvantaged backgrounds, Aboriginal and Torres Strait islander people, women (particularly in non-traditional areas of study), people from non-English-speaking backgrounds, people with disabilities, and people from rural and isolated areas. Subsequent research shows that two groups in particular have not improved their participation in post-secondary education: people from rural and isolated areas and people from lower socio-economic backgrounds (James et al. 1999).

The increased participation of women in post-secondary education that occurred in both countries during the 1990s was presented as a 'good news, bad news' story. Despite national stay-in-school policy initiatives in both countries, more young women than young men completed Year 12: in Australia in 1991, the proportions were 77 per cent of females, compared with 66 per cent of males; in Canada they were 83 per cent compared with 75 per cent (Anisef and Andres 1996; Department of Employment Education and Training 1993). From a post-secondary education perspective, the good news part of the story was that by 1983 in Canada approximately equal proportions of women and men had earned bachelor's and first professional undergraduate degrees, and by 1985 more women than men were enrolled in undergraduate programs. These milestones were also achieved by Australian women, albeit somewhat later (by 1986–87, just over 50 per cent of women had earned bachelor's and first professional undergraduate degrees, and in

1989, 51 per cent of women were enrolled in undergraduate programs). Since these dates, in both countries the proportion of women attending and completing undergraduate studies continued to escalate.[6] However, in both countries, women remained under-represented in the traditionally male-dominant, high-prestige disciplines. Except in the social sciences, little change has occurred since the late 1970s (see Andres and Adamuti-Trache 2006 and 2007 for a detailed analysis of Canada and a comparative analysis of Canada, Australia, and the United States).

The nature and structure of Canadian and Australian post-secondary education systems were identified as disadvantaging certain groups from participating and completing their studies. In Australia the lack of sufficient university places in relation to demand and the lack of transferability between the TAFEs and universities were identified as barriers to access. In Canada, on the one hand, 'articulated' post-secondary education systems, such as the one in place in British Columbia, were lauded as 'democratizing' in that they offered opportunities 'for the previously disenfranchised' (Dennison and Gallagher 1986, 162) to pursue post-secondary studies, including university-degree completion (Dennison and Gallagher 1986; Education 1984; Fortin 1987). On the other hand, it was alleged that accompanying a democratization effect in such systems was a strong diversion effect (Brint and Karabel 1989). Based on research studies and policy analyses of the day, Marquardt (1996, 38) predicted that 'the trends on the two sides of the labour market – the polarization of demand into good and bad jobs, and the reduced accessibility of post-secondary education – will lead to sharper class divisions in Canadian society, and these divisions will be reproduced through the education system.' In Canada and Australia the two key policy documents – again, strikingly similar in their titles and content – were aimed directly at potential post-secondary students of the late 1980s and early 1990s, hence directly affecting both the *Paths on Life's Way* and *Life Patterns* respondents.

In Canada a report entitled *Access to Advanced Education and Job Training in British Columbia*, known as the 'Access for All' Report (British Columbia 1988b), had an enormous impact on post-secondary education policy and practice. It acknowledged that opportunities for advanced education were not equal for all people in all parts of the province.

---

6 In a recent publication (2007, 79) the Canadian Council on Learning indicates that 'males have replaced females as an underrepresented group in PSE participation and completion at the undergraduate and graduate levels.'

Although services to under-represented groups have vastly improved over the past twenty-five years, the report indicated that 'it is unacceptable that significant groups should remain under-represented for long in higher learning activities, unless by free choice rather than by lack of opportunity' (8). Of particular relevance to this study, low participation rates, including the transition of high school graduates to the post-secondary education system and transfer within the system, prompted the British Columbia Ministry of Advanced Education to adopt some of the recommendations of the committee charged with addressing these issues (British Columbia 1988b). Five priority concerns – admissions, transfer, and articulation; institutional capacity and program quality; literacy and adult basic education; university degree programs outside the main metropolitan areas; and under-represented groups identified above – were addressed through policies aimed to strengthen transfer from non-university institutions to universities. These policy initiatives included enhancing access to sufficient and appropriate information for students, such as the publication of a yearly transfer guide that specified course and transfer credit equivalencies among all public post-secondary institutions in the province, and the transformation of four existing community colleges into university colleges, which, for some students, eliminated the need to transfer to another institution in order to complete a university degree.

In Australia a change in government in 1983 launched the beginning of a shift in focus in education policy in terms of participation and equity. A myriad of policies were set in place to enhance retention at the secondary level and to expand the range of post-secondary offerings by amalgamating small colleges of education. By specifying disadvantaged groups, the 1988 White Paper led to further educational reforms intended to ensure 'equal access to the range of services and opportunities that can enhance their lives' (Commonwealth of Australia Department of Employment Education and Training and National Board of Employment Education and Training 1990, 6). With the goal of changing the balance of the composition of the student population to more closely reflect the demographic composition of Australian society, the ensuing discussion paper *A Fair Chance for All: National and Institutional Planning for Higher Education* made the following bold statement: 'Achieving social justice in Australia is a fundamental goal of the Federal Government. Through its social justice strategy, the Government is committed to improving equality of opportunity, enhancing the rights of people – especially the underprivileged – and

making sure that the benefits of economic growth are distributed equi-
tably. A fairer society is both a primary objective of social policy and
an indispensable element in achieving economic policy objectives'
(Commonwealth of Australia Department of Employment Education
and Training and National Board of Employment Education and
Training 1990, 6). This long-term strategy initiative detailed targeted
funding for programs that would increase participation by disadvantaged groups; requests for the development of statements of intent and
related institutional profiles that specified 'equity goals, strategies,
priorities, and performance measures' (Commonwealth of Australia
Department of Employment Education and Training and National
Board of Employment Education and Training 1990, 7–8); and funding for 49,000 additional student places in post-secondary education.
In addition, numerous strategies to identify, target, and monitor the
progress of disadvantaged groups into and through the post-secondary education system were specified.

Conclusion

These educational policies set the stage for our young participants as
they completed their secondary education and made their decisions
about the next steps of their lives. Against a backdrop of a rapidly
changing economic order in both countries, the policies were specifically designed to produce the type of human capital that would ensure
national prosperity and individual security in a new globally competitive world. We have identified striking similarities in the rationales for
expanding post-secondary education and the desire to create a labour
force with the capacity to be flexible and capable of undertaking lifelong learning. We have also identified strong similarities in the social
composition of post-secondary participants and in the development of
policy initiatives to combat inequality. However, Australia has tended
to place a greater focus on vocationally oriented education than has
Canada. The significance of these policies and circumstances for the
lives of young people and their families should not be underestimated.
Our analysis of the policy and economic environment that framed the
lives of our young participants through their early twenties and into
their thirties suggests that they faced fundamentally new realities that
marked them as being very different from the previous generation.

First, the expansion of post-secondary and tertiary education in
both countries allowed an unprecedented proportion of young people

to attend higher and further educational institutions (especially in Australia). In both countries this expansion was accompanied by two goals. The dominant goal (epitomized by the discourse of the knowledge society) was to ensure that young people had the skills and capacities to serve the goals of new and changing economies. The second goal was to expand opportunities for a wider range of young people based on a rhetoric of social justice (expressed through the idea of social cohesion).

Our longitudinal studies allow us to follow the trajectories of this 'education generation' and to analyse how new educational opportunities have affected different groups – especially those who were previously under-represented in higher education. The expansion of educational opportunities in the early 1990s had the potential to give women, young people from rural backgrounds, and young people from low socio-economic backgrounds opportunities to gain the educational credentials and skills that would position them favourably in the labour market. Indeed, by the mid 1990s, predictions of a new gender order were being made, accompanied by claims that boys were the 'new disadvantaged.' Our research explores the extent to which the 'opportunities' that were taken up have produced enduring change for social groups. It also documents the ways in which some groups of young people took on the project of developing their own capacities through informal learning, adding a new dimension to the government's goal of enhancing human capital.

Second, the increases in participation in post-secondary education have implications for other spheres of life, especially personal relationships and family life. Few studies have actively explored the impact of mass tertiary education on the personal lives of individuals. Our research enables us to explore the possibility that, faced with the need to invest in education and to support their children for longer, families have forged new intergenerational relations. We also explore the ways in which the emphasis on educational achievement has fostered the emergence of new intergenerational strategies for securing life chances while financial and social support by families for extended educational pathways has become more important.

Third, educational policies were explicitly designed to interface with labour-market needs. Despite the fact that the educational policies were intended to foster efficient transition pathways from education to employment, many young people found the road to employment to be a long one. Our longitudinal research is able to trace the often messy and sometimes unpredictable pathways taken by individuals over time, to explore the question of which groups of young people have benefited from their educational investment, and to examine the different ways in which young people have used their education. We are also able to analyse their attitudes to work, career, financial security, and lifelong learning in order to document the unintended consequences of these policies.

In British Columbia, policies promoting a generalist education had already successfully created 'universal' post-secondary education, laying a solid foundation for the kinds of human capital required in its emerging knowledge economy. For young Canadians entering further education in the early 1990s, their generalist secondary educational qualifications enabled them to make relatively smooth transitions to the next level of their education. During this period, free-standing vocational institutions were merged into more comprehensive post-secondary institutions. This was different from the Australian context where universal post-secondary education had not yet been achieved. Faced with the urgent need to link Australia's education systems to the production of new skill sets to serve the country's changing economy, the government made vocational education a policy priority, but it also created a more complex structure in terms of articulation between secondary and post-secondary education.

In the following chapters we take up these themes and explore in detail how circumstances have shaped the lives of young people and how they themselves have developed distinctive responses to these circumstances.

4 Hopes and Dreams

The policy frameworks described in the previous chapter had a direct impact on the young people in our studies. They were the first generation for whom it was normative to extend education beyond the secondary level, and in one sense they were the pioneers of the new mass education sector of post-secondary education. Those members who invested in their education were positioned by policies as the hope for the prosperity of their respective nations. They were to play a key role in enabling knowledge to become a crucial resource as well as a commodity and an industry. Their participation in education and their uses of knowledge facilitated the move to the contemporary 'globalising knowledge economies' that are connected locally and globally and which characterize our economies today (OECD 2007, 11).

This context framed the possibilities for being and becoming that informed the generation's decisions. Their 'transition to adulthood' coincided directly with the 'transition to the knowledge economy,' so they were experiencing both personal and social change. For example, the expansion of post-secondary education had the effect of opening up opportunities for groups that had previously been under-represented in higher education; young women were especially responsive to these opportunities. As we will see in chapter 5, in Australia the expansion of post-secondary education also enabled a significant number of young people from families where no one had previously extended their education to this level to gain a university degree or a technical and further education (TAFE) qualification. While the context of social change brought uncertainty, it also offered opportunities, and in both countries these young people had every reason to be optimistic about their futures.

Yet, for those who were embarking on the next steps of post-secondary education and those who were entering the workforce directly after leaving secondary school, the context was also one of unpredictability about the nature of emerging economies. Australia and Canada were among the countries that experienced the full effects of recession in the early 1990s. As we discuss in chapter 6, labour markets in both countries became increasingly unstable, and working conditions began to deteriorate. Stable full-time work was being replaced with part-time, contract work, and the nature of jobs was also changing. There would be fewer jobs in manufacturing and industry and more jobs requiring skills in the service sector, and people would be expected to reskill several times throughout their working lives.

Our young participants developed their life narratives against this backdrop. These narratives would inform their decisions and judgments about education, work, and relationships. As Bauman (2001, 7) points out, narratives about future life are inextricably interwoven with how life is lived. He comments that 'one lives one's life as a story yet to be told, but the way the story hoping to be told is to be woven decides the technique by which the yarn of life is spun.' He adds that the way people construct their narratives of life and existence is determined by conditions of which they are generally not aware. Echoing Bauman, we argue that life narratives are generated by individuals, but they do not have endless possibilities. Life narratives are circumscribed by subjectivities, or sets of ideas about possible ways of being that have salience at particular points in time. We also draw on Bourdieu's ideas about the relationship between individual choice and social context (Bourdieu 1987; Bourdieu and Passeron 1977). Bourdieu argues that actions or practices are neither mechanically predetermined nor produced by creative free will. Instead, practices are 'determined by past conditions which have produced the principle of their production' (Bourdieu and Passeron 1977, 73). In other words, individuals are located in an historical, economic, and social context that sets the stage for their subsequent actions. This is how generations come into being – through shared, distinctive, but often unconscious forces that shape the possibilities they see for themselves. Bourdieu's work is especially useful for understanding how, even within a social generation, individuals draw on different resources and see different possibilities for themselves. Hence, we begin our analysis of the making of a generation by exploring the ways in which our young people took up the subject positions that they saw as being available to them.

The young people in our study are introduced through their views on the good life that they would strive to achieve for themselves, as well as their goals, hopes, and dreams for their futures. This enables us to gain an insight into the possibilities that shaped their decisions, that framed their assessments of success or failure, and in terms of which they felt regret or satisfaction, over the fourteen to fifteen years that we have been following their lives. Over the years we have asked these and similar questions, producing a complex picture of the ways in which individuals and groups navigated their lives, held on to or abandoned their dreams, and faced realities they had not anticipated. We have documented the ways in which the hopes and dreams of individuals were actualized in relation to education, work, relationships, family life, and other life events, and this is presented in the chapters that follow this one. We start by exploring their expectations, goals, and values through the thoughts they shared during interviews. Next, we analyse the survey data on their goals over time and on the extent to which life over the years of our study has delivered what they expected.

The Good Life

'All I want is a room somewhere
Far away from the cold night air,
With one enormous chair.'

(Lerner and Loewe 1956)

We quote these lines from a 1950s musical because the dominant theme to emerge from our interviews with our participants in both Canada and Australia was at first sight more compatible with the expectations for modest comfort and a place to call one's own that were prevalent in the 1950s than with those in the 1990s. In 1990, when the forty-six individuals comprising the Canadian interview sample were around eighteen years old and in their last term of high school, they were asked to describe what 'the good life' meant to them. While a handful of respondents equated the good life with a happy or independent life ('Just to be happy and enjoy what you're doing and be around people that you like'; '[Not] hav[ing] to listen to anybody except for yourself ... Have everything you've wanted, money, a good car, freedom'), almost all other respondents described the good life in similar ways: to them it meant 'comfort,' 'beyond the bare necessities,' and generally a life free from strife. The following quotes are representative of about 77 per cent of the responses:

> Having a happy job, a good family, a good income so you don't have to worry about anything, you've got your house paid off and everything, and you've gotta really nice career that you really enjoy, and you've got a husband, and that's probably the good life. Just having everything set, good – very organized and paid for . . . that'd be the good life. No worries. (female)

> The really good life would be to have a suburban home with the lawn, the two-car garage, and two floors, and kids. Basically it's just a comfortable lifestyle, no real rigid social pressures. Enough money to keep my children clothed and fed and to be able to put them . . . into the school. Basically just to be able to support my family . . . being able to live and not having to [think] . . . 'How am I ever going to pay for the mortgage this month?' . . . or 'We don't have enough money to make it to the end of the month.' And get bogged down in debts and mortgages and student loans and this and that. I guess just basically to be happy. Not to come and go, 'Oh no, the work day's over, I have to go home and face my squalling kids, the overbearing wife, the rundown house, and the car that starts 25 per cent of the time.' Not to have to really struggle. (male)

Many of the interviewees' comments were tempered with phrases like 'more than the bare necessities,' but 'not too extravagant':

> The good life for me: well, some place to live, . . . good medical, good dental, and a young RRSP [registered retirement savings plan] to mature over. Just not too much extravagant things. (female)

> The family with two cars: one for mom, one for dad. An average-sized house. Being able to go on your holidays once a year. Two kids, dog, just average, but I don't want to have to worry about money, that's for sure. And I do want to be able to spoil myself and my family – if you want to call it that. I just don't want to have the bare necessities. But I also don't want to be living in this big $500,000 house and have the Corvette outside. I mean, if it happens that way, great, but I'm not really worried about it. (male)

In essence, these comments reflected that they had come to expect the lives that they had experienced so far in their parents' homes. Bare necessities included comfortable accommodation, at least one and often more than one vehicle, children to indulge, and family pets to join along in a happy life.

Several interviewees mentioned work as part of their vision of the good life, but it was by no means central. Work should be interesting and challenging, but not too demanding or routine.

> The good life would be a job that I don't have to bring home with me – well, not all the time – and that I don't have to live for my work, but that gives me a good standard of living, a husband, maybe a kid or two. (female)

> A secure job that's challenging and not too stressful, and a nice home to go home to, and a family. That's it. Just everything and not too big of problems. (male)

None of the respondents described their preferred life worlds as being organized around their jobs or careers. However, one young woman did articulate a more altruistic vision of work: 'Having people, having people acknowledge you for what you're doing. Pleasing people with your work. Being able to help people.'

A few women anticipated the relationship between work and raising a family. As described in more detail elsewhere (Andres 2005), they envisioned an unproblematic transition from completing their education to settling into careers, to establishing families while staying at home or working part-time, through to re-entering the labour force when the time was right.

> Well, finishing university and getting a job and then eventually getting married and then having a few years before I have kids. And I wouldn't work when I had my kids when they were young 'cause I think it's important that there's someone at home to be with your children while they're growing up. (female)

For three individuals their vision of the good life, although similar to those cited above, was tempered by either their own family experiences or the anticipation of trouble down the road. Clearly, some did not grow up in the same comfortable conditions as described by the majority of interviewees above. Their comments have a corrective tone that would re-establish 'the good' in their future lives. For them, quality of family life was central to their vision of the good life.

> A good family that doesn't fight all the time, and with a mother and a father; not just a single parent. That has a fairly comfortable lifestyle, a nice house, at least one car that works, that'll get you around. Able to support two kids so kids can do things like soccer and baseball and take swimming lessons, and do what they want to do, just as long as everybody is happy and has what they want. Then that'd be good. (female)

> Having a family that isn't divorced parents, having kids, living in a good part of town . . . I'm going to make sure [my kids] go to church 'cause that's something that I do, and make sure they go to school . . . Have a job so I can support them. Help them if they want to go to college, be able to give them that. If they want to play sports, be able to give them that . . . When I have a wife – get a car, just being able to live. Not having millions; it's not something I'm interested in. I guess that would be a really good life, but being able to live comfortably and the nice places to live. (male)

> [I] would be free of any problems that I have . . . The sort of feeling where you can go out and do anything, and there is nothing hampering you down, and nothing making you sad all the time . . . I don't have that great of a situation, but I'd be free and I'd be able to think about things more clearly. I'd be able to have a more tactical mind . . . I don't want to have . . . a big house or anything like that; just a place that could be mine. Like a few interesting things . . . things to look at that I collect over a period of time as to what I do. (male)

Four participants ventured beyond the standard dream and described less traditional and material goals:

> I wouldn't mind being known for something . . . I don't like being anonymous. I wouldn't mind . . . writing a book or being in a play or something. Just so you know who I am. (female)

> I wouldn't be living in Vancouver or Canada; I'd be maybe [in] a simple country – not necessarily a third-world country but somewhere where . . . technology's not influencing it. Like when I was back in the Caribbean, that's what I thought was the good life because it was small and very simple. (male)

To me it means finding contentment and doing what you want to do. Basi-
cally what you feel is right for you to do. Other people, of course, would
say it means money and lots of wealth and things like this. I have no time
for money in life, but I realize I'm unusual in that. . . . I want to be able to
live and take care of myself, but I'm not going to worry about going out
and making lots of money for the sake of buying certain cars or certain
houses and things like this. I don't want any. (male)

Maybe going down to Africa and South Africa and maybe doing some
relief work . . . I'm a believer in that you've got to stir things up . . . I'm a big
believer in youth in the environment and Youths for Amnesty and Youth
for Greenpeace . . . I wouldn't mind being known for something . . . My
vision right now is just not to get caught up in the rat race. (male)

Yet, as one young man's comments revealed, even when they were in
high school, the sense of societal acceleration was present: 'You can
never attain all your goals . . . unless you're super rich, and then usually you don't have very many goals. But you can never do everything
in life that you actually want to do. I just find that kind of depressing
sometimes.'

The hopes and goals of the Australian participants were remarkably
consistent with those of their Canadian counterparts. In 1998, when they
were aged about twenty-four, forty-eight of the Australian participants
were interviewed about their hopes, dreams, and aspirations for the
future. Like the Canadians, their goals were for a life with a modest but
sufficient amount of money, involving stable personal relationships, a
place to call home, and a good job or self-sufficiency. For both young
men and women, being in a stable relationship with their partner took a
high priority, as did owning a home. Being self-sufficient also featured,
as did having enough money. However, because they were first interviewed when they were six years older than the Canadian sample, many
of the young Australians already had steady partners and were thinking
about making long-term commitments to them; some were married, and
some had children. About 50 per cent expressed goals that reflected the
wish to be living in modest material comfort with personal and financial
stability. The following quotes are a sample of this group's responses:

I want a better car to drive (got a crappy old Commodore at the moment),
a better home to live in. Started thinking about family and stuff, but really
haven't talked to my girlfriend about it. (male)

Have a home of my own, with my own car and my own dog and a wife and family. And this will be paid for with my own business. (male)

Marriage is at the back of my mind; my boyfriend seems pretty interested. Having a family and raising them while still having work would be nice. (female)

Like their Canadian counterparts, a small minority wanted to contribute to making a difference for others:

I would like to be living somewhere comfortable with my girlfriend and to be in work where I would be satisfied that I am making a contribution to people's lives and making the world a better place. (male)

I would like to get my house built and feel secure and do as much as I can for the Maltese community in a voluntary capacity. (female)

Four were keen simply to leave the place where they grew up, without having a clear sense of what they might do beyond that, as the following quotes illustrate:

Get out of [my country town], get out of Victoria, get out of Australia! Have a look at the World! (female)

In the long term I would like to move out of the area. It's just the dumps. Things are so down you can see it on people's faces when you go to the downtown shopping centre. (male)

My goal is to not have to return to [my country town]. (female)

A very small minority expressed a desire to achieve at a more exceptional level. For example, one young man said that he was not 'greedy for success, just keen. I would like to be the next [large successful family-owned business] in the cabinet-making industry.' A few others shared similar goals for achievement:

My goal is to get first-class honours and have my thesis published. I hope that my family and friends will continue being supportive of me. (female)

> I want to move up the ladder and be an executive, which would take me away from retail. I would like to be 'counter manager of the year,' which would build up my profile with [cosmetic company]. (female)

Another small group was feeling lost or even a bit desperate. The following quotes are illustrative:

> I haven't been thinking about goals – just getting through every day, then every week, then every month, and then take some time out at the end of the year to recover. (male)

> Working such long shifts and coming home at all hours, the only goal is to get by from day to day. Sometimes we can sit back and look at where we are going. Hopefully things will level out and we can have more children. (female)

One young woman explicitly drew attention to the acceleration of time:

> I want to make more time to enjoy myself. Sometimes I look around and I wonder where time goes. I feel like I'm getting older and I'm not making the most of my youth – it's spent trying to make ends meet.

Comments about time foreshadow the competing demands that our samples were about to experience. For some of the Australian participants, Rosa's characterization of 'accelerated rates of social change in all spheres of life' (Rosa 2003, 11) is an apt description of their experiences, and this was emerging as a challenge to achieving the good life. We discuss this in more detail in chapter 8.

However, there was a large group of Australians whose responses differed from the Canadians' hopes and dreams. Of those interviewed, 29 per cent expressed their goals for the future entirely in terms of work. There are two explanations that we would offer for this difference. First, being six years older than the Canadians were when they were interviewed on this topic (that is, around twenty-four years old rather than eighteen), the young Australians were at a point in their lives where work was taking a more central place. Second, the two groups were asked slightly different questions. The young Canadians were asked to describe the good life whereas the Australians were asked to describe their goals for the future. The former may have elicited a more 'rounded' response, and the latter may have been taken to refer to more instrumental things, although this was not always the case. One young Australian woman's goal was to have a farm, and she had a 'dream of walking through the paddocks with my husband'; another saw her goal as to 'just enjoy myself and not let things get me down. Find a man and settle down.'

Those who focused on work as their goal in life had different reasons for doing so. The majority focused on work as their main goal because they saw this as a strategy for achieving security and financial independence. Some wanted to achieve financial security in order to take care of their parents, and others wanted to be successful in order to make their parents proud of them. The work-focused responses were made by slightly more young women than young men, so we do not interpret the focus on work as simply an expression of traditional gendered approaches to life. To the contrary, we would see the emphasis on work as a direct outcome of the opportunities that educated young women saw for independence and autonomy. The following quotes illustrate these responses:

> My study is my means of securing my future. I would like to find work in the academic field if I can, and in the meantime I will work as hard as possible. (female)

> I want to make my parents proud of my achievements. To have my own paradise and make a thriving business. (male)

> Financial independence and job security are very important to me. I would like to be able to take care of my parents in their retirement. I would like to know that they spend the rest of their lives in comfort and happiness. (female)

In bringing to life the personal stories of our participants, these quotes illustrate the common threads that run through their narratives, as well as highlighting the differences among them. Their stories reveal strong lines of convergence between the young Canadians and Australians in terms of what they want from life. For the majority, the good life is focused on living in comfort with sufficient resources, establishing long-term relationships, and having a home. However, young Australians were more likely than their Canadian counterparts to focus on work in order to reach this dream. They were also more likely to put the achievement of the good life on hold in order to travel.

We attribute these differences to a number of factors. The first has to do with the labour market. In Canada (recent history aside) the worst economic recession since the 1930s occurred between 1981 and 1986 (Boyd and Pryor 1989; Myles, Picot, and Wannell 1988). The Canadian sample were too young to experience its effects directly and instead were embarking on the first part of their adult lives on a upswing of the economy. After the 1990 recession in Australia, the government de-regulated many industries, resulting in a period of rapid change as companies downsized or foundered, and when the conservative government was elected in 1996, new industrial-relations legislation created an era of adverse conditions for workers. By 1998–99, this would have heightened the Australians' awareness of the precariousness of employment and may have influenced many to focus on getting employment in their chosen area. Compared with the Australians, the Canadian cohort were less anxious about getting work. In chapter 6 we provide a detailed analysis of the work experiences of our participants. The second factor is cultural. Australian youth have traditionally sought to explore the world beyond the shores of their continent, and for many of the participants in our study, travelling before 'settling down' would have been seen as an expectation by their families and as a reward for the years they put into study.

We continued to ask our participants questions about the good life and their goals and dreams over a fifteen-year period. The interview data has highlighted nuances and differences in their responses. We now turn to the survey data that enables us to go into detail in a different way and to explore the extent to which they feel they have achieved what they set out to do. For our analysis of the survey data we have chosen to present their responses in terms of two key dimensions: (a) the earning, or not, of university credentials and (b) gender.

Divergent Pathways

In analysing their views on how they fared, we begin with the Australian cohort. In 1996, when they were around twenty-two years old, the Australians were asked to describe their state of well-being since leaving high school five years earlier. The analysis is conducted by gender and a two-category variable of post-secondary completion status in 1999. Overall, their responses show the emergence of different groups within the cohort, based largely on educational level and on gender as

Table 2
Characteristics of life since leaving high school, at age 22, in Australia, 1996

	Females		Males	
	Often %	Not at all %	Often %	Not at all %
Less than university degree				
Happy	74	1	63	0
Anxious	20	12	17	17
Unpredictable	17	24	18	33
Smooth	21	18	30	17
Dull	4	53	5	42
Unrewarding	5	60	7	48
Exciting	43	5	34	6
Much as I expected	23	27	16	15
Different than I expected	17	21	17	25
Better than I expected	27	17	17	18
Worse than I expected	8	50	5	49
University degree or greater				
Happy	74	0	73	0
Anxious	23	6	13	8
Unpredictable	16	28	18	25
Smooth	26	16	31	11
Dull	2	56	4	46
Unrewarding	4	68	6	48
Exciting	45	3	39	4
Much as I expected	22	23	20	21
Different than I expected	17	18	23	16
Better than I expected	28	11	30	11
Worse than I expected	6	47	4	54

well as national differences. Although they held very similar hopes and dreams early on, their experiences have diverged over time. The group that found it the most difficult to achieve their expectations comprised young men with less than a university education.

Table 2 portrays their responses to words that describe their subjective experience of life, such as *exciting, dull, smooth, happy, anxious,* and many others. They were asked to rate their responses to these terms on a three-point scale: *often, sometimes,* and *not at all.* The table describes the responses for *often* and *not at all.* However, we note that *sometimes* stood out for some groups. Almost all respondents described themselves as happy often, and over 40 per cent remarked that life was

indeed exciting. The young men who had less than a university education were the exception. Women were considerably more inclined
to indicate that life was not at all dull or unrewarding. The majority in
all groups experienced anxiousness, unpredictability, and smoothness
sometimes rather than in the other two extreme categories. Around
50 per cent in all groups reported that life was not at all worse than
they had expected, and only a small proportion said it was often so.
University-educated males responded the most positively to this
question. However, around 40 per cent indicated that sometimes life
was worse than they had expected. The majority reported that life
was sometimes different than they had expected. Around 29 percent
of university-educated young women and men, compared to only
27 per cent of non-university-educated women and 18 per cent of
non-university-educated men, indicated that life was often better than
expected, and the university-educated groups were less likely to say
that it was not at all better than they had expected.

Although the patterns are similar across groups, it is notable that
Australian males with non-university credentials were clearly the least
content. They reported considerably lower levels of happiness and
were less likely to say that life was not at all dull or unrewarding and
often exciting. In addition, they were the least likely to say that life was
better than they had expected.

One year later, at around age twenty-three, the Australians were
asked to describe their feelings about the extent to which they were
achieving their main priority in life. Their responses, as reported
in table 3, were rather lukewarm. Although most refuted the statement
that 'it's proving difficult to feel fulfilment,' relatively few claimed
that they were finding real fulfilment about what they were doing.
In this regard, university-educated females were the most positive.
Males were more likely than females to report that they did not feel
like they were achieving what they wanted. Surprisingly, only 20 to
25 per cent overall reported that they expected things to improve in the
near future, and only 16 per cent of university-educated males agreed
with this. The responses of this group of young men had a ring of pes-
simism about them.

In the following year, 1998, when they were aged around twenty-
four, the Australians were asked to rate the extent to which several
statements about work and earnings, family, relationships, and participation in other spheres of life were important. In describing their
responses, we report the extreme categories *low* and *very high* of a

Table 3
Feelings about main priority, at age 23, in Australia, 1997

| | Non-university or less | | University degree or greater | |
	Females % yes	Males % yes	Females % yes	Males % yes
I'm happy enough with where I've reached	23	15	28	18
I feel real fulfilment about what I am doing	20	15	20	16
It's proving difficult to feel fulfilment	6	7	4	7
I don't feel yet that I am achieving what I want	19	32	20	31
I expect things to improve in the near future	20	22	25	16

four-point scale.[1] Here we see the beginning of a pattern of placing an emphasis on steady work but not on either earning a lot of money or having a career, which continues through to the last phase of the study for the Australian sample in 2006 (see table 4). As we will see, this is not the case with the Canadian sample, who tended to place approximately equal value on such elements. Within this pattern there was some variation. For example, Australian women put more emphasis than did men on having a steady job, but considerably less emphasis on earning a lot of money. There is added complexity in the pattern for men with university credentials to place the least importance on steady work and for women in the same category to place the most importance on steady work. University-educated women in Australia were the most likely of all groups to rate involvement in work as a career as *very high*.

In other studies we have attributed the apparent disjuncture in the Australians' attitudes to work, money, and career to a shift in the meaning of *career* (Dwyer and Wyn 2001). As we have discussed above, the young Australians at this stage were facing the full effects of workplace restructuring, and this created considerable uncertainty. In this context, having steady employment is an understandable priority. The uncertainty around workplaces and the trend for employers to want 'flexible'

---

1 The categories of the four-point scale for this question are *very high, high, medium,* and *low*.

Table 4
Elements of personal importance, at age 24, in Australia, 1998

	Females		Males	
	Low %	Very high %	Low %	Very high %
Less than university degree				
Having a steady job	3	61	4	55
Involvement in work as a career	4	23	5	27
Earning a lot of money	3	16	4	26
Owning your own home	14	44	8	45
Marriage or living with a partner	16	36	14	30
Having children	32	25	36	12
Family relationships	3	62	1	43
Developing friendships	1	42	3	41
Staying in my local area	33	13	26	7
Involvement in leisure time activities	0	28	3	47
Involvement in community activities	31	7	31	7
Travelling to different places	7	42	8	23
Working to correct social problems	30	7	40	4
University degree or greater				
Having a steady job	1	65	1	51
Involvement in work as a career	2	35	2	27
Earning a lot of money	8	12	9	21
Owning your own home	12	40	14	38
Marriage or living with a partner	10	38	16	27
Having children	26	23	30	15
Family relationships	1	65	0	51
Developing friendships	0	47	2	38
Staying in my local area	39	10	44	5
Involvement in leisure time activities	0	39	6	41
Involvement in community activities	21	7	28	5
Travelling to different places	5	38	11	33
Working to correct social problems	18	11	24	9

work practices meant that the idea of a career became problematic. It also fostered a fairly pragmatic approach among many of the educated participants, encouraging them to focus on other areas of life experience, including travel, and to take a strong interest in personal development because they experienced workplaces as relatively unstable.

As reported in table 4, around 30 per cent of men and just under 40 per cent of women rated marriage or living with a partner as very high. However, all groups rated travel considerably higher than having children. This is consistent with childbearing patterns over time, as described in chapter 7. Developing friendships was important, as were family relationships. 'Staying in my local area' was considered not important by at least a third of the entire sample, which suggests at least being open to being geographically mobile; geographic stability was least important for the university-educated young women and men. This finding relates to Bauman's claim (2001) that the class of workers who are able to continuously and quickly reinvent and readjust themselves is rewarded with many opportunities and choices. In chapters 6, 7, and 8, we determine whether, indeed, those who are able and willing to be mobile and flexible 'find the new lightness nothing but a fertile and thoroughly enjoyable condition' (Bauman 2001, 12). Also, we demonstrate whether this 'lightness and flexibility' leads to precariousness and misery for those who are immobile, have little or no ability to reinvent themselves, or both.

Another trend that we see in table 4 and subsequent tables is the lack of interest in community activities and social problems. The importance of community involvement and working to correct social problems was rated as very high by less than 10 per cent of all groups. Conversely, involvement in leisure activities was rated as very high by over 30 per cent of all groups. However, there are differences in the response to the statement 'working to correct social problems' between those with and without university degrees, with the former group slightly more likely to rate this statement as very high but less likely to rate it as low. However, at best, only 10 per cent considered social problems a very high priority.

In summing up where our Australian participants have reached by the age of twenty-four, we can point to the emergence of some very clear patterns and quite distinctive attitudes. For many, their hopes of creating a stable life were proving difficult to achieve. They bore the imprint of the changes to working conditions that were implemented by the government of the time. For university-educated women, these effects are seen in their determination to remain in careers that they have worked hard to achieve. University-educated males, like all other groups, were more likely to respond to employment uncertainty by acknowledging that 'a career' would be difficult to achieve, and focused instead on having steady work. The effort of managing these aspects of their lives left them little time to be involved in civic life, but even so, this generation of Australians have focused on their own development and especially on investing in learning (both formal and informal) to

enable them to work. We also see the emergence of distinctive differences between some groups of young men and women and in terms
of their educational qualifications. These patterns recur throughout
the different topics that we consider in this book. Here we highlight,
compared with all other groups, the high levels of dissatisfaction that
the young men with no university education had with what they had
achieved.

We now turn to the Canadian sample to discuss the next phase of our
participants' lives. When they were around twenty-eight years old, the
Canadian participants responded to a survey that asked similar questions to those described in table 4. Their responses show the emergence
of national differences between the Australians and the Canadians
in their values and expectations in relation to work. Unlike the
responses reported by the Australian sample (who were around four
years younger when they responded to these questions; see table 4),
the Canadians placed importance on 'having enough money to live
well' (see table 5). This value was more or less equal in importance to
'succeeding at work or a career.' Almost none of the Canadians rated
either statement as unimportant, and around 50 per cent rated both
values as very important. Canadian university-educated women, like
their Australian counterparts, were most likely to rate the importance
of succeeding at a career as very high.

All groups rated relationships highly, that is, time spent with a
spouse or partner, children, parents, and friends. They also rated living a physically and psychologically healthy lifestyle highly. However,
men were considerably less likely to rate the latter as very important.
Women with university degrees were the most likely (48 per cent) to
rate 'developing an independent lifestyle' as very important, compared
with 39 per cent of men with the same educational credentials and
40 per cent of women and 35 per cent of men who had not completed
university studies.

Similar to the Australians, few Canadian respondents rated 'involvement in community affairs' as very important. Few valued the importance of 'living in a culturally diverse community.' Participation in
religious activities was rated as not at all important by 26 to 37 per
cent of the sample.

When asked to rate which value was the most important (table 6),
the highest proportion from all groups considered time together with
a spouse or partner as most important. Twenty-six percent of women
without a university education considered quality time to spend

Table 5
Importance of personal values, at age 28, in Canada, 1998

	Females		Males	
	Not at all important %	Very important %	Not at all important %	Very important %
Less than university degree				
Succeeding at work or a career	1	48	2	53
Having enough money to live well	1	56	2	53
Time together with my spouse/partner	1	83	1	69
Quality time to spend with my children	1	63	2	50
A good relationship with my parents	2	78	1	64
Developing and maintaining friend-ships	1	67	5	59
Living a psychologically healthy lifestyle	0	74	1	60
Developing an independent lifestyle	1	40	1	35
Living a physically healthy lifestyle	0	61	1	59
Regular involvement in organized learning activities	1	16	2	16
Involvement in community affairs	3	5	5	10
Participation in religious activities	26	16	36	11
Time for leisure activities	1	59	2	65
Living in a culturally diverse community	5	17	8	14
Respect for the natural environment	1	52	1	56
University degree or greater				
Succeeding at work or a career	0	63	2	60
Having enough money to live well	0	48	1	38
Time together with my spouse/partner	0	77	1	72
Quality time to spend with my children	0	54	4	45
A good relationship with my parents	0	82	1	65
Developing and maintaining friend-ships	1	73	1	71
Living a psychologically healthy lifestyle	0	84	1	65
Developing an independent lifestyle	3	48	1	39
Living a physically healthy lifestyle	1	74	2	68
Regular involvement in organized learning activities	0	26	1	16
Involvement in community affairs	1	9	1	9
Participation in religious activities	26	14	37	12
Time for leisure activities	0	67	1	66
Living in a culturally diverse community	3	20	5	18
Respect for the natural environment	1	58	1	56

Table 6
The degree of importance of personal values, at age 28, in Canada, 1998

	Females		Males	
	Most important %	Least important %	Most important %	Least important %
Less than university degree				
Succeeding at work or a career	4	9	10	7
Having enough money to live well	4	13	6	5
Time together with my spouse/partner	29	3	19	3
Quality time to spend with my children	26	2	10	3
A good relationship with my parents	4	0	6	2
Developing and maintaining friend- ships	13	2	15	1
Developing an independent lifestyle	3	5	4	2
Living a physically healthy lifestyle	3	3	7	1
Living a psychologically healthy lifestyle	5	1	3	2
Regular involvement in organized learning activities	0	6	0	5
Involvement in community affairs	1	9	0	11
Participation in religious activities	4	35	4	45
Time for leisure activities	3	3	9	2
Living in a culturally diverse com- munity	1	6	1	11
Respect for the natural environment	1	3	2	2
University degree or greater				
Succeeding at work or a career	10	6	12	5
Having enough money to live well	1	12	5	8
Time together with my spouse/partner	27	4	24	8
Quality time to spend with my children	9	2	3	3
A good relationship with my parents	4	2	1	0
Developing and maintaining friend- ships	19	2	14	2
Developing an independent lifestyle	4	2	3	4
Living a physically healthy lifestyle	6	3	9	1
Living a psychologically healthy lifestyle	4	1	5	2
Regular involvement in organized learning activities	0	6	1	2
Involvement in community affairs	0	9	1	8
Participation in religious activities	8	34	3	40
Time for leisure activities	4	4	14	2
Living in a culturally diverse com- munity	0	9	1	8
Respect for the natural environment	0	3	1	5

Table 7
Rating of goals to aim for in adult life, at age 30, in Australia, 2004

	Females		Males	
	Low %	Very high %	Low %	Very high %
Less than university degree				
To have financial security	0	73	0	64
To make a lot of money	10	10	9	14
To be better off financially than my parents are	13	24	15	16
To have a special relationship with someone	1	74	0	68
To care and provide for a family	7	68	5	65
To pursue a life of pleasure	8	14	14	18
To live up to religious or spiritual ideals	54	15	54	7
To help people who are in need	13	9	15	10
To be active in working for a better society	18	11	12	10
University degree or greater				
To have financial security	0	74	0	67
To make a lot of money	20	5	15	9
To be better off financially than my parents are	20	17	24	18
To have a special relationship with someone	0	80	1	58
To care and provide for a family	13	65	9	56
To pursue a life of pleasure	15	11	25	8
To live up to religious or spiritual ideals	47	11	54	11
To help people who are in need	6	15	20	6
To be active in working for a better society	10	15	15	4

with children as most important; however, this was not the case for other groups. Developing and maintaining friendships was rated by between 13 and 19 per cent as most important. Participation in religious activities was considered the least important by 34 to 45 per cent of respondents. Almost none of the sample considered involvement in community affairs or living in a culturally diverse community to be their most important value.

Similar questions were posed to the Australian participants when they were around thirty years old (table 7). Consistent with the findings in table 4 but not with the responses of Canadians reported in table 5, most respondents rated having financial security as very high and none as low; however, only a small proportion considered making a lot of money as very high. Men without university credentials valued making a lot of money the most (14 per cent), and women with university credentials the least (5 per cent). Less than 24 per cent of all groups strove to be better off financially than their parents. All respondents rated having a special relationship with someone and caring and providing for a family as very high in importance. Living up to religious ideals was rated as low by 47 per cent or more of the sample. Being civilly or socially minded through helping people in need or working for a better society remained a low priority, particularly for university-educated men.

In tables 8 and 9 responses to questions almost identical to those posed five years earlier to the Canadian participants are reported. Now, at around aged thirty-three, some shifts in values are evident.

Interestingly, across all groups, the importance placed on succeeding at work or a career and having enough money to live well had declined over time. However, as in the earlier time period, almost none of the Canadians rated either statement as unimportant. Unlike for the Australians, succeeding at work and earning money to live well continued to go hand in hand. Relationships with partners, children, parents, and friends continued to be rated as very important by the vast majority. And, although they rated living a physically and psychologically healthy lifestyle highly, men were considerably less likely to rate psychological health as very important. Participation in religious activities continued to have a low priority with 26 to 40 per cent of the sample. The majority of university-educated women (56 per cent) rated 'a socially just society' as very important (compared with no more than 42 per cent of the other groups).

It is especially noteworthy to single out the shifts in values over time by women with university credentials. In 1998, when they were aged around twenty-eight, 63 per cent of women from this group rated succeeding at work or a career as most important; five years later this figure had declined to 52 per cent. Similarly, there was a significant shift in the importance of spending quality time with children by women with university credentials – from 54 per cent in 1998 to 72 per cent in 2003 – and of living an independent lifestyle – from 48 per cent in 1998 to 37 per cent in 2003.They were much more likely than other groups, especially men, to rate achieving a balance between work and non-work activities as very important. These findings suggest that their interest in work as

Table 8
Importance of personal values, at age 33, in Canada, 2003

	Females		Males	
	Not at all important %	Very important %	Not at all important %	Very important %
Less than university degree				
Succeeding at work or a career	2	37	1	40
Having enough money to live well	1	46	2	38
Time together with my spouse/partner	1	76	1	70
Quality time to spend with my children	4	73	4	67
A good relationship with my parents	1	71	2	51
Developing and maintaining friendships	0	65	2	60
Developing an independent lifestyle	1	27	5	28
Living a physically healthy lifestyle	1	61	2	49
Living a psychologically healthy lifestyle	3	67	1	49
Achieving a balance between work & non-work activities	1	61	4	54
Regular involvement in organized learning activities	2	8	6	10
Involvement in community affairs	2	6	4	7
Participation in religious activities	33	13	40	16
Time for leisure activities	1	46	1	45
Living in a culturally diverse community	4	14	8	12
Respect for the natural environment	1	40	1	40
A socially just society	1	38	2	38
University degree or greater				
Succeeding at work or a career	1	52	1	50
Having enough money to live well	0	44	0	35
Time together with my spouse/partner	1	76	1	71
Quality time to spend with my children	2	72	6	64
A good relationship with my parents	0	72	1	60
Developing and maintaining friendships	0	76	1	55
Developing an independent lifestyle	1	37	1	26
Living a physically healthy lifestyle	1	68	1	54
Living a psychologically healthy lifestyle	1	77	1	61
Achieving a balance between work & non-work activities	0	78	1	66
Regular involvement in organized learning activities	1	14	5	7
Involvement in community affairs	0	10	4	9
Participation in religious activities	26	16	40	9
Time for leisure activities	2	53	1	54
Living in a culturally diverse community	1	21	5	18
Respect for the natural environment	1	46	1	40
A socially just society	0	56	1	42

Table 9
The degree of importance of personal values, at age 33, in Canada, 2003

	Females		Males	
	Most important %	Least important %	Most important %	Least important %
Less than university degree				
Succeeding at work or a career	3	4	7	5
Having enough money to live well	4	6	3	6
Time together with my spouse/partner	23	4	25	3
Quality time to spend with my children	39	3	22	2
A good relationship with my parents	2	1	4	1
Developing and maintaining friendships	6	2	10	1
Developing an independent lifestyle	1	4	1	2
Living a physically healthy lifestyle	2	2	4	1
Living a psychologically healthy lifestyle	8	1	6	1
Achieving a balance between work & non-work activities	4	5	7	3
Regular involvement in organized learning activities	1	7	1	5
Involvement in community affairs	1	9	1	12
Participation in religious activities	3	40	2	47
Time for leisure activities	0	5	2	1
Living in a culturally diverse community	0	4	1	5
Respect for the natural environment	0	1	1	1
A socially just society	0	0	0	0
University degree or greater				
Succeeding at work or a career	4	6	8	3
Having enough money to live well	1	6	3	4
Time together with my spouse/partner	21	4	24	2
Quality time to spend with my children	31	2	23	1
A good relationship with my parents	1	1	2	1
Developing and maintaining friendships	13	2	6	1
Developing an independent lifestyle	2	2	1	2
Living a physically healthy lifestyle	5	4	6	4
Living a psychologically healthy lifestyle	4	2	3	1
Achieving a balance between work & non-work activities	6	4	10	5
Regular involvement in organized learning activities	0	4	0	11
Involvement in community affairs	1	7	1	6
Participation in religious activities	6	37	2	48
Time for leisure activities	1	4	6	4
Living in a culturally diverse community	0	6	0	4
Respect for the natural environment	0	4	0	1
A socially just society	0	0	0	0

Table 10
Rating of what would be needed to enhance well-being, at age 33,
in Canada, 2003

	Females		Males	
	Strongly agree %	Strongly disagree %	Strongly agree %	Strongly disagree %
Less than university degree				
More leisure time	37	1	35	1
More family time	34	2	35	1
More time to devote to work	1	15	4	15
More money	41	1	36	4
More supportive workplace	12	5	12	2
More supportive immediate family	8	11	6	12
More supportive extended family	3	5	4	10
More help with child care	7	3	3	5
More help with elder care	3	1	4	6
More post-secondary education	9	9	12	15
University degree or greater				
More leisure time	38	1	41	1
More family time	24	1	38	1
More time to devote to work	3	13	2	20
More money	29	1	26	5
More supportive workplace	10	3	8	5
More supportive immediate family	4	13	4	23
More supportive extended family	4	11	3	22
More help with child care	8	1	6	6
More help with elder care	1	4	3	5
More post-secondary education	4	14	5	17

a career was being eroded by an increased focus on family. In chapter 7 we explore family formation patterns and the realities of juggling work and family in more detail.

In 2003, respondents were again asked to rate which value was the most important (table 9). Quality time to spend with children was the most important for the largest proportion of women, whereas time together with a spouse or partner was the most important for men. The second most popular answer for women was spending time with a partner; for men it was quality time with their children. Over time, developing and maintaining friendships lost its importance; still, 10 per cent of men without a university background and 13 per cent of women with university credentials reported that it was their most important value. Over time, religious activities too lost ground with all groups, and few considered involvement in community activities as their most important value. Not one single Canadian rated 'a socially just society' to be her or his most important value. Also, 'living in a culturally diverse community' fared almost as poorly.

Finally, in 2003 the Canadian sample was asked the following question: 'In order to enhance your well-being, what would you need?'

Table 10 shows that no more than 4 per cent indicated that they would need more time to devote to work. In fact, 13 to 20 per cent strongly disagreed with this statement, and the university educated males were the most likely to strongly disagree. Instead, more leisure time, more family time, and more money were the ingredients identified as being important to their well-being. We examine these dynamics more closely in the next chapters.

Conclusion

These hopes and dreams are a fitting point of departure for our quest to understand the way in which these young people have shaped their generation. Their views set the scene for the deeper analysis of their attitudes and their actions in the following chapters, but it is important to reflect on the emerging story at this point. Our young participants set out in the late 1980s and early 1990s in a time of rapid social change as the economies of Canada and Australia were shifting gear and the role of education took on unprecedented significance. Their personal goals and visions of the good life at the outset reflected relatively modest expectations, but in the act of reaching for these goals they have shaped a new generation.

They share some very clear characteristics within and across the two countries, including the impact of processes of 'individualization' (Beck and Beck-Gernsheim 2002) – which is evident in their focus on fulfilling their personal goals and development – and an orientation towards family life and friendships, at the expense of community or political involvement. However, there are differences and complexities within and across groups. Some groups felt more satisfied with where they had arrived than did others, even if their definition of the good life has changed along the way. This difference between groups is a theme that develops in greater depth as we progress through the book, but which warrants further consideration here.

The goals and achievements of one group of our participants – young women with university education – show the most significant effects of the policies discussed in chapter 3. In one sense, they provide the best evidence of the success of these policies. Although all groups have increased their educational participation, the young women who gained university degrees are literally 'trailblazers' who established new patterns of life based on educational achievement and the establishment of careers. In achieving these goals, they, more than any other group, have placed a high priority on maintaining their careers, especially during their mid twenties. They are not in the majority, but their presence in the professions and in the new globally connected service sector has given them visibility, which also gives them a symbolic role. They are the 'can-do' girls (Harris 2004) whose capacity to embrace education and learning, and whose determination to adjust to changing labour-market demands, aligns them very closely with the kind of person that the education and labour-market policies aimed to create. Their relative success and sense of satisfaction with what they have achieved are based in part on their capacity to reinvent themselves and respond to the need for 'flexible' labour. This is what Bauman (2001, 12) describes (perhaps over-optimistically) as a 'new lightness' that is 'nothing but a fertile and thoroughly enjoyable condition.' Their capacities to engage effectively with the new employment opportunities and conditions also align closely with the workers that Rosa (1998) describes in a discussion of the relationship between individuals and neoliberal states. His study argues that the ideal neoliberal subjects must see themselves – and be taught to see themselves – primarily as consumers and producers and thus strive for the dual purposes of working in professional careers *and* continuing to increase their levels of consumption. Rather than their choosing to focus on, for example, artistic pursuits or religious endeavours, 'the collective definition of the good society *must* be such that economic efficiency is given the highest priority' (1998, 203). To the extent that this group epitomizes such qualities, we could call this group *generation-makers*.

While young women with university education are seen as generation-makers, the young men who have not achieved a post-secondary education are positioned over time as *outsiders* who feel a lack of satisfaction about what they have been able to achieve. We see this pattern as especially strong among the Australian males, who were the least likely of all groups to say that they were content and who were often unsatisfied with their lives – but it is also visible in the Canadian data. Early on, this group of young men was the only group that did not find life 'exciting.' The importance of educational credentials and changes in labour markets have disadvantaged this group more than any other. Far from being empowered by these circumstances, its members have become outsiders within their own generation because of their lack of capacity to reinvent themselves and respond in a flexible way to the precarious nature of labour markets. In one sense they are refugees from the changing world. As the policies predicted, this group has become structurally dislocated – unable to move with the times and unable to get work in occupations that have become outmoded. The struggle that they have faced to achieve their hopes, and which is evident by the early 2000s, underlines the predictions made in the late 1980s by writers such Coleman and Husén (1985). They forewarned that, without the protection of educational credentials, some groups would become the 'new underclass.' Our research does support the view that the demand for new types of labour-market skills has indeed led to disadvantage for some groups of young people as they struggle to find their way through structures and policies that are not designed to help or support them, and who, like their more educated peers, need to find gainful employment to support themselves and their families. As Bourdieu (1987, 14) points out, it is critical to examine the implications of the 'performative power of naming' because 'the symbolic struggle between agents is for the most part carried out through the mediation of professionals of representation' who 'have the power to make groups and . . . institute them.'

We find Bourdieu's work useful for highlighting the differential use of resources that produces these outcomes. By focusing on the two groups we are drawing attention to the way in which, against the social and economic conditions of the early 1990s, gender and class have powerfully shaped the possibilities for being. As we will see in detail in chapter 5, education was a resource that young women from higher socio-economic families could access readily, and their existing social capital aligned well with the highly individualized subject of neoliberalism. Other studies have highlighted the way in which this process works, emphasizing the 'highly honed reflexivity' of middle-class girls (McLeod and Yates 2006, 7). This capacity enabled them to self-monitor, to be aware of how their actions in the present positioned them for desired futures, and to construct their own biographies that fit closely with the 'entrepreneurial Self.' This is a form of subjectivity that produces young people whose actions will be 'rational, autonomous and responsible' and whose dispositions are 'free, prudent and active' (Kelly 2006, 18). The group that has least been able to draw on resources comprised young men without a post-secondary education, which has arguably been a barrier to enabling them to achieve the goals that they shared with their peers.

Nevertheless, this picture is partial and leaves many question unanswered. Has the investment in education delivered the benefits they expected? What are the unintended consequences of the focus that many of this generation have placed on work? What has been the impact of the passing of time on the trajectories and outcomes for the different groups? For example, while the young women who are generation-makers have clearly managed the transition from education to the labour market, how well do they manage the transition to parenthood? How do national circumstances have an impact on their lives? In the following chapters we look more deeply into their generational patterns, commonalities, and exceptions by exploring in detail the way in which their lives unfolded in terms of education, work, and family life. Finally we return to some of the themes raised in this chapter to look at how our generation are faring through a consideration of their well-being.

5   Education: Changing Structures and Changing Opportunities

In this chapter we focus on young people's pathways through post-secondary education by comparing their experiences in the context of the secondary and post-secondary systems of British Columbia and Victoria. Within the changing policy and economic contexts that we outlined earlier we trace the educational trajectories of these young people and reveal how individuals' choices and options are directly affected by the distinctive educational structures of each country and by other forces, including economic climate and family background. At the same time we show how individuals shape their own lives within these structures and contexts. This chapter shows the direct effects of global policy and economic forces, which are reflected through the remarkable similarity in rates of post-secondary participation. It also shows the effects of local conditions, which are reflected in the experiences of young Victorians as they attempted to negotiate a poorly articulated post-secondary system, experiences that are relatively chaotic compared with those of their British Columbian counterparts. Young people's beliefs and reflections on the importance of education reveal an overwhelming belief in the necessity of education, but here too there are striking differences based on their experiences within distinctive post-secondary systems. Class and gender have had a significant impact on the 'choices' that young people can make about their educational 'options.' We explore the significance of families in the processes that create different outcomes for young people. As Bourdieu famously identified in his studies in the early 1970s, families provide resources, both material and cultural, that support and equip young people differentially to manage the opportunities and risks of their times, including formal and informal learning. Our analysis enables us to draw conclusions about the social processes, institutional structures, policies, and practices that promote access to and completion of post-secondary studies. We capitalize on the intricate detail of our survey and the interview data sets to explore the complexities of negotiating post-secondary education and reveal the impact of government policies, local economic conditions, and history.

In chapter 3 we highlighted the policy directions that have set the stage for post-secondary participation of both Canadian and Australian young adults, but it is important to reiterate the specific policies that have had an impact on the options of the young people in our studies. Although policy documents in both countries have been strong in advancing a neoliberal ideology and have clearly identified specific groups for enhancing their access, neither country has invested extensively in data collection endeavours to evaluate the extent to which their policy goals have been met. (See chapter 9 for a discussion of data collection strategies and the limitations of existing databases.) In general, the nature of post-secondary participation and attainment remains unanalysed.

The First Steps: Tracing Patterns of Change and Continuity

We have drawn attention to the declining rates of early school leaving and the overall increasing rates of high school graduation in both Canada and Australia (see chapter 3). However, it is important to acknowledge that these common patterns occurred against a backdrop of structural and organizational differences at the secondary level in each country. In Canada curricular differentiation was and is not the result of early and rigid selection, tracking, or sorting schemes. At the end of junior secondary school (Grade 10), students choose courses based on their interests, abilities demonstrated to date, and planned educational paths as formulated to this point in their high school careers. Courses taken and completed in the final two years of secondary school (grades 11 and 12) are contingent on previous educational successes and evolving educational and career interests. The articulated or 'seamless' structure of the post-secondary education system for young Canadians in the late 1980s meant that the Canadians in this study were able to embark on a variety of routes into and through the post-secondary education system (Andres and Adamuti-Trache 2008). By contrast, the Australian participants entered a post-secondary education system that was relatively fragmented (Australian Education Council 1991). 'Careers education' was relatively undeveloped in schools in the late 1980s (Stokes,

Wierenga, and Wyn 2004), and there was poor articulation between the final years of school and a post-secondary sector that included universities, colleges, and technical and further education (TAFE) institutions. Indeed, a report on student pathways in the early 1990s found that the structure of secondary schooling created barriers to the TAFE option being available to school students in their final years, because of the emphasis on students achieving a Year 12 Certificate that was oriented towards university entry (Dwyer, Poynter, and Tyler 1997). Articulation across different sectors of the post-secondary education system was poor, and it was not until the late 1990s that a more effective means of articulating TAFE and university studies was introduced. For the Australian participants, once the decision was taken to go to university or a TAFE institution, it appeared to be final. The Australians who completed their secondary education had to contend with a tradition of school completion leading 'naturally' to a university pathway. Furthermore, to make matters even more complex for the young Australians in our study, the Australian system of allocating a set number of government-subsidized places to each university meant that in 1991 the demand for these places outpaced the supply, and many were forced to enter the TAFE sector instead in order to have a post-secondary education. Although the Australian participants ultimately took up a variety of routes, they were largely required to work out these pathways for themselves.

Despite these differences in the structure of the secondary and post-secondary systems, almost identical participation patterns in some form of post-secondary education by Canadian and Australian young adults within one year out of high school are evident. Table 11 shows that the vast majority of our respondents from both countries, with a slight bias towards females, attended post-secondary institutions within one year following high school graduation.

It portrays the profound shift in post-secondary participation rates that was identified as desirable in policy documents in the 1980s and suggests that the messages espoused by both governments were heard. The message in Canada of 'higher levels of education are good; the more education the better,' and in Australia 'planned government intervention,' to boost post-secondary participation rates was effective.[1]

---

1 Our figures may be higher than other published statistics for two reasons: (1) both the *Paths on Life's Way* study and the *Life Patterns* study have experienced attrition over time with a slight bias towards post-secondary participation (see appendix A), and

Table 11
Post-secondary participation within one year of secondary school
completion, by sex, in Canada and Australia

	Canada, 1989		Australia, 1992	
	Females %	Males %	Females %	Males %
Post-secondary participant	85	79	88	86
Non-participant	15	21	12	15
Total number	441	292	377	167

The Contradictions of Increasing Participation and Inequality

Despite the overall picture, inequalities in participation remained a problem. According to the government of Australia, 'reservoirs of untapped intellectual talent exist in underrepresented groups such as children from working class backgrounds. The nation's stock of human capital will expand as more of these able students are helped to overcome obstacles in the way of their participation in higher education' (Commonwealth of Australia 1993, 194).

In Canada it was argued that 'if our human resources are not to be underdeveloped, policies related to higher education must ensure that all students who have the requisite capability also have the opportunity to develop their intellectual, aesthetic, ethical and practical capacities through higher education' (Watts 1987, 4).

When we analysed the socio-economic backgrounds of our participants, we expected to find that post-secondary participants in both Canada and Australia would be considerably more likely to come from households with parents (and particularly fathers) with university credentials; indeed, this was the case (see tables 12 and 13). With one exception, children of fathers who had earned university degrees were twice as likely (and in the case of Australian males, over three times as likely) to be post-secondary participants rather than non-participants. In addition, as would be expected by historical demographic trends (Andres and Adamuti-Trache, 2007), mothers of our participants were less likely to have completed university degrees; yet, as with fathers,

(2) our data are not constrained by provincial or state boundaries and jurisdictions, because our studies follow individuals.

there is a relationship between maternal degree attainment and post-secondary participation. However, closer analysis of these tables tells a different and remarkably multifaceted story.

A comparison of the intergenerational patterns of educational participation within and between our countries reveals some distinctive trends, as can be seen in tables 12 and 13. In Canada, a very small proportion of parents (19 per cent of mothers and 26 per cent of fathers) had completed less than high school graduation, and 26 per cent and 15 per cent respectively had completed high school only. Conversely, well over 50 per cent of parents had completed some level of post-secondary education, with 20 per cent of mothers and 27 per cent of fathers having completed a bachelor's degree or greater. According to Trow's classic typology (1972), completion of post-secondary studies had already surpassed the threshold of 'universal' for the parents of the Canadian respondents; that is, more than 40 per cent of parents of the Canadian participants in our study had completed some form of post-secondary education. In Australia, the proportion of parents who had *not* completed high school was dramatically higher than in Canada: 58 per cent of mothers and 46 per cent of fathers had completed less than Year 12, and an additional 12 per cent and 7 per cent, respectively, had graduated from Year 12. Overall, fewer Australian parents (30 per cent of mothers and 47 per cent of fathers) than Canadian parents (54 per cent of mothers and 60 per cent of fathers) possessed post-secondary credentials. Also, the proportion of parents of the Australians who had completed university degrees (as opposed to other post-secondary studies) was somewhat lower than that of their Canadian counterparts; that is, 15 per cent of mothers and 21 per cent of fathers of the Australian sample, compared to 20 per cent of mothers and 27 per cent of fathers of the Canadian sample, had earned university degrees. These findings concur with OECD data (OECD 2009, chart 1A.2).

It is apparent that the shift from mass to universal post-secondary education was achieved through the generation of young people of whom our Australian participants were a part. The timing of this shift to universal post-secondary education occurred in the preceding generation for the Canadians, and the universal threshold had been solidly surpassed by the parents of the Canadian sample. This point is important because it draws attention to a significant difference between the positioning of the participants in our respective studies in relation to the dynamics of intergenerational change. We have found it useful to draw on Rosa (2003) to highlight these intergenerational differences

Table 12
Mother's educational level by post-secondary status and sex, in Canada and Australia

| | Canada | | | | | Australia[1] | | | | |
| | Non-participants | | Participants | | | Non-participants | | Participants | | |
	Females %	Males %	Females %	Males %	Total %	Females %	Males %	Females %	Males %	Total %
Less than secondary graduation	19	25	20	15	19	63	72	59	50	58
Graduated from secondary school	26	32	25	27	26	7	14	10	16	12
Apprenticeship, trade, or vocational school	9	5	14	14	13	9	0	4	2	4
Post-secondary non-university	31	23	21	20	21	10	10	10	15	11
Bachelor's degree or higher	16	14	21	23	20	12	3	17	16	15
Total number	58	56	296	197	607	59	29	289	134	511

[1] A very small proportion of respondents reported 'other' as their mother's highest level of education. They were excluded from the analyses.

Table 13
Father's educational level by post-secondary status and sex, in Canada and Australia

	Canada					Australia				
	Non-participants		Participants			Non-participants		Participants		
	Females %	Males %	Females %	Males %	Total[1] %	Females %	Males %	Females %	Males %	Total %
Less than secondary graduation	42	36	22	24	26	53	74	45	41	46
Graduated from secondary school	11	12	17	14	15	10	0	8	6	7
Apprenticeship, trade, or vocational school	30	24	24	21	24	21	15	13	15	15
Post-secondary non-university	4	10	10	9	9	5	4	11	13	11
Bachelor's degree or higher	13	17	27	32	27	10	7	24	25	21
Total number	53	58	299	197	607	58	27	294	134	513

[1] A very small proportion of respondents reported 'other' as their father's highest level of education. They were excluded from the analyses.

in the following way. The young Canadians' consolidation of the post-secondary participation rates that were established by their parents represents a pattern of *generational* acceleration that is consistent with 'classical modernity.' By contrast, the pattern that we have identified for Australia is more consistent with the rapid *intergenerational* acceleration that Rosa identifies with 'late modernity' (8). Hence, our data show the unevenness of processes of social change and highlight the disparities that can exist within a social generation across nations.

The patterns of participation by our young people show the impact of three confluent forces: (1) an overall intergenerational increase of post-secondary participation directly after high school completion, which suggests the impact of higher education policy and educational structures, (2) a strong trend towards increased educational participation by young people with university-educated parents (particularly for Australian males), and (3) a tendency towards greater participation by socio-economic groups that previously had low participation rates in post-secondary education. These patterns are represented in tables 12 and 13. They seem at first sight to be contradictory and reflect an ongoing debate about the extent to which the expansion of post-secondary education in both countries has benefited all social groups equally.

If we use fathers with bachelor-level credentials as a proxy for 'upper middle class,'[2] over 90 per cent of the Canadian and Australian respondents from this class background entered post-secondary education within one year of high school graduation. Taking the measure of those whose fathers' highest credential was the completion of high school or less as a proxy for 'working class,' participation rates were 60 per cent for the Canadian respondents and a much higher 77 per cent for the Australian sample. These figures lend weight to the claim by the Australian government that there was relatively little difference between socio-economic groups in their propensity to go on to higher

---

2 The correlation between father's education and father's occupation in the Canadian sample is 0.50, and in the Australian sample is 0.37. There are many ways to operationalize the concept of family socio-economic background. In this book we have used parental education as described above. Compared to other measures (for example, income, occupational status), we expect that the level of parental education, in the form of cultural capital (Bourdieu 1986), would play a more direct role in the transmission of cultural capital, which in turn would influence their children's educational choices and eventual occupational status. Also, compared to other measures, our respondents were more likely to possess reasonably accurate knowledge about their parents' education.

education once they had reached Year 12 (Commonwealth of Australia 1993, 194). On the other hand, increased participation rates for all social groups is an indication that growth of the post-secondary sector and related changes in policy promoted equity. At least in terms of post-secondary participation following high school, Australia surpassed its goal to obtain 'substantial and sustained reductions in the mismatch between the composition of society and the social composition of tertiary institutions' (194).

For some groups, however, participation in post-secondary education remained low. As we have described in more detail in chapter 3, the trend for non-metropolitan youth to have lower participation in post-secondary education was identified by both Canadian and Australian governments. In its 1993 report the Australian Department of Education noted that post-secondary educational institutions were still concentrated in metropolitan areas. An urban resident – whether male or female, across all age groups and states – was more than twice as likely as a rural resident to enrol in higher education. However, between 1981 and 1989, the government claimed that due to an increase in the number of post-secondary places outside of metropolitan areas, the gap in participation in higher education was closing. According to the Australian Department of Education and Training (Commonwealth of Australia 1993, 211), 'once rural pupils get to Year 12, their chances of going on to higher education are now close to those of urban pupils.'

In Canada, young people in participation in non-urban areas were also identified as being under-represented in post-secondary education (Ontario 1984; Fortin 1987; British Columbia 1988b; Stephenson 1982). Like Australia, the post-secondary system located universities or their satellites in rural areas, expanding the reach of the community college systems and developing distance- or open-learning forms of educational delivery. However, earlier comparative analyses demonstrated that, compared with their urban counterparts, rural youth had lower aspirations and participation and completion rates (Andres and Looker 2001).

In table 14 we demonstrate that, in Australia, higher proportions (87 per cent) of those living in metropolitan[3] areas participated in post-secondary studies directly after completing secondary school, compared

3 In the Canadian study, the categories *metropolitan, urban/rural,* and *remote* correspond to ministry designations of school districts. In the Australian study, *metropolitan* was defined as 'a capital city,' *urban/rural* as 'a large country town,' and *remote* as 'a small country town' (not regional centres).

Table 14
Community of origin by post-secondary status and sex,
in Canada and Australia

	Non-participants		Participants			% Post-secondary Participants		
	Females	Males	Females	Males	Total	Females	Males	Total
Canada								
Metropolitan (%)	29	29	33	38	34	85	81	83
Urban/rural (%)	43	36	43	39	41	83	78	81
Remote (%)	28	36	25	23	26	81	69	76
Total number	65	62	320	205	652	83%	77%	81%
Australia								
Metropolitan (%)	52	45	70	72	62	86	87	87
Urban/rural (%)	25	16	16	16	17	75	81	78
Remote (%)	24	39	15	12	17	75	59	69
Total number	64	31	298	139	532	81%	82%	82%

with 78 per cent in urban/rural areas and 69 per cent in remote areas. Gender differences are also evident with 75 per cent of females and 81 per cent of males from urban/rural areas, and 75 per cent of females and only 59 per cent of males from remote areas, making the transition to post-secondary education. Higher proportions of metropolitan females (86 per cent) and males (87 per cent) participated directly following Year 12.

The Canadian data demonstrate similar but less pronounced patterns. Participation in post-secondary education directly out of high school by metropolitan and urban or rural youth was high. Like rural Australian males, remote Canadian males were the least likely to continue to post-secondary studies. However, regardless of urban or rural differences, in both countries post-secondary participation for all groups following high school completion is well beyond the 40 per cent level that demarks universal participation.

Family Influences and Support

There are a number of influences that have contributed to these patterns of participation, including availability of financial resources, the impact of debt, and traditional beliefs about gender roles, as well as economic trends and government policies. Family is also a very significant influence that works through and across all other dimensions. Systematic inequalities in the patterns of participation suggest that the constellation of factors that are routinely summed up as 'family influence' is significant.

Although there is a wealth of literature and research evidence that identifies the connection between family (or socio-economic background) and educational participation and attainment, there is less evidence on the nature of family influences on young people's educational achievement and trajectories. For example, writing about the United States, Schwartz (2008, 14) points out that 'class origin' is a predictor of adult socio-economic status; 'it does not reveal the mechanisms that facilitate achievement.' Similarly, reflecting on research in the United Kingdom, Witz (1995, 45) comments that, in educational research on class, 'families appear like phantoms, clearly implicated in the intergenerational transmission of social and economic advantage, and yet assuming a unitary status lacking in real world content.'

We gain some insights into the multiple and complex ways in which families (including parents, siblings, and grandparents) influence young people's education, through their interviews and comments on the surveys, as well as from the survey data. For both the Canadian and Australian samples, the role of family has been very significant. In chapter 7 we use questionnaire data to demonstrate the relationship between our samples and their parents. In this chapter we use interview comments, which, perhaps, are the most revealing.

While still in high school, the Canadian sample were asked about the extent to which their families were influential and supportive in their educational decisions. In total, thirty-nine of the forty-six individuals interviewed in both 1989 and 1990 responded to questions about family. Elsewhere, Andres (1992, 1993) has provided an extended account of families as sources of cultural or social capital. The majority were positive about the encouragement and support provided by their families. In many instances, the type of support was direct and often had financial strings attached:

I've probably been spoiled by [my parents] a lot . . . I have an easy life, but they had to work to get where they are right now, so they want me to do the same. What they tell me is if I don't go to [post-secondary] school, I'm not going to have anything, unless I marry rich or something, which is kinda hard to do sometimes. And I agree with them . . . I think my parents want me to go so bad . . . it's really up to them that I go to college, so it's the least . . . they'll pay off in the end for me, I think. (female)

My dad's always wanted me to go to school. I have always done well in school so I guess that's why he's always wanted me to go. They're glad that I'm going away to university right away. They think it's going to be very beneficial to me. So they're really happy about it. Pleased with my decisions. (female)

They want me to go straight to school . . . I just don't feel like doing that, so [my parents are] making me pay money if I don't go straight to school. So that's a bit of a problem but not major. (male)

[My parents] like my plans. I'm not to go out and be a hooker or anything. They're parents, they like this university business and the college and all that. (female)

Others described the support and encouragement received by their families as present but less direct:

And well, they're encouraging me to go to school too, but they say it's okay if I take time off, and they're just helping me decide what I want to do. They're leaving it all up to me, like they're not going to say, 'Oh, you should be this, or that'; they're really good that way. (female)

My parents aren't pressuring me to go to university or anything. I mean they'd be happy for me with whatever I choose. (female)

No, they said, 'You just do whatever you like to do, but just do your best.' (male)

Yet, a small minority reported that they felt they were completely responsible for making decisions about the future:

It doesn't matter. So it's totally up to me. Like, [my parents would] prefer it 'cause . . . there's more job opportunities and stuff to . . . go on to some kind of post-secondary education or whatever, but if I don't want to, I don't have to. (female)

They don't care. They just say it's up to me. They don't like it too much, but I don't know, they don't want to force me to go to school if I'm not going to like it. It's just a waste of money, right? (female)

One young man described the advice he received from his parents as 'Just do things right; don't screw up. Graduate and just keep – get a good education. That's about it.' When asked if his parents encouraged him to continue to post-secondary studies, he said, 'Not yet. They haven't been saying much about it. 'Cause they don't look forward to paying for it, so they're not saying much.'

A few of the Canadian interviewees highlighted how their parents exerted pressure on them to excel in their studies:

Well, my dad wanted me to go to university and for him. Last year actually, there was no say for me like 'It's either you go to university or not.' And this year I kinda sat down and talked with them and told them that, well, I think there's no way that I can get into university right now, and I explained to them that I'd go to [a community college] for a year, maybe two years, and use the science transfer and go to university. And I guess they really talked it over with themselves and they thought about it, and they finally agreed that I could go to college. Because, well, college to my mom is a waste of time, really, 'cause I guess she thinks you can't learn anything in college, and I kind of explained that you can, you know, so she's for it now. (female)

They're pretty upset [about my high school grades] . . . Both [my parents] graduated from university, and my brother and sister are geniuses – I wonder what happened [to me]. But they're really upset about it. My mom is, and my dad doesn't actually know about it. I haven't showed him my latest report cards. (female)

For two young people, the lack of parental support was palpable:

[My father and stepmother want] to get me out of the house. Get luggage for my graduation present . . . My dad doesn't even think I'm going to grad-uate, so he hasn't really put much into my education. I don't know about my mom, though; I haven't lived with her for a while. It's my choice what I want to do; they really don't get in the way of what I want to do. (male)

I think [my dad] wants me to get out – push me out the door. But my mom wants me to stay . . . Well, my mom . . . she always supports me in my decisions, so she said that she would help, you know, if there were ways that they could help. But there would be no way they could help completely, and so I have to do most of it on my own, and I don't think I could make it . . . I know they could [help me financially] if I needed the money to actually go to school. But I don't know if they would pay, like, for my rent or anything. (female)

The relationship between cultural and social capital and educational outcomes has been documented in numerous studies (Andres 1993; Bourdieu 1979). Although they do not use theoretical language, the Canadian interviewees clearly understand the concept of transmission of cultural capital and the importance of networks of social capital.

Yeah, I think [I will attend] McGill or Laval, either one, 'cause my parents' friends have relatives there that I can stay with. (male)

Chances are if [your] parents [have been] talking to [you] since [you] were three years old, 'You've got to be a lawyer, you've got to be a lawyer,' chances are, 'Oh, I'm going to be a lawyer because my parents want me to.'(female)

However, the transmission of capital, as this young man describes, does not always come in the form of pointing children to the path to university.

Ever since I've been small, [my family] expected me to go into military because that was always what I did. I was in cadets and stuff so they sort of expected me. All my whole family, not just my parents, but my relatives also always thought I was going to be in the military. All my aunts and uncles, it's just like, 'Oh yeah, so how's the military going? So when are you going to go join, or how are things going here?' For instance, I had a birthday once, and . . . one of my uncles, who's a baker, put on the cake 'May the Force Be With You,' meaning the armed forces, you know. This is what they figured I was going to be doing. So, like, it won't be a surprise for anyone in my family; it'll just be, 'Okay, he finally did it.' (male)

In 2002 when they were aged thirty, the Australians were asked to reflect on what had facilitated and what had obstructed the achievement of their goals. Of the fifty-one young people who were interviewed, 50 per cent mentioned family as the most positive influence on their lives with regard to their education. The majority of these (90 per cent) said that family support had been essential – 'My family have been the backbone of what I do; I always fall back on them.' This support included providing direct financial support, enabling young people to live in the family home with their parents, and providing guidance and advice.

> I knew I'd go to uni. Thought I'd do a degree in advertising. My parents wanted me to do a tertiary course; they've always placed a high regard on tertiary education, and they instilled those values in me. (male)

> My parents have always been very supportive. In the past eight years I have moved out of home a total of three times, and they have always been there for me. (female)

> My grandparents paid the $7000 for my course. (male)

Some made direct reference to their family context as one in which certain understandings of the importance of education were influential, even when families were not able to provide financial support:

> Family – the goals they have instilled in me, 'Do the best you can, but do it properly; no half-heartedness accepted here.' (female)

> My parents always wanted me to finish a tertiary degree, and have given me money when times were hard. (male)

> I began working in my father's company after encouragement from the family. I was encouraged to work full-time and study part-time as the family said they could not afford to support me through study. (male)

However, for a few, family influence was negative because it was a source of pressure or advice that proved to be unhelpful or because the family connection was undesirable:

> My family pressured me to be involved in a science-related area, my sister is a doctor, and that also put pressure on me, and it didn't work out. (female)

> I had to put in special consideration as my father was imprisoned. I have to be careful who I deal with – many [people] worked with my father, and he is still in jail – and I don't want them to make the connection. (female)

I thought about uni, but I wouldn't burden my parents with the financial responsibility What if I didn't like it or couldn't finish it? (male)

These comments underline the significance of family to the educational careers of the Australians. We know from the strength of the data for both our Australian and our Canadian participants that family background is one of the most significant elements that structure their experiences, especially with regard to their educational careers. Yet we agree with Ball's assessment (2006, 6) that 'it is often difficult to read classed individuals as though their experiences were transparent concomitants of the social category they are allocated to.' His study draws our attention to the nuances and ambiguities of class positionings through education. Ball comments that Bourdieu's view (1987) that social boundaries of theoretical social classes are not clear cut should be thought of as 'lines or imaginary planes' and suggests that 'a flame whose edges are in constant movement, oscillating around a line or surface' (Ball 2006, 13), is a more appropriate metaphor. The planes on which class dynamics are played out are specific to space, place, and time because 'class gets done' differently in different places and times (Ball 2006). While the profile provided by our survey data reveals the strength of class processes, it is important to acknowledge the complex dynamics that produce these patterns. We agree with Ball that class is productive and reactive, it is a 'longitudinal process rather than a cross-sectional one,' it is 'achieved and maintained and enacted,' and it is also 'realised and struggled over in the daily lives of families and institutions, in consumption decisions, as much as in the processes of production' (Ball 2006, 6). The twenty-five Australians whose quotes acknowledging the importance of their families to their educational progress are represented above are among those who have been able to draw on the various kinds of capital that their families provide and who over time have continued to sustain a positive narrative about their lives in relation to family support.

The absence of family support in some of their narratives also underlines the nature of social capital as a relationship and a process. While it is very likely that these young people drew unconsciously on understandings about education that derived from their family context, it needs to be kept in mind that various forms of capital can only be realized if they are accessed by individuals. The point is that we gain a partial insight into the processes whereby patterns of inequality are produced through the ways in which young people draw, over time, on social, cultural, and material support.

In the following section we explore the beliefs that our young Canadians and Australians expressed about the benefits of education. This section provides further insights into the social dynamics of higher-education participation, as attitudes derived from family background are mediated by messages circulating through the government policies of the time and by the very structure of secondary and post-secondary education.

Beliefs about the Benefits of Education

As Trow (1972, 69) points out, the movement from mass to universal higher education is concomitant with the notion of 'involuntary atten-dance.' He argues that whereas attendance in a mass system was a voluntary privilege or even a right, participation in a universal system becomes an obligation. He states that for young people, 'everyone they know goes on to college, . . . [and] as more and more college-age young-sters go on to college, not to be or have been a college student becomes increasingly a lasting stigma, a mark of some special failing of mind or of character, and a grave handicap in all the activities and pursuits of adult life' (Trow 1972, 69–70).

An examination of the beliefs that the Canadian survey sample held one year following high school graduation, when they were around nine-teen years old, supports Trow's claim that young people have bought in to the notion of universal education. A full 79 per cent of women and 76 per cent of men reported that they believed a post-secondary educa-tion would *definitely* lead them to become better educated, 69 per cent of women and 63 per cent of men said it would *definitely* prepare them for a job, 62 per cent of women and 56 per cent of men said it would *definitely* increase their income, and 65 per cent of women and 59 per cent of men said it would *definitely* give them a wider choice of jobs. However, only 36 per cent of women and 30 per cent of men believed that post-secondary education would make them more informed citi-zens, and 6 per cent and 26 per cent, respectively, said it would provide them with recreational or social opportunities.

In their written responses to an open-ended question at the conclusion of the 1989 questionnaire, fifty Canadian respondents commented spe-cifically on their beliefs about post-secondary education. Twenty-eight per cent of the comments suggested that post-secondary education is at worst a 'waste of time' and at best one option out of many.

Post-secondary education is too expensive. It's highly overrated. Employment opportunities are highly unavailable for people with specified degrees. (male)

While I am not presently attending college, I have learned many aspects of life, specially where they concern me. I feel post-secondary is important but not absolutely essential. (female)

Who needs more than a Grade 12 education? I don't, 'cause I'm a QUALIFIED HOG [motorcycle] TECHNICIAN and I make quite a bit of cash. Personally, an education in further years than [Grade] 13 isn't gonna help a guy a whole hell of a lot. (male)

Education takes up a lot of personal time. That is, at times, it's just not available. Jobs are just not guaranteed along with post-secondary education – so there's a question of if it's really worth all the time and effort. (female)   .

A slightly smaller proportion (24 per cent) described post-secondary education as a means to an end, or a 'necessary evil.'

I believe that education is highly over-rated; however, to get a decent and respectable job, it has become obvious that it is necessary to have that useless piece of paper stating that I wasted four years of my life at university. (female)

I do believe that there is too much emphasis on an education. If you wish to succeed in life and can't afford an education that could land you a good job, you're out of luck! (male)

Unfortunately, post-secondary school must be attended in order to obtain a decent job. If this were not the case, I certainly wouldn't be continuing my studies. I am not learning anything worthwhile for the amount of money which is being spent. (female)

Post-secondary education is a must in order to get a well-paying job. Society socializes us into believing we must have post-secondary education in order to maintain a sufficient standard of living. Education forces us to know exactly what we want to do and will enjoy doing for the rest of our life. (female)

Almost half (46 per cent) of the comments cast post-secondary education, the experience of studying at a post-secondary institution, as extremely positive.

> Although I am not sure in what direction my post-secondary education will lead me, I feel it is important to complete at least a bachelor's degree . . . Education is very important, and I don't feel it has been stressed nearly enough or made available to anyone who wishes to utilize it. (female)

> I would like to say that, when your survey is printed, encourage future graduates, counsellors, etc., not to look for the easy way out of school. I did and I have regretted that I did so. The importance of a good education cannot be underestimated. (male)

> Life has taught me a valuable lesson . . . I realize that 'a little knowledge is a dangerous thing,' and my 360[-degree] turn to continue my education was the smartest move I've made. (female)

Not only did Canadian young adults in this study believe in post-secondary education, but also the vast majority of survey respondents in 1989 – 70 per cent of females and 69 per cent of males – expected to earn a bachelor's degree or greater. Expectations varied somewhat by parental educational status. Of those having one parent or more with university-level credentials, 83 per cent of females and 89 per cent of males expected to earn a bachelor's degree or greater. For females and males who came from non-university-home backgrounds, expectations were somewhat lower, at 67 per cent and 66 per cent, respectively. Post-secondary aspirations were even higher, with 90 per cent of females and 88 per cent of males wanting to earn a bachelor's degree or greater. This figure ranged from a low of 86 per cent by males from non-university-educated homes to a high of 97 per cent by females with university-educated parents.

A somewhat different question was posed to the Australian sample. While they were still in Year 12 in 1991, they were asked about their plans following high school. Eighty-eight percent indicated that they intended to study full-time, 6 per cent said they would study part-time, and 7 per cent indicated that they did not expect to study. Differences by gender and parental educational background are much greater than for the Canadian sample. Only 73 per cent of males, but 91 per cent of females, from homes with non-university-educated parents expected to study full-time following Year 12; 12 per cent and 4 per cent, respectively, planned to study part-time; and 15 per cent and 5 per cent, respectively, did not plan to study at all. Conversely, 94 per cent of males and 98 per cent of females from homes with at least one university-educated parent planned to study full-time; 3 per cent and 1 per cent, respectively, planned to study part-time; and 3 per cent and 1 per cent, respectively, did not plan to study at all.

The Australians' comments about post-secondary education are taken from interviews and open-ended sections on surveys in 1996 and 1997. They also reveal a strong belief that having some form of post-secondary education was highly desirable. As one student put it, 'You thought, like, the more education you had, the better chance you had of getting work.' It needs to be remembered that the Australian participants in this study were in a unique position. Never before had so many young Australians set their sights on completing secondary education and entering post-secondary education. As we have pointed out above, compared to their Canadian counterparts, fewer Australians had the benefit of parents who themselves had experienced post-secondary education to help them make decisions. These young people were also among the first to enter a new system of certification, called the Victorian Certificate of Education (VCE), which produced a single score upon the completion of secondary education. This 'entry score' was the basis on which they would compete for limited places in universities. The change to this system strained resources in Victoria's secondary schools at that time, leaving less time for careers education, and students understandably tended to focus on their studies in the final years of secondary school, with little real sense of the implications (apart from a score) for further education or employment. Hence, although they believed in post-secondary education, many were ill-informed about the next steps. As one young person put it, 'I had no idea; I just wanted to get through the year, no careers advice, and no real thinking. VCE was a hard year, and the change meant that the teachers didn't know what they were doing.' Another participant, looking back in time to when she had left secondary school, summed up the experiences of many: 'When I left school in 1991 there was a lot of emphasis placed on getting a tertiary place. I believe there still is. I was almost devastated when I didn't get a place in 1992. Since then I've come to realize, as have my peers, that there is no need to be in such a hurry. There is plenty of time for study.'

Pathways, Journeys, and Educational Destinations

In tables 15 through 20 we examine the educational outcomes of the *Paths on Life's Way* and *Life Patterns* respondents. Tables 15 and 16 portray the credentials earned by our two samples at fifteen and ten years out of high school, respectively, according to parental education. Most noticeably, the non-participation rate is extremely low in both countries, with no more than 16 per cent in any socio-economic group never having attended a post-secondary institution (tables 15 and 16). However, despite the low rate, those from homes where neither parent had completed a university degree are much more likely to fall into this category.

Among the participant groups there is a stronger class effect in Canada; that is, respondents from university-educated homes were considerably more likely to complete at least undergraduate degrees. A similar pattern is evident in the Australian data, but the magnitude is less. Gender patterns are uneven, with approximately the same proportion of Canadian females and males from non-university-educated homes earning bachelor's degrees or higher. In Australia, females from similar backgrounds were somewhat more likely to do so. Overall, however, the proportion of respondents earning university-level credentials is impressive – no less than 49 per cent in any socio-economic or gender group had accomplished this level of post-secondary education.

Tables 17 through 20 provide a glimpse into the complexity of the educational pathways upon which our respondents embarked. In these tables we distinguish between those who did and those who did not commence their post-secondary studies within a year of high school completion, at two points in time – at five and fifteen years out of high school for the Canadian sample, and seven and ten years for the Australian sample. Direct comparisons are constrained by the lack of availability of data points that match exactly. However, the overall patterns provide a reasonably robust portrayal of the pathways taken by our respondents and highlight differences by gender and socio-economic background. The findings are clear and more or less consistent for both Canada and Australia. Most importantly, those who commenced post-secondary studies directly following high school completion were much more likely to have completed some post-secondary credential both within five years after high school completion and over a more extended period of time.

Table 15
Highest credential earned by 2003, by sex and parental educational attainment, at age 33, in Canada

	Neither parent with university		One or both parents with university	
	Females %	Males %	Females %	Males %
Non-participant	6	7	1	3
Non-completer	10	12	3	9
Certificate	17	10	11	12
Diploma	18	12	13	14
Associate degree	0	1	2	0
Ticket	2	8	0	2
Bachelor's degree	26	31	39	38
Professional degree	15	11	19	14
Master's degree	7	8	11	9
Doctoral degree	1	1	1	0
Total number	320	219	88	58

Table 16
Highest credential earned by 2002, by sex and parental educational attainment, at age 28, in Australia

	Neither parent with university		One or both parents with university	
	Females %	Males %	Females %	Males %
Non-participant	15	16	9	6
Some apprenticeship	0	0	0	0
Trade qualifications	1	9	2	6
Other (unspecified)	8	7	5	11
Some TAFE	5	4	6	0
Some university	5	5	1	3
Undergraduate diploma	6	8	4	14
Bachelor's degree	13	12	12	17
Post-graduate diploma	42	36	53	34
Master's degree	3	4	7	6
Doctoral degree	2	1	2	3
Total number	291	132	86	35

As we noted earlier, the vast majority of our Canadian and Australian respondents were post-secondary participants following high school completion. This includes 84 per cent of Canadian women and 77 per cent of men, from non-university-educated families; the comparable proportions for Australia are 85 per cent and 79 per cent, respectively. By comparing the four quadrants of tables 17 through 20, a class effect is also evident; that is, those from non-university-educated homes were the least likely to undertake post-secondary studies initially, and of those who did, they were less likely to have earned university-level credentials either within five to seven years or over a longer time horizon.

However, these tables also demonstrate a considerable agency on the part of our respondents in relation to structural effects. The nature of the post-secondary education system in each country is arranged in such a way that allows for upward educational mobility over time, despite social-class background. However, the British Columbia system was much more highly articulated than the Victoria system of post-secondary education was at that time. Yet the majority of respondents in both Canada and Australia where neither parent had university-level credentials and who did not enrol directly into post-secondary studies (upper right quadrant of tables 27 to 20) eventually earned post-secondary credentials. In other words, against socio-economic and structural odds, these individuals managed to negotiate their way into and through the system. The pattern is similar to that of initial non-participants from university-educated homes; however, the fact that this proportion is so small (less than 3 per cent) is telling in and of itself.

Gender effects are not strong. In Canada, from non-university family backgrounds, women are more likely than men to have earned non-university-level credentials, whereas in Australia, women in this group were more likely than men to earn university credentials. The large proportion of non-completers at five years out of high school in Canada is most likely due to (1) a shorter time frame than that of the Australian sample (that is, five rather than seven years) and (2) a more strongly articulated higher education system that allows students to transfer with credit from non-university institutions to universities.

Evolution of Beliefs over Time

Over the time spans of our two studies the Canadian and Australian participants were asked about their progress. We end this chapter by

Table 17
Initial engagement in post-secondary education in 1989, by post-secondary completion status, parental educational attainment, and sex in 1993, at age 23, in Canada

	Neither parent with a university degree			
In 1989, of those who were	Non-participants		Participants	
	Females %	Males %	Females %	Males %
No credentials	31	35	1	1
Non-completer	41	37	32	44
Certificate	12	8	22	14
Diploma	10	6	16	13
Associate degree	0	0	0	0
Ticket/apprenticeship	2	12	1	5
Bachelor's degree	4	2	21	20
Professional degree	0	0	7	1
Master's degree	0	0	0	1
Doctorate	0	0	0	0
Total number	49	49	271	170

	One or both parents with a university degree			
In 1989, of those who were	Non-participants		Participants	
	Females %	Males %	Females %	Males %
No credentials	0	33	0	0
Non-completer	33	44	30	51
Certificate	22	11	14	12
Diploma	22	0	14	10
Associate degree	0	0	0	0
Ticket/apprenticeship	0	11	0	0
Bachelor's degree	11	0	34	25
Professional degree	11	0	8	0
Master's degree	0	0	0	2
Doctorate	0	0	0	0
Total number	9	9	79	49

Table 18
Initial engagement in post-secondary education in 1989, by post-secondary completion status, parental educational attainment, and sex in 2003, at age 33, in Canada

	Neither parent with a university degree			
In 1989, of those who were	Non-participants		Participants	
	Females %	Males %	Females %	Males %
No credentials	22	22	3	3
Non-completer	18	14	8	11
Certificate	16	14	17	9
Diploma	18	8	17	13
Associate degree	0	0	0	1
Ticket/apprenticeship	2	14	2	6
Bachelor's degree	10	18	29	34
Professional degree	8	6	17	12
Master's degree	4	2	7	10
Doctorate	0	0	1	1
Total number	49	49	271	170

	One or both parents with a university degree			
In 1989, of those who were	Non-participants		Participants	
	Females %	Males %	Females %	Males %
No credentials	0	11	1	2
Non-completer	0	0	4	10
Certificate	11	11	10	12
Diploma	22	33	11	10
Associate degree	0	0	3	0
Ticket/apprenticeship	0	11	0	0
Bachelor's degree	11	22	42	41
Professional degree	44	0	17	16
Master's degree	11	11	11	8
Doctorate	0	0	1	0
Total number	9	9	79	49

Table 19

Initial engagement in post-secondary education in 1992, by post-secondary completion status, parental educational attainment, and sex in 1998, at age 24, in Australia

	Neither parent with a university degree			
In 1992, of those who were	Non-participants		Participants	
	Females %	Males %	Females %	Males %
No credentials	51	44	23	30
Trade qualifications	5	17	1	5
Undergraduate diploma	16	17	5	5
'Other' credential[1]	16	22	37	45
Bachelor's degree	5	0	18	10
Post-graduate diploma	5	0	14	5
Master's degree	0	0	2	1
Doctorate	0	0	0	0
Total number	37	23	254	107

	One or both parents with a university degree			
In 1992, of those who were	Non-participants		Participants	
	Females %	Males %	Females %	Males %
No credentials	50	0	13	27
Trade qualifications	13	0	0	6
Undergraduate diploma	25	0	8	9
'Other' credential	13	0	41	50
Bachelor's degree	0	0	22	6
Post-graduate diploma	0	100	15	0
Master's degree	0	0	1	3
Doctorate	0	0	0	0
Total number	8	1	78	34

[1]The 'other' category includes vocationally oriented certificates and credentials offered by private institutions.

Table 20
Initial engagement in post-secondary education in 1992, by post-secondary completion status, parental educational attainment, and sex in 2002, at age 28, in Australia

| | Neither parent with a university degree | | | |
| | Non-participants | | Participants | |
In 1992, of those who were	Females %	Males %	Females %	Males %
No credentials	38	26	11	13
Some apprenticeship	3	0	0	0
Trade qualifications	5	21	0	7
Other unspecified	11	13	7	6
Some TAFE	8	9	5	3
Some university	3	4	5	5
Undergraduate diploma	11	13	5	6
Bachelor's degree	5	4	15	14
Post-graduate diploma	16	9	46	42
Master's degree	0	0	4	5
Doctorate	0	0	2	1
Total number	37	23	254	107

| | One or both parents with a university degree | | | |
| | Non-participants | | Participants | |
In 1992, of those who were	Females %	Males %	Females %	Males %
No credentials	50	0	5	6
Some apprenticeship	0	0	0	0
Trade qualifications	13	0	1	6
Other unspecified	13	0	4	12
Some TAFE	0	0	6	0
Some university	0	0	1	2
Undergraduate diploma	13	0	3	15
Bachelor's degree	0	0	13	18
Post-graduate diploma	13	100	56	32
Master's degree	0	0	8	6
Doctorate	0	0	3	2
Total number	8	1	78	34

focusing on their beliefs about education at ten to fifteen years out of high school. In 2003 at around age thirty-three the Canadian survey sample was asked to provide any final comments or thoughts about education, work, and life. About one third of the respondents did so. Many of their comments addressed multiple issues and topics simultaneously, attesting to the interrelationship among education, work, family, health, the economy, and society in their lives. The following comment is an example.

> [Regarding prospects for children's future:] Dark, which is why we're assuming we won't have any! We can't responsibly afford to have children anyway! I felt high school did not prepare me adequately for determining how to follow an educational process. I therefore spent too much time exploring courses at College, which obviously put me into higher levels of debt as I did not have the financial background to pay my own way. I also did not have the 'fortune' of good health to aid me in taking a heavier course load so as to complete my post-secondary education faster. Said education did not provide access to an adequately paying employment position after graduation, so I almost feel it was all a waste of time and money! (female)

Because of the intertwined nature of their comments, it is difficult to provide a precise indication of how many individuals held strong beliefs about the importance of post-secondary studies. However, around fifty individuals provided more direct comments about education and higher education, and we will focus on their words.

Overall, there is a shift in tone from the comments they had provided when they were around nineteen years old. Compared with the comments reported earlier in this chapter when the Canadian sample had been out of high school for only one year, by 2003 only a small proportion was unabashedly supportive of higher levels of education.

> If BC and Canada is going to have a skilled workforce that will be able to differentiate from and compete with our rich First World neighbours, we are going to need to have a broad cross-section of our society highly educated. A good social system can make such goals affordable to a broad and diverse cross-segment of our community. (male)

> I value education greatly and am pleased with my educational choices. (female)

Similarly, a few were extremely negative:

> People are no longer people...they are consumers and automatons,
> myself included. My education leads me to be pessimistic about the future,
> not optimistic as I had hoped. (female)

> I found the equation of good education = good job = good money = happi-
> ness wasn't always true or relative to each other. (female)

However, many discussed their educational pursuits and education in
general in relation to the reality of their own lives and their observations about society as a whole:

> You need education nowadays to get anywhere in the employment ave-
> nue, yet it does not guarantee you a decent earnings/wage. (female)

> Even though I am involved in a specially trained 'industry,' I see the
> 'highly specialized' training requirement in many 'help wanted' ads as a
> reason for concern. I wonder if, in our desire to be trained/specialized, are
> we creating a closed environment where people entering the job market
> cannot gain experience in an industry unless they are trained (specialized)
> but cannot get training unless they are experienced...In our 'must go
> university' society, are we leaving room for those that don't? Or have we
> overqualified ourselves beyond practical usefulness? (female)

> In many respects it is too easy to get a post-sec[ondary] educ[ation]. Its
> value has been lessened. There are all kinds of people not using their edu-
> cation. Also, the degrees being earned often don't help people in their jobs.
> Too often post. sec. schooling is more about jumping through the correct
> number of hoops and less about learning skills. Education is not just a
> means to an end. Today to most that is what it is. (male)

> Education is an excellent opportunity to broaden one's perspective on
> global issues. I would recommend it to all high school graduates. On
> the other hand I believe that it doesn't prepare one for the 'real' world
> in the sense that only life can teach you about life. One's values + ethics
> are not learned in school. I believe they are to a large degree learned at
> home. (male)

Many of the comments focussed on the pressure to attend university rather than non-university institutions. According to some respondents, this pressure was unnecessary and inappropriate:

In 1988 there was a huge emphasis on getting a university education, and now I think I would encourage people to investigate trades and other options. Not all smart people necessarily need to go straight to university. (female)

People shouldn't be pressured into the high-paying important (lawyers, doctors) [jobs] when they are inclined to a trade, etc. ... I now make more money and I am happier than half the unemployed computer tech people. (male)

University is getting more expensive, yet a degree doesn't guarantee a good paying job. Trades right now seem to be the place to be – plumbers make more an hour than I do! (female)

I am concerned that society is moving towards a university-degree require-ment for more and more jobs. I see so many people with bachelor degrees who are working in dead-end jobs that have nothing to do with their degree. It seems there is a kind of snobbery going on in regards to other forms of post-secondary education such as technical schools. (female)

In the late 1990s and early 2000s the Australian survey sample was asked similar questions. In the variety of views expressed about the benefits of education several themes stood out. The overwhelming majority of young people saw post-secondary education as a tool for gaining a secure and fulfilling job, but, for some, the links between edu-cation and the labour market were not as straightforward as they would have liked. Similar to the comments made by the Canadians above, the theme that education was a prerequisite for employment but the 'real world' was different was expressed by approximately 40 per cent of those interviewed:

The biggest obstacle was that university was all theory and no practice. (male)

It is difficult to link training, expectations for the future and work upon leaving school. The 'world out there' didn't seem open to opportunity, ran-dom decision making, or flexibility. (female)

My course of study failed to deliver what it promised so now I'm in a dead-end job, finding many barriers to progressing to a more interesting, fulfilling career. (male)

Nonetheless, many who felt that education did provide a pathway to employment were also a significant group of around 30 per cent:

> The compulsory work experience program at my university made a significant difference to my post-university work. The university has contacts. You tell them your area of interest, and they set up an interview. (male)

> Life has some unexpected twists. The university course I took (and completed) led to very limited opportunities. Now, through starting at the bottom, I have managed to step up a few rungs in an indirectly related field, but it was my degree that enabled me to do this. My future is now looking very promising. (female)

> I believe that the additional studies that I have completed since leaving high school have been a definite advantage in helping pursue a great career. (male)

> For me, education is everything. It has opened up many doors and allowed me to do what I want to do. (female)

The importance of education for this group was emphasized by those who did not participate to the extent they would have liked because of financial barriers. This was particularly the case for a group of around 15 per cent of interviewees who would have liked to undertake some additional education beyond their first degree or diploma so that they could change their field of employment. The following quotes were recorded in 2002 when the participants were aged around twenty-nine.

> I work in my field of study; however, it is not all I thought it would be. I would like to study again; however, finances don't allow it. (male)

> I would have liked to have studied at uni, but I can't afford it. (female)

Finally, a third theme to emerge over the years was that education was of benefit for personal development.

> My TAFE diploma certainly helped me out with the whole discipline of working life and gave me a clearer, better understanding of the big wide world, but you don't grasp it until you're out there. I think studying and

socializing with people who share similar goals and passions is extremely helpful, inspirational. (male)

These data show that while the overall patterns of educational participation for both countries are similar, and our respective study participants agree on the importance of education, it is clearly only one component of the dance of life. And, as their comments reveal, policies and structures only teach a few of the moves.

Conclusion

Our analysis of the educational trajectories, experiences, and attitudes of our participants reveals a complex story. On the surface, the similarities in the patterns for Australians and Canadians in higher education over the 1990s suggest that global processes have had an impact on the lives of these young people in exactly the same ways. However, a deeper analysis reveals significant differences between the Canadian and Australian experience – and differences within each country – and provides insights into the dynamics of social change.

First, this chapter provides insight into the processes of institutional change within the period known as late modernity. We have drawn attention to the uneven progress of intergenerational change between Australia and Canada. In Australia we see evidence of an acceleration of generational change in the significant increase in post-secondary participation by our respondents, compared with their parents; in the space of one generation, educational levels of young Australians were transformed. In Canada the pattern was less dramatic, representing a consolidation rather than a transformation between generations.

Within the broad framework of writing about social change provided by Beck and Lau (2005) and Giddens (1991) this chapter raises some interesting questions. The Australian pattern of intergenerational change resonates with the understanding that in late modernity social institutions are subject to more rapid change and as a result are less stable. Rosa (2003) argues that institutional stability is on the decline in late-modern societies, which his study characterizes in terms of 'high-speed' societies in which temporalities have sped up. However, the institutional 'project' of engineering universal higher education on which both Canada and Australia embarked in the 1990s speaks to a reinforcing of institutional processes and their extension into new areas of life (that is, post-secondary education). It also speaks to a modern temporal sequence in which investment in education in one phase of life (student) is rewarded in the next phase (worker) through remuneration in a well-paid job. The assumption of a lockstep sequence is in contrast to a post-modern temporality in which the links between education and employment are less well defined and are more likely to involve active work by individuals than to evolve through established processes.

Although the outcomes for our participants suggest that the government policies of both Canada and Australia were successful, we identify systematic differences between groups because some have benefited from the investment in their education, others have benefited less, and some have not invested in education. Hence, while increases in participation in post-secondary education have meant that in both countries some groups have increased their participation, a complex pattern of inequalities continues to exist. Young people from higher socio-economic backgrounds navigate access to and participation in higher education better than do any other group. But there are also complexities within these patterns, especially in terms of gender and geographic location. These complexities call for a closer reading of the social processes of intergenerational capital, and we have drawn on the writing of Bourdieu in order to do this. Our brief discussion of the ways in which our participants perceived the role of their families in their education opens up the issue of the interaction between resources and their use. Although family support in all its dimensions is clearly significant for the young people in our studies, it is not available to all. We suggest that in times of change the role of families becomes increasingly significant and complex.

Our research has shown that the systems in place in the 1990s were negotiated and navigated most effectively by young people whose parents had some experience of post-secondary study. In one sense, the inadequacies of one institution (education) were being addressed by another institution (family), but only for those who could bring knowledge based on their own experience of education. The patterns we have documented could be seen as a failure by post-secondary education systems to support the educational careers of those who are most disadvantaged.

Finally, the experiences of those who did invest in post-secondary education suggest that educational systems today are required to offer flexibility in order to meet the demands that young people make for better articulation across systems (secondary and post-secondary) and across types of study. Our research participants have largely accepted the need to be responsive to changing labour-market demands and to chart their own course through formal and informal learning opportunities in order to develop their own talents and capacities. Their experiences should be seen as a challenge to policymakers to design educational pathways that will enable subsequent generations to access the kinds of learning they need and to build their educational careers over their lifetimes.

These observations about social and institutional change, the role of families, and the use of resources are taken up in different ways in the chapters that follow, as we explore the relationships between education, gender, class, employment, and other aspects of life.

6 Gaining a Foothold in the World of Work

The relationship of our participants to the labour market and their attitudes to work have become a defining feature of their generation. In chapter 3 we highlighted the policy discourse since the 1980s on the changing nature of work. The authors of those policy documents advanced compelling arguments that individuals as workers and citizens require sophisticated skill sets for an increasingly knowledge-based society. Recently, Mills and Blossfeld (2003) echoed the sentiment that over the past several decades the transition to adulthood for young people in industrialized nations has changed dramatically. They account for this change by 'globalization, via (1) the internationalization and importance of markets, (2) intensified competition, (3) accelerated spread of networks and knowledge via new technologies, and (4) the increasing dependence on random shocks' (Mills and Blossfeld 2003, 189).

Labour markets are increasingly described as precarious, unstable, unsafe, and uncertain, or *Unsicherheit*, a noun that, according to Bauman (2001), captures all of these dimensions. Mills and Blossfeld (2003) point out that because young people lack experience and seniority, they are particularly vulnerable to the factors affecting the labour market. According to Bauman (2000), while uncertainty has always been part of employment, in the past the workplace allowed for more collective protection and action. He argues that 'the present-day uncertainty is a powerful *individualizing* force' (Bauman 2000, 24) where 'individualization is a fate; not a choice' (Bauman 2000, 44). Labour markets have had a significant impact on this generation because the rules of the game of work as experienced by previous generations – long-term employment and related relationships and connections, and systems for promotion – have been reduced or eliminated and have been replaced with weak and transient forms of association. Today's labour force is described as flexible, mobile, disordered, and even chaotic. As a result of capital becoming, in Bauman's terms, 'exterritorial, light, disencumbered and disembedded to an unprecedented extent' (Bauman 2000, 25), related jobs have changed in terms of availability and conditions.

Bauman (2000, 2001) advances the argument that for those who are 'disencumbered,' who are able to reinvent themselves as necessary, who thrive in chaotic and creative disorder, and who work regardless of location or relocate as necessary, the freedom of flexibility is ideal. However, those who find themselves immobile (for example, owing to limited or outdated skills, family ties, or other constraining forces such as a disability), flexibility leads to precarious employment, vulnerability, and lack of freedom.

According to Wyn and Woodman (2006), in Australia, changes in educational policies coincided with changes in labour-market policies and the dismantling of collective bargaining. The term *flexible* work is a trope (Rhoades and Slaughter 1998) that more accurately describes the replacement of stable full-time work and related benefits with ' "just in time" employment, short-term contracts and part-time positions' (Wyn and Woodman 2006, 505). The latter study argues that while today's educational policies 'focus on essential human capital to feed the new Australian economies, labour market policies position young people as disposable and dispensable items in the economic management of workplaces' (Wyn and Woodman 2006, 506). This argument is supported by Bauman (2001), who claims that today's workers must make choices without any guarantee of returns for their investments and that in 'a *Risikoleben*, it is the acting person who is bound to pay the costs of the risks taken' (Bauman 2001, 44).

The impact of the new industrial relations regulations that were implemented in Australia in 1995 was significant for all Australian workers (Todd 2004), but they had particular implications for young workers. Changes to legislation had the effect of withdrawing previously negotiated Industrial Relation Awards, which had covered multiple employers and ensured minimum standards for workers across substantial sections of occupations. They were replaced by a regime in which individual employees negotiated their conditions (such as rates of pay, and working hours and conditions) with their employer. This meant that many groups, including young workers, became vulnerable to worsening working conditions. However, even before the 1996 Workplace Relations Act, working conditions in Australia were

different from those in Canada. The main difference was that employment for most workers did not carry benefits or fringe benefits.

In Canada, employment has traditionally included a range of both
mandatory (for example, Employment Insurance and Canada Pension) ·
and discretionary non-wage benefits (for example, dental health and
medical insurance schemes, and life insurance). Moreover, an increase in
the number of dual-earner families in recent years has led to an increasing number of family-related benefits (for example, child or parental care leave, and fitness facilities). According to Marshall (2003, 5),
over the past fifty years non-wage benefits have increased, currently
'account for one-third of total labour costs,' and 'are used as 'indicators of job quality.' Non-wage benefits packages, together with wages
and salaries, are used by employers to attract and retain employees
(Akyeampong 2002). However, in a recent Statistics Canada study
on income inequality in Canada, following a period of stability in the
1970s and 1980s, an increase in the inequality of family after-tax income
in the 1990s was attributed to 'a reduction in the generosity of several
income transfer programs, including the Employment Insurance and
Social Assistance Programmes ... and decreases in income tax rates.
This potentially reflects a weakening of the redistributive role of the
Canadian state' (Heisz 2007, 5).

Despite differences in the specifics of wages and non-wage benefits,
both Canada and Australia rank among the highest of the thirteen most
developed countries in terms of the Gini index of the inegalitarian distribution of disposable income, which according to Mahler and Jesuit
(2006, 489) is 'more as a result of limited state redistribution rather
than of a highly inegalitarian distribution of private sector income.'
Furthermore, this study reports that Australia and Canada rank second
and third from the bottom in terms of the average size of public social
benefits relative to total household incomes (11.1 per cent and 12.2 per
cent, respectively) compared to the highest ranking countries (Sweden
at 27.3 per cent and France at 24.4 per cent).

Despite the different context of their workplaces, a global pattern that
could be described as 'acceleration' of work (Rosa 2003) appears to have
had an impact in a similar way on both countries. In 2001, 65 per cent of
working Canadians reported that they experienced a medium or high
level of work-family conflict (Duxbury and Higgins 2003). For Australian
workers, 'work intensity' rose in 1995, with 28 per cent of employees
experiencing increased levels of work-related stress, putting more effort
into their jobs, and working at a faster pace, according to a report by
Morehead, Steele, Alexander, Stephen, and Duffin (1997). This report

also showed that in households where both spouses worked, 70 per cent of full-time employed mothers always or often felt rushed, as did 56 per cent of fathers and 52 per cent of women with no dependent children.

This research sets the backdrop against which the young people in our studies struggled to establish a livelihood within labour markets that are described as having increasing levels of *Unsicherheit*. We analyse their experiences and ask whether the promise of educational investment has paid off for all our participants. Since our data are longitudinal, we are able to assess the extent to which the theory and rhetoric advanced in the body of literature on labour-market precariousness explain the long-term outcomes and experiences for the young adults in this study. In subsequent chapters we go beyond the statistics on labour-market destinations to explore the dynamics of our respondents' actual labour force experiences in relation to other adult life events such as forming relationships and establishing families over time. We begin by using our respondents' own words to describe their expectations in their last year of high school about future work and careers.

Work and Career Plans and Goals

When interviewed in November of their final year in high school in 1989 and at age eighteen, fifty-one students from three different geographical areas in British Columbia were asked about their career plans and goals. About one-third had a specific goal in mind. They responded by identifying career goals such as 'working in a hospital...sterilizing things or something,' 'law,' 'translator, interpreter,' and 'I want to become a child psychologist.' An equally large proportion of the interviewees had a career area in mind, but these plans were tentative.

I think I'm joining the army. (female)

[I] just thought of the idea of getting into day care. (female)

Something along the lines of kinesiology...Maybe a physiotherapist or a sports medicine consultant or something. (male)

Approximately one-quarter of respondents had multiple ideas about their future careers:

Psychiatrist...or something to do with business...like manager of a something. I...don't really know though...Maybe working in some sort of office job. I don't know exactly what those people do. You always see them on TV; there's people in office, big high executive people – don't know what they do or how they get there, but that looks kinda interesting. I'll have to find that out. I'm interested in languages too. (female)

I was thinking of going on an exchange somewhere, to maybe Japan or even the States or something...I'm not going to take anything major, just...easy courses and learn another language, probably Japanese or something. If I went to the States, maybe Spanish, and that's just a thought, but before that I wanted to take a year off. I used to be a gymnast, so I'd want to get my coaching levels and everything, and just take other things, 'cause I sing and I wanted to take voice lessons and piano lessons and just things like that for my own personal pleasure kind of thing, and after a year go back to college and start from there. (female)

Yet, around 20 per cent had no idea about their future careers:

I really don't know. I'm just really undecided, so that's like I say, I'll probably take a year off. Finally get down to what I really want. Hopefully it won't take more than a year to decide what I want to do. (male)

No, I don't really have a set goal. There's just so much to pick from . . . Hard to decide. (female)

For several interviewees, the notion of career was inextricably linked to post-secondary study, and they responded to questions about career goals by clarifying their plans for study after high school:

Something that interests me is going into legal secretary, so I might as well get more education on that. (female)

As soon as I graduate...hoping that I'll be accepted...into one of the architectural engineering programs. Then hopefully later into the two-year program, where I can get – I think it's a degree, an architectural degree. (male)

For those with multiple ideas about possible careers, there was a strong sense of contingency and 'keeping their options open':

I'm interested in three areas, because of things that I do best...I'm good helping people, like counselling people...And then again I'm also into fashion . . . I'm very good – coordinated with fashion and ideas and things like that. And then I'm very into my entertainment world, acting, singing, dancing . . . And stick to those three, because you know, I feel like if you just focus on one thing and that doesn't work out for you, or you decided to change your mind, you know, you should always have something to go to. (female)

I'd like to write, but I don't know whether I'll be able to do that . . . I'm not sure . . . For a few years I was planning to go into law school, but I've sort of gone off that a bit. My step-dad's a lawyer, and it seems fun sometimes, but it seems like an awful lot of drudgery. So, I'm just going to sort of keep my options open and see what I want to do in a couple of years. (female)

While some respondents anticipated work to be hectic, several others emphasized that they did not want to work excessive hours, and a few even indicated that they did not want to work for many of their adult years.

Hopefully it's pretty lenient and flexible . . . I'd like to be doing some travelling and I don't want really structured hours . . .Working with other people, serving the public some way. But I don't want anything really structured or analytical. A moderate stress job is okay, but I don't think I want to be in something that's really stressful. (female)

Not that strenuous. A little laid back, sort of, you know. But there'd be a lot of work . . . Maybe full-time, I think. In an office, I think. (female)

In 1997 when they were twenty-three, a subset of eighty young Australians were asked about their intentions when they had left secondary school in 1991. Their retrospective answers reveal very similar patterns to those of the young Canadians. As we have discussed in chapter 5, their transition from secondary school into post-secondary education bore the effects of changes to the Victorian education system of secondary school certification, and of more demand for post-secondary education places than could be met. If the pathways into and through the post-secondary education system were intended to be 'smooth,' their transitions would have to be described as 'rough'; relatively few understood how to reach their employment goals, and a short-term focus on certification was at the expense of careers planning. Despite this, most young people emerged feeling optimistic about their future prospects.

Just over half of the respondents had had a specific career goal in mind when they left school, which gave them a definite direction to take in terms of either post-secondary studies or employment. The following examples are typical of this group:

> I always wanted to do a teacher course (Primary). In primary school I had a really good teacher and I wanted to be like that. (female)

> I wanted to go on to university and do an accounting degree. I was doing well in that area at school and thought I might as well keep going with it. I enjoyed business studies. (male)

> I wanted to get an apprenticeship in Year 10 in carpentry through the army. I liked working with wood, and my sister had already taken this path. (male)

> I wanted to get into uni to do physical education. I was always interested in sport. (female)

A quarter of these young people had multiple options that they wanted to follow, some of which were related (for example, 'primary teaching or domestic science teaching') and some of which were in quite different directions or focused on their levels of satisfaction with their future job rather than on what the job would be ('I hoped to gain as much satisfaction as possible from what I would be doing'). The following quotes are illustrative:

> I was interested in doing a forestry management course, or computing. (male)

> I wasn't sure where to go, but I thought accounting or marketing. (female)

> Either a nurse or a fashion designer. (female)

A quarter simply had no idea about what to do.

> I had no idea. My school was structured in science and maths. My school wasn't very helpful – careers advice was no help; they just focused on marks. (male)

> I had no idea about what I wanted to do. It took me all my energy just to get through the VCE. I saw the careers advisor, but they were no use.

I challenged the assumption that it is automatic to go straight on from school to uni. (female)

I wanted to get out of school as quickly as possible. Dad's a mechanic, and I was interested in that, but Dad said, 'Mechanics don't get paid enough' – it was a prick. (male)

Analyses of survey data over a fourteen-year (Australia) to fifteen-year (Canada) period following high school graduation reveal that the actual experiences of respondents were somewhat different than they had anticipated. Moreover, differences by country are evident. In this chapter we use gender and post-secondary-completion status (no post-secondary credentials; non-university credentials; and university credentials) as key moderating variables. Although the proportion of those who never completed post-secondary education over the course of our research is very small, they are likely to be the most vulnerable (Saunders, 2003) and hence warrant specific attention.

Five to Seven Turbulent Years of Labour-Force Participation

Almost all survey respondents had participated in the labour force within five to seven years of leaving high school. As portrayed in table 21, Canadian young women and men were far more likely than their Australian counterparts to have held more jobs. Even though the Australians had been in the labour force for almost two years longer than the Canadians had been, just 33 per cent had held only one job, and only 3 per cent had worked at six jobs or more. In contrast, very few Canadian young women and men held only one job, and 36 per cent of both women and men had worked at six jobs or more. The number of jobs held also varied by post-secondary-completion status. When compared to the other groups, those who had not earned any post-secondary credentials in five to seven years out of high school were most likely to hold only one job. However, in both countries, most young women and men in this category held at least two jobs, suggesting that the job market for those heading directly into the labour force was less than stable for this group. For the Australian cohort it also represented an emerging belief that moving jobs was a good thing to do. Between 1996 and 2002, over half of the Australians who changed jobs did so in order to have better opportunities. In 2002, as many as 44 per cent of the Australians were hoping to change jobs in the next two years.

Table 21
Number of jobs held in five and seven years out of high school, by sex

| | Age 23, Canada, 1993 | | | | | | | Age 24, Australia, 1998 | | | | | | |
| | Females | | | Males | | | | Females | | | Males | | | |
	No PS %	Non-univ. %	Univ. %	No PS %	Non-univ. %	Univ. %	Total %	No PS %	Non-univ. %	Univ. %	No PS %	Non-univ. %	Univ. %	Total %
None	0	0	1	0	0	0	0	1	6	3	2	0	6	3
One	27	3	1	15	6	6	5	36	30	31	44	19	33	33
Two to five	62	59	58	65	58	59	59	57	55	64	48	81	56	61
Six or more	12	38	40	20	36	34	36	6	9	2	7	0	5	3
N	17	212	141	20	143	70	603	91	33	233	45	31	84	517

PS = post-secondary education

Table 22
Current or most recent occupation, at age 24, in Australia, 1998

| | Females | | | Males | | | |
	No PS %	Non-univ. %	Univ. %	No PS %	Non-univ. %	Univ. %	Total %
Casual/irregular paid job	17	18	15	13	13	17	15
Unemployed, looking for work	1	6	4	7	7	4	4
Part-time job	11	6	10	9	7	6	9
Unemployed, not looking for work	1	6	4	0	0	6	3
Full-time job	61	58	64	67	68	63	63
A number of jobs	3	3	2	0	0	2	2
Voluntary work	1	0	0	2	3	0	1
Family/home commitments	2	3	2	0	0	1	2
Self-employed	3	0	0	2	3	1	1
N	92	33	233	45	31	84	518

In 1998, aged twenty-four, the majority of Australian young women and men indicated that they were employed full-time, with another 15 per cent reporting that they were employed in casual or irregular jobs (table 22). Those who had been in the labour force since leaving high school were no more likely than those who continued their studies to hold full-time positions. Few indicated that they were unemployed and looking for work; however, males with no post-secondary or non-university credentials were the most likely to be unemployed. Few reported that family or home commitments constituted their major activity. This is not surprising, given that so few respondents were married or had children by this time (see chapter 7).

Around two-thirds of the Australian sample described their current job status as permanent; those with non-university credentials were the most likely to do so. Those who had graduated from university were slightly less likely than average to hold permanent positions, which may reflect the fact that their university studies had delayed their job entry. Another 13 per cent indicated that they were employed on renewable contracts. However, 19 per cent indicated that they were seasonally or casually employed or were working on limited-term contracts (table 23). Both females and males with non-university credentials were least likely to belong to this category, once again reflecting the relative advantage at this stage of their lives of earlier engagement with the labour market. University graduates, at around 38 per cent, were the most

Table 23
Status of current job by sex, at age 24, in Australia, 1998

	Females			Males			
	No PS %	Non-univ. %	Univ. %	No PS %	Non-univ. %	Univ. %	Total %
Permanent	66	75	61	72	82	63	65
Renewable contract	13	0	16	8	11	11	13
Limited-term contract	0	4	8	5	4	5	5
Seasonal/casual	15	14	13	13	4	17	14
Other	6	7	1	3	0	4	3
N	84	28	210	39	27	75	463

likely to hold non-permanent positions, which is understandable given that they would have studied full-time for the equivalent of four years during this seven-year span. Those with non-university credentials were the least likely to do so, suggesting that they had managed to experience some job stability. At this stage, as graduates moved from the part-time work that had provided financial support for their studies into their careers, the patterns are mixed. However, the most significant point emerging from these data is the overall uncertainty of the labour market. Precarious work was the only option available for 34 per cent of women and 29 per cent of men with no post-secondary education history, who remained in non-permanent jobs. Since it was often all that they could get at first, graduates also took precarious work or continued with the jobs they had been doing to support themselves while studying, while they sought more permanent work.

No directly comparable data to tables 22 and 23 are available for the Canadian sample. However, five years out of high school, inequalities in labour-market outcomes by gender were becoming apparent. Canadian respondents were asked to report specifically the type of jobs in which they were employed (Andres 2005). Overall, despite the fact that women (63 per cent) were much more likely than men (48 per cent) to have earned a post-secondary credential, and more likely than men to have completed a bachelor's degree or greater (29 per cent versus 20 per cent, respectively), the largest proportion of women were employed in semi-skilled jobs. Men were more likely to work in the skilled/semi-professions or in management or professional positions. Only 4 per cent of women overall held management or professional positions.

Canadian women were four times more likely than Canadian men to be married and three times more likely to have had children (see chapter 7), which may explain gender differences in occupational status.

The picture for university graduates reveals further complexities in gendered patterns. Almost 20 per cent of university graduates held unskilled jobs. It could be argued that upon leaving university, graduates held few skills that prepared them for high-status jobs, and therefore entry-level service work provided them, as 'outsiders' (Mills and Blossfeld 2003), with a gateway into the labour market. However, analyses by gender reveal that although the proportions of university-educated men and women employed in semi-skilled jobs were similar, men were more than three times as likely as women in this group to be employed as professionals; that is, only 5 per cent of women, compared with 17 per cent of men, with university degrees were employed as professionals or managers. Just under half of the men with non-university credentials were employed in semi-skilled or skilled jobs, with the other half being approximately equally divided between lower-level and higher-level jobs. About 60 per cent of non-university-educated women held unskilled or semi-skilled jobs. Not surprisingly, over 70 per cent of young women and men who had not earned post-secondary credentials were concentrated in unskilled and semi-skilled jobs. Men in this category tended to be in semi-skilled manual work, and the women to be in semi-skilled clerical and sales positions.

When interviewed in the last year of high school, none of the Canadian respondents commented on the possibility of being unemployed or underemployed. Finding work and remaining employed was perceived as relatively unproblematic and was described as the logical follow-up to post-secondary completion. Many of the women foresaw that they would enter the labour force as full-time employees, take leave when they had children, and then re-enter, either full-time or part-time, according to their own desires. We asked the Australian respondents to describe their goals in retrospect, and by this time (1996 and 1998) they were very aware of the possibilities of being unemployed. Their strongly employment-focused goals and labour-market experiences to date may well reflect this awareness. Both the young men and the young women, like their Canadian peers, foresaw little problem in leaving the workforce for family reasons. Across the Australian cohort, child-rearing was almost exclusively seen as something that the women would manage, juggling work and child-rearing or taking time out of work.

We conclude that the Canadian and Australian survey respondents were not prepared for periods of unemployment, underemployment, and part-time work. Table 24 describes the patterns they experienced around these dimensions.

Approximately one-third of both Canadian and Australian young adults collected unemployment benefits at some point within five years of leaving high school, with women and men without post-secondary credentials twice as likely as the average to do so. The clear incremental decline in collecting unemployment insurance benefits across post-secondary completion categories suggests that those with higher levels of education were able to stave off unemployment.

The labour-market experiences of those who did maintain employment were not universally positive. Data available for the Canadian sample show high levels of underemployment across all categories except women with no post-secondary credentials. Those who had earned some level of post-secondary credential struggled to find full-time employment, as did men without post-secondary credentials. Very few Canadian respondents collected social insurance and welfare benefits, largely due to the limited availability of these benefits as an option for support. The overall proportion of Canadians who received childcare subsidies is also low; however, 38 per cent of women with children, most of whom had only high school credentials, collected such subsidies.

Our analysis reveals that job entry within five to seven years of high school completion was indeed turbulent. These patterns were complex as young women took different pathways from their male counterparts, and as those with no post-secondary qualifications took up different strategies in relation to their options than did those with post-secondary qualifications. However, when asked about their views about their current or most recent jobs, both Canadian and Australian young adults were relatively optimistic. In tables 25 and 26 we have collapsed the categories 'strongly agree' and 'agree' into one category labelled 'A,' and 'strongly disagree' and 'disagree' into one category labelled 'D,' to report responses to several attitudinal statements about work.

Canadian women and men were particularly positive that their jobs paid well, they were able to use their skills and abilities, the work was interesting, their work gave them a sense of accomplishment, and they enjoyed coming to work. Negative responses were related to the freedom to decide what to do in their jobs, chances for promotion, and the fact that their work was not related to their education and training. Women were generally less likely than men to respond positively to these items, which suggests that they were somewhat less satisfied than

Table 24
Unemployment history, by sex

	Females			Males			Total
Replied 'Yes'	No PS %	Non-univ. %	Univ. %	No PS %	Non-univ. %	Univ. %	%
Canada (September 1989 to April 1993, up to age 23)							
Unemployed when you wanted to be employed	29	50	59	60	49	47	51
Unemployed for at least three consecutive months	42	47	41	45	50	50	47
Working part-time when you wanted to be working full-time	29	48	43	15	43	29	42
Received unemployment insurance benefits	53	32	13	55	32	10	26
Received social insurance or welfare income	0	9	6	20	6	4	7
Received childcare subsidy (MSSH)	6	4	1	0	0	0	2
Australia (1991 to 1996, up to age 22)							
Had drawn unemployment benefits	35	33	30	35	35	20	30

Table 25
Views about work, by sex and 1993 post-secondary-completion status, at age 23, in Canada

	Females (%)						Males (%)						Total (%)	
	No PS		Non-univ.		Univ.		No PS		Non-univ.		Univ.			
	A	D	A	D	A	D	A	D	A	D	A	D	A	D
The pay is good	74	24	66	26	65	29	85	15	61	25	69	19	65	26
I have the freedom to decide what I do in my job	54	48	47	38	49	36	60	20	51	31	56	25	50	34
The fringe benefits are good	48	36	46	38	45	43	55	25	53	29	49	41	48	37
The job lets me use my skills and abilities	76	24	65	22	67	27	85	5	59	27	73	19	65	24
The chances for promotion are good	53	30	38	44	32	40	50	20	39	36	41	40	38	40
Job security is good	70	18	59	26	50	37	50	30	60	24	44	30	55	29
The work is interesting	83	6	67	21	70	19	75	20	63	25	81	10	69	19
The job gives me a feeling of accomplishment	71	24	63	23	61	25	80	20	61	22	74	12	70	16
The job is directly related to my education and training	30	48	49	44	51	46	45	25	44	50	62	34	49	44
This is the kind of job I expected to have at this stage in my life	18	47	39	43	43	40	45	35	40	31	49	33	38	41
I look forward to coming to work	71	18	56	23	59	20	70	15	59	25	75	14	61	22

A = 'strongly agree' and 'agree' combined
D = 'strongly disagree' and 'disagree' combined

Table 26

Views about work, by sex and 1999 post-secondary-completion status, at age 25, in Australia

	Females (%)						Males (%)						Total (%)	
	No PS		Non-univ.		Univ.		No PS		Non-univ.		Univ.			
	A	D	A	D	A	D	A	D	A	D	A	D	A	D
The pay is good	57	40	54	32	58	33	68	25	56	16	62	27	59	32
I have the freedom to decide what I do in my job	60	25	53	36	63	29	60	15	48	34	62	27	61	28
The fringe benefits are good	41	29	36	39	30	45	60	23	60	8	44	30	39	35
The job lets me use my skills and abilities	82	16	93	7	87	8	78	10	89	4	86	7	85	10
The chances for promotion are good	42	37	46	33	38	40	38	38	52	22	45	34	41	37
Job security is good	68	16	78	11	60	28	40	18	73	12	70	20	66	22
The work is interesting	81	14	93	7	84	9	75	15	81	8	86	10	84	10
The job gives me a feeling of accomplishment	75	15	82	11	78	12	73	15	78	8	79	4	77	12
The job is directly related to my qualifications	53	36	79	11	73	20	60	23	74	11	80	18	70	22
This is the kind of job I expected to have at this stage in my life	59	33	53	25	63	27	48	25	65	16	61	15	60	25
I look forward to coming to work	64	18	57	11	61	16	60	13	75	11	69	12	64	15

A = 'strongly agree' and 'agree'
D = 'strongly disagree' and 'disagree'

men overall with the conditions of work. Almost 50 per cent of women without post-secondary credentials disagreed that they had the freedom to decide what to do in their jobs, and none strongly agreed that she looked forward to coming to work.

Women and men who had earned university degrees were the least likely to agree that the fringe benefits were good, and around 40 per cent of those with some type of post-secondary credential disagreed that their chances for promotion were good. This concurs with the finding that only approximately 16 per cent of Canadian male respondents and 12 per cent of Canadian female respondents with university degrees had medical insurance, and 13 per cent and 11 per cent respectively had dental insurance, during this period in their lives, suggesting that in the early 1990s it was not necessary for employers to woo university graduates with non-wage benefits as has been suggested in the literature (Akyeampong 2002; Marshall 2003). Those without post-secondary credentials fared slightly better, reflecting longer periods spent in the labour force. Around 40 per cent of women and men in this group had medical insurance, but only 23 per cent of women and 32 per cent of men had dental insurance. Relatively high proportions across all categories disagreed that this was the kind of job they expected at this stage in their lives.

Australia does not have a tradition of aligning welfare provisions such as health care or unemployment payments to employment. This means that what are called employment 'benefits' in Canada do not exist in Australia. Instead, since the 1970s, Australians have had access to universal 'welfare' measures that provide for the cost of medical care through a system of reimbursements by the government for consultations with general practitioners, a public hospital system where health care is free, and unemployment benefits. Working conditions have been the subject of ongoing negotiation. Traditionally, working conditions were negotiated on an occupational basis through trade unions. These ensured that workers had access to sick leave, parental leave, and annual leave and included other conditions such as the right to strike and protection from unfair dismissal. These conditions were eroded during the workplace legislative changes that occurred during the 1990s.

In some respects, Australian young adults were more positive than Canadians about their current jobs (table 26). Across all post-secondary-completion categories, the vast majority agreed that their employment let them use their skills and abilities, the work was interesting, and it gave them a feeling of accomplishment. However, 40 per cent of Australian women without post-secondary credentials disagreed that the pay was good (compared to 25 per cent of men in the same category). Similar to the Canadian sample, 39 per cent of women with university degrees tended to disagree that the fringe benefits were good (compared to 30 per cent of Australian men with university degrees). The question has a somewhat different meaning in Australia because there is no system of workplace fringe benefits for workers, as we have discussed above.

Finally, we can directly compare the extent to which Canadian and Australian young adults had formulated their career plans within the five to seven years following high school completion. Table 27 indicates that only around 10 per cent of respondents claimed to have a well-established career at this point in their lives.

Here we see some strong trends among groups and across countries. With one exception, those with university degrees were most likely to stay on course with their high school plans. This is in stark contrast to those without post-secondary credentials. Comparing across categories, Australian men were more likely than any other group to have not formulated plans in high school and to still have none seven years later, and in most instances they were less likely to have changed and chosen new careers. Very few from any group reported having well-established careers, indicating that their place in the labour market was not characterized by stability and permanence.

Ten Years of Slow Change

By comparing our respondents' work histories and future plans for employment from five to seven years following high school departure to around ten years, we are able to determine the extent to which their lives, as influenced by their work conditions, remained precarious. Despite the contingency and precariousness of employment, it is clear that work is central to the lives of the young people in our studies. All but six women and five men from Canada, or 99 per cent, indicated that they had been in the paid labour force during this period. Similarly, in Australia only three men and two women reported in 2000 that they had not worked over the past five years. However, as table 28 indicates, job turnover remained high, with only about one-fifth of both Canadian and Australian young people occupying a single job during this period. However, it is noteworthy that, when compared with the first

Table 27
The extent to which career plans have been formulated

| | Age 23, Canada, 1993 | | | | | | | Age 24, Australia, 1998 | | | | | | |
| | Females | | | Males | | | | Females | | | Males | | | |
	No PS %	Non-univ. %	Univ. %	No PS %	Non-univ. %	Univ. %	Total %	No PS %	Non-univ. %	Univ. %	No PS %	Non-univ. %	Univ. %	Total %
No planned career when I left high school, and still have none	6	6	5	5	6	6	5	10	9	6	17	7	12	9
I discarded my original career plan but have not chosen a new career yet	35	13	6	10	10	4	10	7	15	5	14	0	7	7
No planned career when I left high school, but have now chosen a new one	12	18	15	15	23	13	18	9	15	15	12	18	15	14
I have changed and chosen a new career	18	26	25	15	28	21	25	27	12	23	17	18	7	19
I have retained the career plans that I had at high school graduation	12	25	36	25	22	44	29	31	21	40	26	46	45	37
I already have a well-established career	12	10	6	15	5	9	8	8	21	8	12	7	12	10
Other	6	3	6	15	6	3	5	8	6	3	3	4	2	4
N	17	214	143	20	148	70	612	88	33	226	42	28	83	500

Table 28
Number of jobs held during ten years out of high school, by sex

| | Age 28, Canada, 1998 | | | | | | | Age 26, Australia, 2000 | | | | | | |
| | Females | | | Males | | | | Females | | | Males | | |
	No PS %	Non-univ. %	Univ. %	No PS %	Non-univ. %	Univ. %	Total %	No PS %	Non-univ. %	Univ. %	No PS %	Non-univ. %	Univ. %	Total %
One	58	31	10	28	22	13	19	24	24	20	29	22	27	23
Two to four	37	49	56	53	52	55	53	65	63	66	62	70	58	64
Five to eight	5	21	34	20	26	31	28	12	13	13	10	8	15	12
N	21	178	225	20	110	150	704	86	33	229	47	34	83	512

time period (see table 21), the number of jobs held by both groups in this latter period had declined.

Canadian women without post-secondary credentials show the most stability, at least in terms of job turnover, with 58 per cent remaining in one job during this period (compared to 24 per cent of Australian women in the same category). The proportion of men in this category was around 28 per cent in Canada and 29 per cent in Australia. Most of those with post-secondary credentials held two or more jobs during this period. The exception is Australian men, where 27 per cent stayed in one job.

Considerably more Canadian females (38 per cent) than males (18 per cent) reported that they did not currently hold full-time jobs at around 28 years of age. The opposite is the case for part-time work: more males (83 per cent) than females (62 per cent) indicated that they were not currently employed part-time. Most respondents reported that they currently held one full-time job. Among women, those with university degrees were most likely (72 per cent) to work full-time (compared with 63 per cent of those with no post-secondary credentials and 58 per cent of those with non-university credentials). Over 80 per cent of men across all post-secondary categories reported working full-time. Of those respondents with full-time jobs, 20 per cent of females and 13 per cent of males reported that they were also employed part-time. Six percent of Canadian women and 5 per cent of men indicated that at the time of the survey in 1998 they were not working full-time or part-time. The vast majority of Canadians (83 per cent of women and 84 per cent of men) claimed that their jobs were permanent rather than temporary; however, university graduates (72 per cent of women and 83 per cent of men) were slightly less likely to do so than those without university credentials.

In contrast, when asked about their main current work situation, 74 per cent of Australian women and 79 per cent of Australian men indicated that they were employed in full-time work, and around 12 per cent indicated that they were engaged primarily in regular part-time work, casual work, or a number of jobs. Eleven percent of Australian women, but no Australian men, identified family or home commitments as their primary occupation. Approximately equal proportions of women (75 per cent) and men (74 per cent) described their positions as permanent, with an additional 9 per cent indicating that they were employed under renewable contracts. There is very little variation across post-secondary completion categories, with women and men with non-university credentials more likely than average (77 per cent and 80 per cent, respectively) to be in permanent positions, and less likely (8 per cent and 7 per cent, respectively) to be working under renewable contracts. Yet, over 40 per cent of both Canadian and Australian females and males planned to leave their jobs within two years. Canadian women (8 per cent) and men (6 per cent) were much more likely than Australian women (1 per cent) and men (2 per cent) to indicate that they were currently unemployed.

Ten years following high school graduation, 59 per cent of Canadian women and 67 per cent of men received medical insurance benefits, and 59 per cent and 64 per cent respectively had a dental plan. However, large differences among post-secondary-completion status groups continued to exist. Only 38 per cent of men with no post-secondary credentials, compared with 75 per cent of those with non-university credentials and 65 per cent with university degrees, had medical insurance. The comparable figures for women are 53 per cent, 58 per cent, and 63 per cent. Dental insurance followed a similar pattern. Most notably, men across all groups were more likely than women to receive childcare benefits. University-educated men were the most likely to be granted parental paid leave (compared with 33 per cent of university-educated women and less than 32 per cent in all other groups).

Findings at the ten-year mark demonstrate that unlike the expectations expressed by interviewees at the beginning of this chapter, establishing a career was not as straightforward as both the Canadian and the Australian samples had expected. Although almost all respondents had been in the paid labour force, job turnover and planned job mobility remained high at ten years after having left high school. Indeed, for a majority of the Australians, the difficulty of establishing a career had translated into new attitudes about the nature of career. As we will see in the following chapter, for both groups the challenge of making a livelihood had implications for other areas of their lives and, for many, led to reassessments of their priorities.

The Long Road to Job Stability

Fifteen years out of high school for the Canadian sample and twelve to fourteen years out of high school for the Australian sample, there is evidence of greater job stability than at any point earlier. It had taken them a long time to find the security that they had sought when they were leaving school. By the mid 2000s, their job outcomes were assisted by the buoyancy of the Canadian and Australian economies, as well as by their own efforts and gained experience. Around 90 per cent of Canadian women and men indicated that their current employment positions were permanent rather than temporary, and around 90 per cent reported that they were not likely to be laid off or to lose their jobs within the next year. This was consistent across all groups except for women with university degrees, where 17 per cent reported that their jobs were temporary. However, 17 per cent of females and 20 per cent of males reported that they were currently looking for another job, and those with post-secondary credentials were slightly more likely to be searching for new positions. Compared to the ten-year mark in 1998, higher proportions of Canadian females (36 per cent compared to 21 per cent) and males (44 per cent compared to 18 per cent) had held only one job since that time. Women with university credentials were least likely to hold more than one job during this period (for example, 31 per cent compared to 46 per cent of university-educated men), and women with no post-secondary credentials and men with non-university credentials were the most likely to hold more than one job (46 per cent for both groups). Women remained almost twice as likely (30 per cent) than men (17 per cent) to be working part-time in their current or most recent job.

Considerably lower proportions of Australian women (72 per cent) and men (85 per cent) reported that their employment was permanent or on a renewable contract, with 5 to 6 per cent of Australian women and men reporting that they were employed in seasonal or casual employment. Women across all post-secondary completion categories were at least 10 per cent less likely than men to hold permanent or renewable positions.

By 2003, Canadian women had made considerable gains in terms of employer-provided benefits. However, when benefits are disaggregated by post-secondary-completion category, women without post-secondary credentials are considerably disadvantaged; that is, 75 per cent of women with university degrees had medical insurance, compared to only 59 per cent of women with no post-secondary credentials and 61 per cent of women with non-university credentials. This pattern holds for dental insurance, parental leave, and childcare benefits. For men, the patterns vary little across categories, with about 70 per cent having medical and dental insurance. These findings concur with those of Marshall (2003) that higher levels of education were positively associated with better benefit coverage and that smaller proportions of women than men received non-wage benefits. However, our findings demonstrate the interaction of gender and levels of education. Also, it is critical to note that at fifteen years following high school graduation and already with long-term commitments to the labour market, a maximum of 75 per cent of respondents were receiving mainstream benefits such as medical insurance, a dental plan, sick leave, and long-term disability; in other words, the term *universal health care* did not apply to one quarter of the Canadian sample.

Forty-two per cent of women and 25 per cent of men reported that they had received unemployment benefits between 1998 and 2003. University-educated men were the least likely (20 per cent) to collect such benefits; women without post-secondary credentials were the most likely (46 per cent) to do so.

In tables 29 and 30 we are able to compare occupational status levels by post-secondary completion for both the Canadian and the Australian samples. By 2003, when they were around thirty-two, 95 per cent of women and 93 per cent of men in the Canadian sample had earned some type of post-secondary credential, and 53 per cent of women and men had completed university degrees. Table 29 indicates that Canadian women with non-university credentials continued to be concentrated in the unskilled, semi-skilled, and skilled jobs, and just over a third of women in this category were employed as semi-professionals. Women without any post-secondary credentials were much more likely than those with credentials to work at unskilled and semi-skilled jobs.

About 40 per cent of Canadian men who had not earned post-secondary credentials within fifteen years of high school graduation were concentrated in the skilled-jobs category and were half as likely as women in the same category to be employed as unskilled or semi-skilled labourers. This finding indicates that there must be better opportunities available for educationally unqualified men than for women to learn skills on the job. Less than 10 per cent of women and 5 per cent of men in this group were employed as professionals, and almost none were self-employed.

Canadians who had earned university degrees by 2003 were most likely to be employed as semi-professionals or professionals. However, a 10 per cent gender gap remains, with more men than women employed in the professional/managerial category. These proportions changed minimally between 1998 and 2003, indicating that university-educated women continue to be concentrated in the semi-professions. Only 10 per cent of men and 3 per cent of women reported being self-employed, suggesting that 'pull factors' such as independence from

Table 29
Current or most recent occupation (Pineo-Porter-McRoberts), by post-secondary-completion status, at age 33, in Canada, 2003

| | Females | | | Males | | | |
	No PS %	Non-univ. %	Univ. %	No PS %	Non-univ. %	Univ. %	Total %
Farm labourers	0	0	0	0	2	1	1
Unskilled manual	0	1	1	10	8	3	3
Unskilled clerical, sales, services	23	15	4	5	3	1	7
Total unskilled	23	16	5	15	13	5	11
Semi-skilled manual	5	2	0	5	7	1	2
Semi-skilled clerical, sales, services	27	12	3	10	6	3	7
Farmers	0	0	0	0	0	0	0
Total semi-skilled	32	14	3	15	13	4	9
Skilled crafts and trades	0	0	2	33	17	5	5
Skilled clerical, sales, services	9	11	6	0	4	1	6
Forewomen/foremen	0	1	0	0	3	1	1
Supervisors	5	5	2	0	10	1	4
Technicians	0	8	3	5	6	4	5
Total skilled	13	25	13	38	40	12	21
Middle management	5	11	5	24	12	11	10
Semi-professional	18	25	40	5	15	24	27
Total semi-professional	23	36	45	29	27	35	37
High-level management	0	4	5	0	2	2	3
Employed professionals	5	5	26	5	6	33	18
Self-employed professionals	5	0	3	0	0	10	3
Total professional/managerial	10	9	34	5	8	45	24
N	22	177	116	21	116	151	603

an employer and flexible working hours may be less attractive than income security non-wage benefits (Akyeampong and Sussman 2003). The sentiments of one young Canadian female survey respondent reflect this view:

The majority of young adults are finding it harder and harder to find full-time work with a company that provides benefits; we are left to be self-started and self-employed, yet we have little to no support from the government; self-employed small business owners most often have no dental, no pension, and no maternity, no paid vacation – 'no nothing.'

Table 30
Current or most recent occupation (ANZSCO) by post-secondary-completion status, at age 30, in Australia, 2004

	Females			Males			
	No PS %	Non-univ. %	Univ. %	No PS %	Non-univ. %	Univ. %	Total %
Labourers	2	1	0	7	2	0	2
Machinery operators and drivers	0	1	0	10	3	0	2
Sales workers	5	4	3	7	6	0	4
Clerical and administrative workers	34	16	10	12	12	10	15
Community and personal service workers	10	9	4	10	5	2	6
Technicians and trades workers	2	6	3	12	18	12	8
Professionals	39	54	72	33	40	67	55
Managers	8	9	8	10	14	10	9
N	85	113	165	42	87	51	543

Although the job classification scheme for Australia (table 30) is somewhat different, a similar pattern emerges. By 2004,[1] when they were thirty, 78 per cent of women and 77 per cent of men held post-secondary credentials; 46 per cent and 32 per cent, respectively, had earned at least a bachelor's degree. About 53 per cent of women and 58 per cent of men without post-secondary credentials were employed in non-professional and non-managerial jobs. Conversely, only 20 per cent of women and 24 per cent of men with university degrees were employed in similar positions. Over 50 per cent of those with non-university credentials worked as professionals or managers, with women somewhat more likely to do so. Women without post-secondary credentials remained concentrated in the clerical and administrative worker category, and men without post-secondary credentials worked as labourers or clerical and administrative workers. Unlike the Canadian sample, however, women with university degrees were more likely than their male counterparts to be employed in professional positions; they were slightly less likely than men to be managers. As there is no distinct category for the semi-professions in the Australian and New Zealand Standard Classification of Occupations (ANZSCO), we are unable to tease out gender differences within the semi-professional and professional categories.

---

1 Because of the reduced sample size in 2006, we report 2004 data in table 30.

The situation of *Unsicherheit* (precariousness, instability, unsafeness, and uncertainty) had a particular effect on the young Australians. The instability of the labour market and the degree of uncertainty that surrounded the 'value' of their educational qualifications were reflected in a redefinition of the idea of career. Responding to survey questions in 2004, an overwhelming majority (92 per cent) agreed that a career could be defined as 'a job that offers scope for advancement,' 88 per cent said that 'a career should offer commitment,' and 82 per cent agreed that 'a career was any ongoing role that offered personal fulfilment.' However, less than half equated a career as 'a full-time, permanent job,' which suggests that in some ways they appear to have redefined the rules of the game and to have internalized the contingent, 'disembedded' nature of life that Bauman describes.

Fifteen and twelve years out of high school, most of our study respondents considered themselves adequately qualified for their jobs. Analyses by post-secondary-completion status (table 31) reveal that Canadian female degree holders and men with non-university credentials were the most likely to consider themselves overqualified for their current positions, suggesting that they were underemployed in relation to their post-secondary credentials. Australian men in all categories were much more likely than Canadian women and men and Australian women to consider themselves underqualified for their positions.

In chapter 7 we examine in detail the extent to which Canadian and Australian respondents were satisfied with their lives at fifteen and fourteen years, respectively, following high school graduation. However, because satisfaction levels are inextricably linked to work, we summarize here some of the key findings related to work.

In brief, our respondents were overwhelmingly satisfied with their personal lives and development, their family lives, their careers, and their educational attainments. However, there are a few important differences by gender and post-secondary completion status. Over 30 per cent of those who had not earned any post-secondary credentials indicated that they were dissatisfied with their educational attainments, and around 20 per cent were dissatisfied with their work or careers. A higher proportion of Canadian women than men expressed concern about educational opportunities for today's children. When asked to comment about educational and career opportunities for members of their generation, Canadian women and men without post-secondary credentials were the least enthusiastic, with men voicing more dissatisfaction than did women on educational opportunities. Similarly,

Table 31

Responses to 'Are you qualified for your job?' by post-secondary-completion status and sex

| | Age 33, Canada, 2003 | | | | | | | Age 30, Australia, 2004 | | | | | | | |
| | Females | | | Males | | | | Females | | | Males | | | |
	No PS %	Non-univ. %	Univ. %	No PS %	Non-univ. %	Univ. %	Total %	No PS %	Non-univ. %	Univ. %	No PS %	Non-univ. %	Univ. %	Total %
Underqualified	0	4	2	0	4	1	3	7	6	5	9	8	5	6
Adequately qualified	6	79	76	86	75	85	79	79	85	83	83	81	77	82
Overqualified	5	17	22	14	21	14	18	14	10	12	9	11	18	12
N	22	117	224	21	117	154	715	95	125	193	46	88	62	609

32 per cent of Australian women and 34 per cent of Australian men without post-secondary credentials (compared to 2 per cent of women and 3 per cent of men with university degrees) were dissatisfied with their educational attainments. Also, 20 per cent of women and 32 per cent of men in the same group expressed dissatisfaction with their careers. Such dissatisfaction was much lower for those with university degrees (6 per cent and 12 per cent, respectively).

Conclusion

The evidence of our two studies reveals in stark detail the struggle that many of these young people have waged in order to establish a livelihood. Data sets such as ours permit us to go well beyond an examination of labour-market outcomes at a given point in time in relation to various educational credentials earned. In addition, we have been able to augment the tables with our respondents' voices to provide a much sharper understanding of their expectations. In their late teens and early twenties their lives were dramatically and systematically shaped by the educational policies of the Australian and Canadian governments, but by their mid to late twenties the labour markets had made their mark. The Canadian sample took their first steps into adulthood just as after-tax-income inequality began to rise in 1989 and continued through to 2004, which corresponds exactly with the time span of this study. Similarly, the Gini coefficient that measures income inequality also began to rise in 1989, reached its peak in 2000, and has since stabilized. During the same time period the middle class in Canada declined, as measured by smaller proportions of individuals with incomes 75 per cent to 150 per cent above the median income, compared to the 1979–1989 period (Heisz 2007). In other words, although the Canadian sample spent most of their formative years (1970s and 1980s) in a period of relative prosperity, they entered adulthood and eventually the labour force in an extended period of relative decline.

At the outset of this chapter we claimed that their relationships to the labour market were a defining feature of this generation. In presenting the evidence for how this has unfolded, we have exposed the complex but powerful ways in which it has shaped their lives. The rules of the game of work have indeed changed for this generation. We feel that their experiences can be compared with a game that is commonly found in children's arcades and fun parks in Canada. In this game, gophers' heads pop up randomly, and the players use a mallet to knock them down. However, it is a rather no-win game because the heads just keep popping up. In Australian fun parks there is a similar game, which involves shooting at a row of ducks that never seem to line up. Our participants appear to be locked into one of these games. At one point someone may have a permanent position but no benefits. Each group of our participants (by gender and by educational qualifications) seems to have some advantages and disadvantages simultaneously, but the advantages do not appear to line up fully for any one group.

For example, by the time they were in their early thirties, women with university degrees were the most likely to have benefited (job security, permanency, and, in Canada, work-related benefits), but they were also the most likely to experience job mobility. This may be desirable in terms of upward mobility through successive job changes but, as we will see in chapters 7 and 8, bears a cost in terms of establishing relationships, managing a family, and ensuring positive levels of well-being. The opposite was true for women without post-secondary credentials, who exhibited more stable patterns of employment but in the end had much lower levels of non-wage benefits. These findings may illustrate Bauman's description (2001) of today's educated workers who are able to reinvent themselves as necessary, who thrive in chaotic and creative disorder, and who work regardless of location, or who relocate as necessary. For many of these, at least for a time, the freedom of flexibility was ideal – as long as they worked full-time and did not attempt to push the notion of flexibility to the point that this involved successfully juggling work and child-rearing. While their attitudes may have been flexible, the demands on their lives were less so.

Although women (from higher socio-economic backgrounds) were in one sense the poster girls for the educational policies of the 1990s – breaking new ground as they achieved educational credentials at an unprecedented level – their effort and investments in education have paid off less fully than they have for their male counterparts, while a small but persistent proportion continues to work in the semi-professions. Hence, the story of this generation in terms of breaking gender barriers is not without ongoing challenges. As we demonstrate in the next two chapters, the costs that the 'new' professional women have incurred in their family lives have been the main factor causing Esping-Andersen (2009) to propose that society has failed, so far, to adapt to women's new roles. As educational policies in the 1990s foreshadowed, those who did not invest in education have been restricted to unskilled and semi-skilled positions, especially those categories of women whose unqualified and qualified male counterparts eventually found work in skilled jobs.

The differences between Canadian and Australian young people in terms of their labour-market experiences are less significant than the commonalities. For example, Australian youth experienced a less favourable labour-market climate than did their Canadian peers – their jobs did not involve 'benefits,' and the Workplace Relations Act of 1996 systematically reduced employees' workplace rights. As noted in this chapter, discretionary non-wage benefits were not automatic for Canadians either. However, overall, the similarities in their patterns of employment and in their levels of satisfaction with what they have achieved stand out. They are a generation that has borne the brunt – and some of the benefits – of economic transformation as both countries shifted their dependence on primary industries and manufacturing to service industries and a knowledge economy. The turbulence of their trajectories into their mid and late twenties as they sought to gain a foothold in changing labour markets is evident. Even for those who invested in higher education the patterns were complex. Although education has served to protect many young people from the worst effects of economic transformation, the effort required by individuals to keep pace with change has been plain. However, the vast majority of those with post-secondary credentials were rewarded with careers in the semi-professions, professions, and management. Educated women in our samples, and particularly those with university degrees, were largely spared from being relegated to clerical and sales work, which may have been the case in an earlier time period.

The generation's relatively high level of satisfaction and their eventual success in gaining employment does not in any way diminish the difficulty of their achievements, even for the privileged and advantaged. As they have experienced the effects of individualizing processes, they perhaps rightly take comfort in what they have achieved. In chapter 5 they articulate their understandings of the challenges created for them by educational policies that held out the promise of financial returns for educational investments.

In the following chapter we explore in greater detail the more personal dimensions of how this generation have lived and shaped their lives, through a consideration of relationships and family life.

7   Relationships and Family

The shift in patterns of household formation, marriage, and childbearing between this generation and their parents' has often been noted, but the implications for family and personal life have been relatively unexplored. In this chapter we examine several dimensions of the significance of new patterns of living for the nature and meaning of relationships.

Although there has been relatively little empirical exploration of new patterns of intimate and social relationships among this generation, social theorists have argued that these patterns are one of the most significant aspects of social change. The individualization thesis, for example (Beck and Beck-Gernsheim 2002), has been extensively discussed in relation to family life, intimate relationships, and friendship. This approach, which focuses on the effects of de-traditionalization of personal life, highlights the pressure on young people to construct their own biographies in a context of changing social conditions. One of the most important effects of this process has been the pressure placed on individuals to secure their future through keeping options open, and especially through their shaping of educational and employment pathways. Mobility, a flexible approach, and a disposition towards keeping options open may have served many of these young people very well in terms of their educational and employment 'careers,' but these approaches have possibly been a less functional way of forming and maintaining relationships.

Other researchers (for example, Rosa 2005) have pointed out that one of the consequences of social change over the last quarter of a century has been an acceleration of time, in which many aspects of life are effectively speeded up. This is especially the case in relation to the expectations about what individuals can achieve within the early years of adulthood in the areas of education and work. Rosa (2005) argues that the effects of structural changes are felt in the acceleration of temporal norms and expectations and that people experience 'permanent temporal pressures to an unprecedented degree' (455). In the lives of our young people this is evident in their constant struggle to 'achieve a balance in life.' The emerging norm for young people to gain (increasingly costly) educational credentials that will provide a pathway into secure, meaningful, and well-paid work, to support themselves financially, and to demonstrate that they have work experience has arguably contributed to the new reality of temporally pressured adult life.

One of the distinctive features of this generation, and one of the first to be widely reported and debated, was the multiplicity of ways in which they shaped new living arrangements (Boyd and Norris 1999; Boyd and Pryor 1989; Holdsworth 2000; Jones 1995; Jones and Wallace 1992; Kilmartin 2000). They became the 'stay-at-home generation,' with significant proportions remaining in their parents' homes until their late twenties or early thirties. This trend, which in Canada and elsewhere began in the 1970s and 1980s (Boyd and Pryor 1989; Mitchell 2006), has been noted extensively in studies of young people across many different countries, and it is now regarded as normative for young people to remain in their family home until their mid to late twenties (Boyd and Norris 1999; Boyd and Pryor 1989; Furlong and Cartmel 2007; Goldscheider and Goldscheider 1994; Heath and Cleaver 2003; Leccardi and Ruspini 2006; Mitchell 2006). The trend by young people in our respective studies to forge new patterns of living reflects the wider trends that were occurring at the same time across many Western countries.

In Australia, Canada, and elsewhere young people tended not only to remain in the parental home through their early adult years but also to have high rates of returning to live in the parental home (Heath and Cleaver 2003; Mitchell 2006). This phenomenon has led to the invention of new terms to describe young people's living patterns, including *the yo-yo generation, boomerang generation*, and *cluttered nest*, referring to the tendency for young people to return to the parental home even after leaving (Mitchell 2006). This pattern represented a break with that established by the previous generation, which tended to mark entry to adulthood through becoming 'independent' financially and residentially by their early twenties.

Some researchers have remarked that the patterns of life established by the baby boomer generation (in the late 1960s and 1970s) were only possible because of the particular social and economic conditions they experienced, but nonetheless their experiences have widely been taken as the standard pattern of transition to adulthood (Boyd and Pryor 1989; Lesko 2001; Mitchell 2006; Wyn and White 1997). Indeed, achieving financial, residential, and emotional independence has been seen as a normative mode of development from youth into adulthood (Gillies 2000).

With a few exceptions (see Mitchell 2006), the tendency to take an ahistorical perspective on young people's transitions has meant that young people's relationships and family life have been subjected to very little research. Heath and Cleaver (2003), for example, found that research on young people living in the parental home was scarce and was mainly focused on young people in training schemes or those who were disadvantaged. Despite the fact that young people living in the parental home until they are well into their twenties is well known, this phenomenon is poorly understood (Coffield, Borrill, and Marshall 1986). Gillies (2000) also supports this view, pointing out that research on youth during the 1980s and 1990s has tended to be framed through one of two dominant conceptual approaches: developmental psychology or school-to-work transitions. Both, her study argues, make the assumption that increasing autonomy is a natural (and necessary) process, and both ignore important developments and processes in family relationships. Mitchell (2006) has adopted the concept of 'the life course' and has employed international comparative historical data to explore how young people negotiate their transitions to adulthood through particular sets of family relationships. Her work extends the body of work in this area that has tended to regard family as simply a set of factors (in addition to economic or political ones) that the individual young person negotiates. Several authors suggest that family relationships need to be understood as a significant point of intersection for family members, including those of different ages, recognizing that 'transition' is a dynamic ongoing process throughout the life course, rather than being relegated to the period of youth (Boyd and Norris 1999; Gillies 2000; Mitchell 2006).

Existing studies of young people's living patterns and family relationships are mixed in the extent to which they claim there has been change. Heath and Cleaver (2003) argue that this generation has significantly reshaped the landscape of family life. Their findings emphasize the role that this generation has played in the 'destandardisation' of household formation. In their study of young people in the United Kingdom, including a comparison with Australian youth, they found that 'former certainties of more or less linear transitions into a house and family of one's own have been displaced by fragmented routes and a proliferation of possibilities' (Heath and Cleaver 2003, 24). Other researchers have raised the issue of the diversity of patterns and the extent to which research on youth transitions has fully recognized this diversity. For example, du Bois-Reymond (1998) argues that the trend to continue living in the family home until the late twenties or early thirties, which is now taken as normative for this generation, was first set by a 'cultural elite' of urban-based, educationally engaged young people. Ball, Maguire, and Macrae (2000) point out that many studies of young people's transitions have a bias towards urban-based youth and fail to account for the full diversity of young people's origins and locations. Our analysis directly explores the diversity and complexity of pathways by providing a long-term view of living arrangements within and outside the parents' home and of marriage, relationships, and family. These patterns are viewed through the lenses of gender, class (as measured by parental levels of education), post-secondary-completion status, as well as geographic location to examine their patterns of living arrangements and relationships over time. However, there is one element of diversity that we acknowledge but are not able to explore as fully as we do these other dimensions. Relationships between same-sex partners are rarely explored in studies such as these. In 1998, 3.5 per cent of Canadian respondents self-reported that they were lesbian, gay, or bisexual. Interestingly, by 2003 this proportion had dropped to 2.5 per cent. The Australian study did not ask the respondents to divulge their sexual preference on the surveys, but some respondents indicated their sexual preference in open responses and during interviews, and the proportion of lesbian, gay, or bisexual participants was similar to that in the Canadian study. As a consequence of the low numbers, neither of our studies can do justice to documenting life transitions of non-heterosexual young adults, and it is vital to acknowledge this limitation in the data.

Esping-Andersen's work (2009) is a notable exception to the tendency to ignore the relevance of family and personal relationships. Esping-Andersen is interested in understanding the implications of social change, drawing on economic and sociological theory and research techniques in an attempt to generate a more holistic conceptual and empirical analysis. His focus on economic activity has led him to highlight the significance of new patterns of women's work and the implications that this has had for other aspects of society. He sees the changing status of women as a 'fount of revolutionary upheaval' (2009, 1), and he places this in the foreground as he analyses the nature of societies that are experiencing major transformation. His 'primary goal is to identify change in the logic of family behaviour' (2009, 44). At the risk of oversimplifying Esping-Andersen's argument: he argues that there has been an uneven social and economic transformation as young women from higher socio-economic backgrounds have entered professional working life in unprecedented proportions. The implications of this dramatic shift, he argues, have yet to be fully completed because workplace policies and the organization of domestic labour remain locked into the past, with family-unfriendly policies, poor childcare, and early-childhood-education provisions and social norms that continue to give full responsibility for domestic work to women. As a result, these women are forced to decide between having children and having a career, and many are deciding on the career. Esping-Andersen could be describing the highly achieving women in our study, and especially the Australian women.

Changing Living Patterns

In 1996, when they were around twenty-two years old, a majority of the Australian respondents (75 per cent) reported that they had been living mainly with their parents since they left high school (see table 32).[1] The uniformity of this trend across all socio-economic groups indicates the extent of a generational shift in Australia related to their levels of participation in education, uncertainty in the labour market, reduced affordability and availability of housing for young people, and the inherent mobility in their life stage. Ten years later when they were aged thirty-two, the proportion living with their parents had dropped to 13 per cent (table 33). Over the ten-year period the young Australians gradually moved out of the parental home and established their own place of residence, through a process that involved a multiplicity of living arrangements. It is important to note that although the strongest pattern in their early twenties was to live with parents, a significant minority (around 10 to 15 per cent) lived with friends. This pattern for

---

1 Data in tables 32, 33, and 34 are not mutually exclusive. For example, respondents could be living with their partners, their children, and their parents.

Table 32
Living arrangements, by sex and parental education, at age 22,
in Australia, 1996

| | Females | | Males | | |
	Parents No university %	Parents University %	Parents No university %	Parents University %	Total %
Parents or guardians	71	83	66	78	75
Myself	6	1	5	3	5
Spouse/partner	7	3	2	3	5
Friends	15	12	9	15	13
Other	4	0	5	5	4

Table 33
Living arrangements, by sex and parental education, at age 32,
in Australia, 2006[1]

| | Females | | Males | | |
	Parents No university %	Parents University %	Parents No university %	Parents University %	Total %
Parents	13	6	14	13	12
Shared household	6	2	2	13	5
Single occupancy household	9	17	11	13	11
Partner	53	63	41	31	50

[1]The data in this table are from 2006 with a sample size of 334.

young people to live with their parents represents a significant shift
from the patterns of the previous generation, who tended to move out
of home in their early twenties to live with their partner. This pattern
has occurred in other countries (especially the United Kingdom) as well
(Heath and Cleaver 2003). However, as they grew older, the patterns
changed, with the trend being to live with partners.

When we explored these patterns in more detail, we found that
there were strong differences between groups. For example, males at
age thirty-two, particularly those from university-educated families,

were the least likely of any group, and half as likely as women from university-educated families, to establish households with partners. Instead, they continued to live in shared households, with parents, or alone. Women from university-educated families stand out as the most likely of all groups to live alone, and they were the least likely to remain in the parental home. Just under 15 per cent of all other groups continued to live with their parents at fourteen years following high school. These patterns among the Australian cohort reflect the complex reworking of class and gender in new times. It shows that young women and young men from university-educated families have quite divergent experiences; in particular, the young women from these groups appear to forge new patterns, such as living alone, that go against the common perception of their generation as 'home-stayers.'

Detailed Canadian data on living arrangements are available at two points in time: ten years (1998) and fifteen years (2003) following high school graduation (table 34). They show distinctively different patterns to those of the Australians. By 1998, when they were around twenty-eight years old, the largest proportion lived in partnerships. Both women and men from non-university-educated households were more likely than those from university-educated households to live with partners, and women in the former group were more likely to be living with children. However, there was a second relatively large group that consisted overwhelmingly of young men who were not living with partners and whose living arrangements were quite diverse, including living alone or with parents, siblings, or friends.

By 2003, when our respondents were around thirty-three years old, the rates of living with partners for the Canadian sample had increased for all groups. Here, gendered patterns are also noticeable, but they contrast with the Australian pattern. Canadian males with university-educated parents were the least likely to be in marriage or marriage-like relationships and were most likely (26 per cent) to be living alone, which contrasts directly with their Australian counterparts, who were more likely to be living in non-partnership arrangements or with their parents, and half as likely to be living with a partner. Except for this group, the proportion of the Canadian sample living with children had evened out to around 50 per cent. Other living arrangements – for example, with roommates or friends, brothers or sisters – declined considerably. In other words, living arrangements for *thirty-something* Canadians consisted of long-term partnerships and family. Men from university-educated households who were living alone were outliers

Table 34
Living arrangements, by sex and parental education, in Canada

| | Age 28, 1998 | | | | | Age 33, 2003 | | | | |
| | Females | | Males | | | Females | | Males | | |
	Parents No university %	Parents University %	Parents No university %	Parents University %	Total %	Parents No university %	Parents University %	Parents No university %	Parents University %	Total %
Alone	14	16	19	22	17	15	14	17	26	16
Female spouse/partner	2	1	48	41	20	1	1	73	66	29
Male spouse/partner	65	58	2	0	39	76	80	2	0	47
One or more children	27	16	15	9	20	58	52	50	41	53
One or both parents	8	13	16	19	12	3	3	6	2	4
Brother or sister	6	3	8	12	7	4	5	2	3	3
In-laws	1	1	1	0	1	1	1	1	2	1
Roommate or friends	10	10	12	19	12	4	1	5	3	4
Other relatives	2	2	2	2	2	2	1	1	2	2

to this dominant pattern. A comparison of tables 33 and 34 reveal that Canadians by their early thirties were much more likely than Australians to be married, have children, and not be living with parents.

Our data enable us to take account of the lives of young people living in metropolitan, urban/rural, and remote areas of British Columbia and Victoria and to explore the classed nature of young people's living arrangements (using the highest post-secondary credential completed as a proxy of the time invested in educational pursuits). We found for the Australian cohort that at age twenty-two not all groups were equally likely to be living in the family home (table 35). Non-participants in urban/rural and remote areas were more likely than those who had earned post-secondary credentials to be living with their parents. Ten years later, in 2006, urban thirty-something Australians were the most likely group to remain in the parental home, with men who had never attended post-secondary institutions the most likely to do so. However, of all groups, university-educated men from urban/rural areas were the most likely to be living with their parents. In this case, we saw a trend for urban-based young people to remain in the family home, but it was young men from lower socio-economic backgrounds who were the most likely to do so – no longer the 'cultural elite' of du Bois-Reymond's study (1998) of Netherlander youth. In the Canadian sample in 1998, in all geographic and post-secondary status groups, men were more likely than women to live with their parents. At the fifteen-year time point, in a pattern that matches the Australian situation fairly closely, males who had never engaged in post-secondary studies were the most likely to be living at home. Women who remained in the family home were evenly spread across geographic and post-secondary-completion groups.

In Canada the social class effect is evident in a different direction than in Australia (see table 36). Ten years following high school graduation, Canadian young adults from university-educated families who originated from metropolitan and urban/rural areas were the most likely to be living at home. Young Australians from non-university-educated families originating from metropolitan areas, and males from similar backgrounds originating from urban/rural areas, were the most likely to remain in the family home.

Patterns of returning to the parental home are also telling. In 1996, when they were aged twenty-two, only 40 per cent of the Australian cohort thought that moving out of home was an important characteristic of adult life, and 28 per cent thought that living with a partner was. The attitudes of the Australian cohort reflect the impact of changing conditions. Although for a short historical period from the 1950s to the late

Table 35
Still at home, by geographic location, post-secondary-completion status, and sex, in Canada and Australia

| | Age 28, Canada, 1998 | | | | | | | Age 33, Canada, 2003 | | | | | | |
| | Females | | | Males | | | | Females | | | Males | | | |
	No PS %	Non-univ. %	Univ. %	No PS %	Non-univ. %	Univ. %	Total %	No PS %	Non-univ. %	Univ. %	No PS %	Non-univ. %	Univ. %	Total %
Metropolitan	0	9	26	67	16	28	20	0	9	4	50	13	11	9
Urban/rural	0	9	7	40	22	12	11	11	3	5	0	2	0	3
Remote	0	2	9	13	14	13	7	0	0	2	11	6	0	2

| | Age 22, Australia, 1996 | | | | | | | Age 32, Australia, 2006[1] | | | | | | |
| | Females | | | Males | | | | Females | | | Males | | | |
	No PS %	Non-univ. %	Univ. %	No PS %	Non-univ. %	Univ. %	Total %	No PS %	Non-univ. %	Univ. %	No PS %	Non-univ. %	Univ. %	Total %
Metropolitan	71	79	74	72	91	77	74	5	16	15	25	18	14	14
Urban/rural	35	50	45	49	65	44	44	13	8	0	0	14	50	12
Remote	40	44	26	40	62	40	35	13	8	0	0	0	0	4

[1]The data in this portion of the table are from 2006 with a sample size of 334.

Table 36
Still at home, by geographic location, parental education, and sex, in Canada and Australia

| | Age 28, Canada, 1998 | | | | | Age 33, Canada, 2003 | | | | |
| | Females | | Males | | | Females | | Males | | |
	Parents No university %	Parents University %	Parents No university %	Parents University %	Total %	Parents No university %	Parents University %	Parents No university %	Parents University %	Total %
Metropolitan	18	21	21	23	20	5	8	13	5	9
Urban/rural	5	19	17	22	10	5	0	1	0	3
Remote	6	5	16	-7	7	1	0	5	0	2

| | Age 22, Australia, 1996 | | | | | Age 32, Australia, 2006[1] | | | | |
| | Females | | Males | | | Females | | Males | | |
	Parents No university %	Parents University %	Parents No university %	Parents University %	Total %	Parents No university %	Parents University %	Parents No university %	Parents University %	Total %
Metropolitan	78	71	86	73	78	16	7	19	15	15
Urban/rural	43	40	65	25	48	8	0	25	0	12
Remote	32	50	44	67	32	6	0	0	0	4

[1] The data in this portion of the table are from 2006 with a sample size of 334.

Table 37

Returned home, by geographic location, parental education, and sex, in Canada and Australia

| | Age 28, Canada, 1998 | | | | | | | Age 26, Australia, 2000 | | | | | | |
| | Females | | | Males | | | | Females | | | Males | | | |
	No PS %	Non-univ. %	Univ. %	No PS %	Non-univ. %	Univ. %	Total %	No PS %	Non-univ. %	Univ. %	No PS %	Non-univ. %	Univ. %	Total %
Metropolitan	80	51	47	25	61	50	51	40	40	35	67	22	35	37
Urban/rural	56	38	35	57	31	26	35	61	58	31	80	33	40	49
Remote	57	40	25	70	45	18	34	30	31	23	0	33	29	28

1970s (Boyd and Pryor 1989; Mitchell 2006), living independently had been associated with achieving 'adulthood,' this generation did not feel that living in their parents' homes was necessarily a sign that they were not adults. By the time they were aged twenty-six (in 2000), 39 per cent of the Australian cohort who had left home previously had returned to their parents' home. Rates of returning varied by geographic region and post-secondary-completion status (table 37). University-educated women were the least likely to have returned home. Men who had not attended post-secondary institutions from metropolitan and urban/ rural regions were the most likely to return to the family home.

Rates of leaving and then returning home are similar for the Canadian sample. University-educated women and men from urban/rural and remote areas were the least likely to return home. This could be an indication of brain drain to larger urban centres (Andres and Licker 2005). Those most likely to return home were women from metropolitan regions and men from urban/rural and remote regions, none of whom had ever studied at post-secondary institutions.

Living at home for short or extended periods throughout their twenties signals the continuation of a trend of a different dynamic from that of earlier generations, between our respondents and their parents. As Boyd and Pryor (1989) point out, adult children living with parents provides increased opportunities for mentoring each other. This may have specific implications for the Australian respondents and their families, given the dramatic increase in educational attainment between the two generations. More highly educated children are likely to increase the levels of social capital in families in ways that are quite different than would be the case for the reverse if the *parents* were more highly educated. The fact that a significant proportion of the Australians were better educated than their parents placed them in a position to be able to contribute to the quality of their family's life through externality or spillover effects rather than in financial ways. Although living arrangements were driven by financial necessity while the young people were studying or during their periods of unemployment, underemployment, and economic downturns, to our surprise, the majority of interviewees described their parents as their friends and even their best friends. The following quotes reflect the sentiment expressed by many of them:

I think I'll stay home forever. [laugh] It's a good place . . . I love 'em. I have a good family. (Canadian female, age eighteen)

I want to do that as much as I can before I die or get old. Spend as much quality time with the people who I love – my parents. (Canadian female, age eighteen)

I have taken a step back and realized that I have been too busy and that one of my greatest pleasures is having a cup of tea with my dad! (Australian female, age thirty)

I am still living at home and very happy about it. (Australian male, age thirty)

However, as we have seen in chapter 5, good relationships with parents were not the case for all of our respondents. A few felt unsupported and even not welcome to stay in the family home.

Tables 38 and 39 further illuminate our respondents' attitudes towards their parents. In 1996, when they were twenty-two, the Australian sample was asked to respond to the following question: 'Since leaving school, what do you see as the most positive aspects of

Table 38
Most positive aspects of life, by sex and parental education, at age 22, in Australia, 1996

| | Females | | Males | | |
	Parents No university %	Parents University %	Parents No university %	Parents University %	Total %
Family	48	47	41	58	47
Closest friend	37	43	22	35	34
Other friends	18	14	11	20	16
My work situation	22	14	14	25	19
My work associates	13	7	11	20	12
My course of studies	18	24	16	28	19
Particular teachers	10	14	9	15	11
What I've learnt about myself	42	38	28	25	36
My social life	24	23	12	18	20
Travel experiences	24	32	19	18	24
Sporting/leisure pursuits	15	23	21	27	19

Table 39
Influences on educational decisions, by sex and parental education,
at age 23, in Canada, 1993

	Females		Males		
	Parents No university %	Parents University %	Parents No university %	Parents University %	Total %
Mother/guardian	18	22	9	20	16
Father/guardian	17	17	13	27	16
Grandparents	4	1	1	20	2
Other family members	5	7	1	20	4
Spouse/significant other	8	7	3	7	6
Friends	4	1	3	4	3
Secondary school teacher	2	3	3	2	3
Secondary school counsellor	2	1	1	6	1
Post-secondary instructor	6	25	4	19	4
Post-secondary counsellor	3	1	1	2	2
Employer	5	5	6	4	5
Career information provided by Canadian government	1	1	1	4	1
Lack of good job opportunities	11	15	11	4	11
Timing of childbearing	4	3	1	4	2
Availability of childcare	3	1	1	2	2
Myself	70	71	70	76	70

your life?' Across all social class groups, parents were ranked highest of any factor as 'most positive' (table 38). When the respondents from the Canadian sample were around the same age, they were asked to comment on the extent to which individuals and structures influenced their educational decisions (table 39). With the exception of males from non-university-educated families, compared with other influences the Canadian cohort rated the influence of their parents as 'very strong,' and males from university-educated families rated their fathers, mothers, grandparents, and other family members as having a 'very strong' influence. Interestingly, the perception that their extended family had exerted a very strong influence was not forthcoming from women from university-educated families and young men from non-university-educated families as they reported receiving minimal levels of family support. This pattern provides an insight into the diversity of intergenerational relationships by gender and class, suggesting that young men from high socio-economic backgrounds may be the most able to access various forms of social capital.

Indeed, tables 38 and 39 show that for both cohorts, from early in their young adulthood, gender and class effects were quite strong in some areas of life. These tables reveal that the greatest divergence in accessing social support from family was between young men from high socio-economic backgrounds and young men from low socio-economic backgrounds. Overwhelmingly, young men from high socio-economic backgrounds were the most able to draw on friends and family for support, and young men from low socio-economic backgrounds were the least likely of any group to draw actively on social support from any source, with fathers being their most significant source. It is also noteworthy that the Canadian participants, and to a somewhat lesser extent the Australian participants, placed high importance on themselves as a strong influence. At least 70 per cent of the Canadian sample stated that 'self' was an important influence, and 36 per cent of the Australians reported 'what I have learned about myself' as a very strong influence on educational decisions.

The heightened awareness of themselves as a source of support, and the emphasis on personal development as an important process, may be one of the reasons that they were relatively unaware of the structural influences on their lives. This is especially noteworthy given that our data show the marked and ongoing influence of both class and gender inequalities in their lives. The tendency to be blind to the structuring of life chances by this generation has been noted widely within the youth research literature (Bourdieu 2000; K. Evans 2002; Furlong and Cartmel 2007; West, Sweeting, Young, and Robbins 2006). The strong awareness of both family support and the role they themselves have played reinforces the influence of individualization processes and, in particular, the sense of having personal responsibility for the risks and opportunities of life.

Eventually, most of our respondents moved away from their parents' home. Although home-buying patterns reflect the cultural beliefs strongly held by both the Canadian and the Australian samples about the desirability and necessity of owning one's own home, differences are evident among groups. In 2000, when they were aged twenty-six, 41 per cent of the Australians had obtained a housing loan (table 40). By 2006 (aged thirty-two), despite a dramatic increase in the cost of housing in Victoria, 57 per cent of the cohort were living in a home that they owned or were buying, and only 14 per cent were renting. In Canada 46 per cent had bought a home by 1998; by 2003 this figure had increased to 81 per cent[2] (table 41). However, in this area too, social divisions are very evident. There is considerable variation in home-buying patterns by gender, post-secondary-completion status, and geographic location.

As table 40 reveals, except for those living in remote areas, university-educated males in Australia were slower than all other groups to get into the housing market. By 2006, when compared with their female counterparts, university-educated males were still somewhat behind as owner-occupiers. In Canada, at ten years following high school graduation, with one exception, the university-educated were less likely than the non-university-educated to own a home.

University-educated women in Canada were more likely to have bought a home than university-educated men. In the five years between 1998 and 2003, more university-educated women and men (except for the urban/rural group) were first-time home buyers. This suggests that in terms of home ownership it took university graduates in both countries at least ten years to catch up with their non-university-educated peers because they had spent longer out of the full-time workforce while they were studying. Also, many had to pay off debts that were incurred by their studies (see Andres and Adamuti-Trache 2009 for an extended discussion of the impact of student loans on adult life-course activities).

Relationships

In 1996, aged twenty-two, the Australian cohort was asked about priorities for life. Their priorities reflected the emergence of new possibilities and options. A significant proportion expressed the desire to follow relatively traditional patterns of living. Although only 6 per cent were married at that stage, 44 per cent said that they would be very unhappy if they never married (39 per cent of males and 46 per cent of females). However, 19 per cent said that they were 'neutral' about the prospect of never marrying, with a greater proportion of males (24 per cent) than

---

2 This figure is cumulative (that is, 1998 plus 2003).

Table 40
Home ownership, by geographic location, post-secondary-completion status, and sex, in Australia

	Age 22, 1996							Age 32, 2006[1]						
	'Have you taken out a housing loan?'							'Are you an owner-occupier?'						
	Females			Males				Females			Males		
	No PS %	Non-univ. %	Univ. %	No PS %	Non-univ. %	Univ. %	Total %	No PS %	Non-univ. %	Univ. %	No PS %	Non-univ. %	Univ. %	Total %
Metropolitan	48	41	39	41	48	19	40	59	43	58	50	68	38	46
Urban/rural	33	48	44	0	50	50	42	50	69	60	0	86	25	40
Remote	23	70	71	33	39	57	54	43	85	75	50	75	67	29

[1] The data in this portion of the table are from 2006 with a sample size of 334.

Table 41

Home ownership, by geographic location, post-secondary-completion status, and sex, in Canada

	Age 28, 1998							Age 33, 2003						
	'Have you bought a home?'							'Since 1998, were you a first-time home buyer?'						
	Females			Males				Females			Males			
	No PS %	Non-univ. %	Univ. %	No PS %	Non-univ. %	Univ. %	Total %	No PS %	Non-univ. %	Univ. %	No PS %	Non-univ. %	Univ. %	Total %
Metropolitan	60	54	36	25	38	24	37	0	19	49	50	18	46	37
Urban/rural	67	63	46	57	68	37	53	30	24	33	29	35	43	32
Remote	100	67	36	60	47	15	46	14	35	37	30	32	53	37

females (17 per cent) expressing ambivalence about marriage. In 1996 they were also asked what they thought was likely to be their status in five years time. Thirty percent of women thought that it was 'very likely' that they would be married, and an additional 23 per cent thought that it was 'likely.' Males were less optimistic, at 15 per cent and 25 per cent, respectively. As we will see below, their predictions were not fulfilled.

Five years following high school departure, only 6 per cent of the Australian sample was married; this is in stark contrast to the Canadian sample at 28 per cent (table 42). For Canadian respondents, the probability of being married is directly related to gender and post-secondary-completion status. The most likely to be married were women who had never attended post-secondary institutions, at a remarkable 85 per cent. With the exception of this group of women where the rate was 31 per cent, rates of childbearing were low for both the Australian and the Canadian samples (see also Andres 1999). Canadian women and men with either non-university or university credentials were least likely to have had children within five years of high school graduation. However, they were much more likely than the Australian sample to be married and have children.

Other researchers have also found that the pursuit of higher education correlates with later marriage and childbearing (Blackwell and Bynner 2002; Heath and Cleaver 2003). However, for the Australian participants, low rates of marriage and childbearing were also evident for those who did not pursue post-secondary education. This was not the case for the Canadian non-participants in post-secondary education.

By 2000 at age twenty-six (Australia) and 1998 at age twenty-eight (Canada), only 37 per cent of the Australian respondents and 41 per cent of the Canadian respondents were married, and another 29 per cent and 17 per cent, respectively were in marriage-like relationships. As portrayed in table 43, about half of Australian men with some type of post-secondary credential reported were single, and Canadian women were much more likely than all other groups to be married and have had children by this point in their lives. Interestingly, the separation and divorce rates were extremely low for all groups.

Variation in relationship types and childbearing was evident at this stage, with differences by post-secondary completion, gender, and country. Table 43 shows that Australian women at the age of twenty-six to twenty-seven were almost half as likely as their Canadian counterparts (at age twenty-eight) to have children, and Australian men were almost three times less likely than Canadian men to be fathers. Men

Table 42

Marital and parental status five years out of high school, by sex, in Canada and Australia

| | Age 23, Canada, 1993 | | | | | | | Age 22, Australia, 1996 | | | | | | |
| | Females | | | Males | | | | Females | | | Males | | | |
	No PS %	Non-univ. %	Univ. %	No PS %	Non-univ. %	Univ. %	Total %	No PS %	Non-univ. %	Univ. %	No PS %	Non-univ. %	Univ. %	Total %
Single	15	52	80	69	78	85	72	91	92	94	97	99	98	94
Married/in marriage-like relationship	85	46	21	25	22	15	28	9	8	6	3	1	2	6
Divorced	0	3	0	6	0	0	1	6	2	0	3	0	0	1
Have children	31	12	1	25	2	0	5	1	2	1	3	0	0	2

Table 43

Marital and parental status ten and nine years out of high school, by sex, in Canada and Australia

| | Age 28, Canada, 1998 | | | | | | | Age 26, Australia, 2000 | | | | | | |
| | Females | | | Males | | | | Females | | | Males | | | |
	No PS %	Non-univ. %	Univ. %	No PS %	Non-univ. %	Univ. %	Total %	No PS %	Non-univ. %	Univ. %	No PS %	Non-univ. %	Univ. %	Total %
Single	5	26	42	35	50	55	41	26	37	31	33	51	48	37
Living in a marriage-like relationship	14	23	16	30	10	15	17	30	28	31	33	22	28	29
Married	81	48	40	35	39	29	41	42	34	35	26	25	23	32
Divorced	0	2	0	0	1	1	1	2	1	3	7	2	2	2
Separated	0	1	1	0	1	1	1	–	–	–	–	–	–	–
Have children	59	43	21	24	21	17	27	17	14	7	4	7	2	10

in both countries were half as likely as women to be parents, which is partly due to a cohort effect.

The stark difference in childbearing patterns between Australia and Canada reflects the way in which social conditions have an impact on people's lives. At the age when their Canadian counterparts were having children, the young Australians were struggling with a relatively hostile workplace environment. Young workers, across all educational levels, were relatively vulnerable within the new industrial relations climate that placed the onus on individual workers to negotiate their working conditions with their employer. Employers gained unprecedented power during this time to set working conditions, with the consequence that family-friendly policies, maternity and paternity leave, and employee preferences for part-time work were not widely recognized (Forsyth and Stewart 2009; Pocock 2003). As Pocock illustrates in her study of Australian workers (2003), family life was a direct casualty of these changes. This means that, in their late twenties, the Australian participants who were working were finding it very difficult to find time to devote to a partner, and, for most, the prospect of having children was out of the question. The lack of parental-leave arrangements and the uncompromising approach to part-time work meant that these young people were faced with the dilemma of working or becoming parents, but most could not see a way to do both. The higher proportion of Canadian participants in our study who were able to make the decision to have children suggests that there are implications of the workplace arrangements that give employees some protection. In chapter 5 we have demonstrated the unevenness of receiving non-wage benefits, particularly by gender and post-secondary-completion status. However, as we pointed out, policymakers in Canada have increasingly recognized that workers and their families require family-friendly non-wage benefits and a work flexibility that suits both the worker and the employer – not simply just the latter. In 1998, when they were twenty-eight years old, the Canadian sample without children were asked if they intended to start a family within five years. Thirty-eight percent of women and 30 per cent of men said 'yes,' with another 34 per cent and 41 per cent respectively stating 'maybe.'

The evidence on family formation provides strong support for Esping-Andersen's assessment (2009) that it is time for policies to catch up with changes in people's lives. Esping-Andersen advocates the need for more holistic policies that recognize the impact that changing patterns of economic (and educational) participation have on family life, relationships, and child-rearing. The marked difference between the 'choices' that Australians and Canadians have made regarding family formation and child-rearing is testimony to the need for more holistic policies that support people to participate in economic activity *and* be parents.

Drawing on interviews, the following comments from Australians illustrate the personal struggles they felt in managing work and home life, and help to explain why so many of the Australians deferred childbearing:

> I am working as a remedial masseur from a gym – no benefits such as sick pay or holiday pay. I want to have a family, because I am not one of these women who want to shove their children in a crèche [day care]. But I feel really drained by the physical nature of the work. Paying off the house is a priority now, because I do not plan to return to work after I have a family. My husband's career will take priority. (female, age twenty-seven)

> What do I want on my tombstone, 'a great worker' or 'a caring family member'? (female, age thirty)

Despite better working conditions, the Canadian sample also struggled with work-life balance issues, but these struggles are not reflected in the same way in terms of having children. We take up this discussion in more depth in chapter 8.

Over time, relationship and family patterns shifted, and by 2003 the majority of both Canadian and Australian women and men were married or living in marriage-like relationships. When comparing tables 42, 43, and 44, this proportion increases dramatically, and we can see that the men have now begun to form long-term partnerships. Here too, though, the Australian cohort reveals a wariness about making long-term personal commitments, particularly the men. Canadians were much more likely than the Australian sample to be legally married. Marriage patterns are, however, only one indication of the ways in which these young people are instrumental in shaping new patterns of living. It is important to acknowledge the ways in which this generation has embraced a diversity of living arrangements and ways of managing significant and intimate relationships. Throughout, a significant proportion of the Australian cohort was living in de facto relationships. For example, while nearly half of the cohort was married by the age of thirty (in 2004), a further 23 per cent were in living together in a de facto relationship,

Table 44
Marital and parental status fifteen and twelve years out of high school, by sex, in Canada and Australia

| | Age 33, Canada, 2003 | | | | | | | | Age 30, Australia, 2004 | | | | | | | |
| | Females | | | Males | | | Total | | Females | | | Males | | | Total |
	No PS %	Non-univ. %	Univ. %	No PS %	Non-univ. %	Univ. %	%		No PS %	Non-univ. %	Univ. %	No PS %	Non-univ. %	Univ. %	%
Single	0	14	23	29	33	22	22		20	34	25	33	24	37	28
Living in a marriage-like relationship	14	13	11	5	8	11	11		23	19	23	26	26	23	23
Married	82	67	63	57	56	66	64		55	47	52	44	49	40	49
Divorced	0	2	1	5	1	1	2		3	2	2	2	1	0	2
Separated	1	4	2	5	3	0	2		–	–	–	–	–	–	–
Have children	86	64	47	48	48	46	52		27	30	24	15	14	13	22

which means that approximately 75 per cent were in an ongoing relationship. On average, 11 per cent of the Canadian sample was in de facto
relationships, which was slightly lower than the national average of 16
per cent reported in the 2001 Census (Statistics Canada 2001, 2003). This
suggests that Canadians may hold more conservative attitudes towards
marriage, particularly in relation to beginning a family. However, like
their Australian counterparts, around three-quarters are in committed
relationships. A relatively new trend for couples to be in a de facto relationship but not living at the same residence was noted by Levin and
Trost (1999) as 'living together apart' and studied by Heath and Cleaver
(2003); this does not appear to be the case for our respondents.

A considerable proportion remained single, but this too varied across
groups. At one extreme, 100 per cent of the Canadian women who had
never participated in post-secondary education were married or in
partnerships, whereas Australian men with university degrees were
the most likely to be single. These extremes show the complexities particular to a generation that can be masked by broad-brush approaches
attempting to characterize a generation in a homogenous way.

Tables 43 and 44 show that by 2003 the proportion of Canadian
women and men with children had increased considerably from 1998,
to 48 per cent and 46 per cent, respectively. In both samples, those with
no post-secondary or non-university credentials were still more likely
than those with university degrees to have children, which concurs
with recent Statistics Canada findings (Zhang 2009). However, these
patterns contradict another study that reports no differences in the proportions who desire to remain 'childfree by choice' between educational
level and gender, suggesting that factors beyond desire influence the
decision to remain childless (Stobert and Kemeny 2003). Indeed, when
asked whether they planned to start a family within the next three years,
39 per cent of both university-educated women and men aged thirty-
two who did not yet have children said 'yes,' and around another 35 per
cent said 'maybe.' Around 25 per cent indicated that they did not plan
to start a family, so they may either be further delaying the decision or
be part of a small proportion of young Canadian adults who intend to
remain 'child free.' It is remarkable, however, that Australian women
in all categories were at least half as likely as Canadian women to have
children, which may explain why somewhat higher proportions of the
former are employed as professionals (see chapter 6). However, just
over a quarter of those without post-secondary credentials have children. Even more remarkably, only 13 per cent of university-educated

Australian men, compared with 46 per cent of Canadian men with degrees, reported having children; Canadian men in each group were three to four times more likely than Australian males to be fathers at this point in their lives.

Clearly, while partnering (in the form of either marriage or a de facto relationship) has been a reality for a significant proportion of the Australian cohort, with the vast majority in one or the other of these categories, having children has been very difficult to achieve, and it was clearly not what they had anticipated. In 1996, when they were aged around twenty-two, 48 per cent of women and 44 per cent of men said that they would be very disappointed if they never had children. Ten per cent of women said that it was 'very likely,' and 15 per cent said it was 'likely,' that they would be parents in five years time; the comparable figures for men are 2 per cent and 8 per cent. In fact, by 2004 and age thirty, only 26 per cent of women and 14 per cent of men had become parents (table 44). For women, the disjuncture between their early expectations and the realities they are encountering is especially strong. In 1996, perhaps as the realities of workplaces were sinking in, more men (22 per cent) than women (14 per cent) said that they were neutral about never having children, and more women (48 per cent) than men (44 per cent) said they would be very unhappy if they were not ever able to become parents.

Many of the Australians expressed regret when they reflected on how long it was taking them to find a partner and to have a family. In 2002, aged about twenty-eight, thirty-nine of the participants were sufficiently concerned that they wrote comments on the surveys about relationships. The following are examples of what they wrote.

> I always hoped to be in a long-term relationship by now. I have made lots of great friends, but nothing intimate has lasted. (female)

> I am seeing a career counsellor right now to work out why I can't do the life-work balance thing. Why don't I have a relationship? The buck stops with me, but I am still not achieving my goals. (male)

> I've really only had one personal relationship, back when I was twenty-three. I'm now twenty-eight. For whatever reason I haven't had a relationship in all that time, and I feel like it's such a missed opportunity. I see my friends in relationships, getting married, having children, and I sometimes

wonder what I've done with my life. I'm not even sure what the answer is, but it sure is time for something new. (male)

I always thought that at age twenty-seven I would have been married with kids, but career, family, and friends have always come first. I feel now that I might never settle down and have a family and get married. This is one area of my life that I am not happy with. (female)

Faced with the challenge of finding a partner, some became resigned and sought alternative ways of being parents; for example:

I want to have a child by the time I am thirty-four. I don't want to miss out. I have always wanted to have children. If there is no partner, I will do IVF at thirty-five. I will have to move to (a country town) if I am a single mum to live with my mother. Lots of girlfriends are doing it! I have spent five years worrying about being single and not enjoying it. It isn't exactly how I imagined my life, but that hasn't stopped me buying two houses, pushing myself at work and at home to make myself happy. I still feel good about the decisions I have made and what I call my 'survival capacity.' I have a female friend who is also sitting there waiting for someone to come and change her life. I just don't understand it! (female)

Conclusion

The personal lives of our young people – their living patterns and their personal relationships – reflect distinctive patterns that have been widely identified with their generation, when compared with the previous generation. These include later partnering and parenthood, a tendency to live in the parental home longer, and more diverse patterns of living, including group households and living alone. Other research has highlighted the association between educational success and childlessness (Blackwell and Bynner 2002), and Heath and Cleaver (2003, 155) note that 'the higher the level of qualification attained by a woman, the less likely she is to marry or to have children.' Aapola, Gonick, and Harris (2005, 101), who explore the experiences of young women in Finland, Canada, and Australia, argue that 'increasingly young women have to choose between having a career or having children.' Beck and Beck-Gernsheim also note (2002) the disjunction between the wish to have children and the dramatic fall in the birth rate in Germany, which their study relates to the difficulty of reconciling personally held values with the challenge of managing an increasing and competing range of life options. Even Canadian government research analysts have recently acknowledged this issue as the 'child penalty' or the 'motherhood earnings gap' (Zhang 2009, 5) and have conducted analyses that demonstrate that such penalties do exist and that they are associated with educational levels. Also, while remaining 'child free' – a term signalling a deliberate conscious choice – is an option for less than 10 per cent of Canadians, for most it is not their intention (Stobert and Kemeny 2003). It is important to interrogate this term, for, according to Esping-Andersen (2009), most people continue to want to have at least two children.

The disjuncture between their expectations and their life outcomes, especially for the Australian sample, shows that the shifts and trends in living arrangements and personal lives pioneered by this generation were in large part an outcome of the conditions of their lives – rather than a result of a conscious choice to live differently from the previous generation. The changing patterns of living and relating that these cohorts have forged raise important questions about what these changes mean for our participants.

Heath and Cleaver (2003, 53) argue that there is evidence that 'the younger generation may ... be engaged in a renegotiation of the bounds of intimacy in a number of spheres, including parent-child relationships, sexual relationships with partners, and platonic friendships.' Our analysis suggests that our participants mainly started out with relatively traditional ideas about relationships and family formation – as expressed in chapter 4 – but that things did not necessarily turn out as they had expected, particularly for the Australians. Although some of our participants have been at the forefront of changing norms for family and intimate relationships, these changes have often been a response to circumstances rather than being actively sought.

Few other studies have been able to explore the diversity of personal relationships and living patterns within this generation, particularly on the basis of an international comparison over time, as we have done. The differences between groups and across countries reveal that underlying these broad generational patterns are diverse experiences that show very clear effects of gender and social class. Our data also reveal the striking impact of government workplace policies on young people's lives.

Gender and class have interacted in complex ways in terms of personal relationships and living arrangements for our participants. On the one hand, young men from university-educated families were slowest to establish their own families and were the most likely to live in their family homes throughout the study, through to their late twenties. By their early thirties the small group of young people who were still living in the family home were urban-based males from non-university-educated families. On the other hand, women from university-educated families were the most likely of all the groups to live independently (a trend noted by Boyd 1989), but they too were very slow to find long-term partners and to begin childbearing. In general, this generation's views on the characteristics of adulthood reveal that leaving the family home early in adulthood is not universally seen as a necessary prerequisite for being adult. It also became clear that for a substantial group, relationships with parents and siblings during this stage of their lives were avenues of support, company, and enjoyment and were highly valued. We would hazard to speculate that, particularly for Australian parents, having their more highly educated children closer at hand enhances the social capital of the entire family. This contradicts assumptions about the 'necessity' of becoming 'independent' as a stage of life and points to a need to understand more about the ways in which family life is about 'interdependence' of the generations.

Over time we saw some significant differences emerge between the Canadians and the Australians in their personal lives. Across the board Australians were much slower to form long-term partnerships, less likely to marry, and less likely to have children than were the Canadians. It is clear that the young people in both countries set out with very similar hopes and dreams for themselves, especially in relation to 'settling down' and 'having a family' (see chapter 3). Although young people in both countries travelled a relatively similar course during their years of study, differences began to emerge once they entered the labour force. At this point, it became clear that already the young Australians were finding it much more difficult to realize these dreams. Australia's newly enacted workplace laws heightened their vulnerability as they struggled to pay off debts incurred during their studies and to achieve the financial security needed to buy a house. They worked longer hours than they would have liked, accepted short-term contracts, and managed their precarious work situations. For a proportion, this situation precipitated a change of heart, as they reconsidered their field of study and changed course – further prolonging their financial insecurity in the hope of making longer-term gains. The impact on their personal lives is woven through this chapter. The effort that many put into work (and often study as well) reduced the time they had for personal pursuits and meant that many did not find a partner until they were into their thirties. Even for those who did find partners, the difficulty of managing the work-life balance meant that they did not feel they could commit to having children while they needed to keep their jobs in order to maintain the level of material affluence they wanted. Their personal lives are a casualty of the acceleration of work (Rosa 2005) witnessed in the sharp focus in the Australian case and of the poverty of policies that elevate education and labour markets while excluding other policy domains such as family.

Family was important across all groups, but our research shows that young men in university-educated families rated family support as more significant in shaping their lives than did any other group. As we have already discussed in chapter 5, this group appear to have drawn on family support more effectively than did any other group, and it may be one reason that they did not rush to move out of the family home. In both countries, young men from families with no university education were the least likely to say that they drew on family support and were the most disadvantaged in terms of their labour-market position (see chapter 6). In a context where education has increasing value, young men from non-university-educated families are not able to access the kind of social capital they need to gain a foothold in changing labour markets. Their disadvantage is compounded by processes of individualization, in which individuals are increasingly required to draw on personal resources to make their way. To put this in another way, in late modernity, families have become more important while institutional processes and traditional ways have disintegrated, and families with higher educational levels are able to provide their children with both the social and the material resources that enable them to 'move with the times' more effectively.

To conclude, this chapter has revealed the ways in which education and employment are interwoven in the shaping of this generation's lives. Hopes and dreams have been unattainable for some and partly achieved by others. The group that has most fulfilled the hopes they held across all life areas as young people just setting out from school are young women from university-educated families in Canada, where the promises held out by education were more able to be fulfilled in the workplaces that offered greater flexibility. Yet, even here, work-life balance has become an issue. The group that has missed out most are the young men from non-university-educated families in Australia, who have borne the brunt of social and economic change.

8 Health and Well-Being: Achieving a Balance in Life

In previous chapters we discussed the ways in which members of this generation have responded to and shaped the circumstances of their lives. Here we explore their health and well-being as both an outcome of and a contributing factor to these elements, drawing out the relevance and meaning of health and well-being for their generation. Their comments reveal a tendency to see well-being as an individual choice, something for which they are responsible and yet something that is difficult for many to achieve in their busy lives as they juggle multiple responsibilities across many life spheres: employment (often two or more part-time jobs), study (keeping up with the need to have credentials), managing personal relationships, and nurturing the lives of their children. We present their views on the implications of social change for health and well-being, and we explore the extent to which health and well-being are indicators of the costs (and benefits) of social change.

Our interest in the health and well-being of these young people is informed by current thinking about the changing meanings of health and well-being during late modernity. Theorists of social change have pointed out that the project of being healthy and managing to be well has emerged as a significant theme over the last twenty-five years. Many argue that a focus on personal development, well-being, and mental and physical health is one of the distinctive features of life in late modernity (Furlong and Cartmel 2007; Giddens 1991; Henderson et al. 2007). This observation is often linked to the idea of individualization (Beck and Beck-Gernsheim 2002), referring particularly to the trend for individuals to bear the risks and costs of living in uncertain times. The increasing significance of health and well-being as an individual responsibility has formed the backdrop against which our cohorts have forged their early adulthood.

A temporal dimension runs through many of our chapters. It is reflected in our participants' struggles to manage the acceleration of time, as life becomes layered with multiple tasks, responsibilities, and options. A temporal dimension is also reflected, in a different way, in the need for our participants to constantly look to the future, an unpredictable future, but one that they are investing in through their engagement in education. As one of the Australian participants commented in the survey in 2004, 'I feel as though my life is always focused on the future, not the present.' Both of these dimensions of temporality can be stressful, and both require considerable management by individuals. As we consider the health and well-being of our participants, it is timely to consider the challenge of the 'project of the self,' which Beck and Beck-Gernsheim (2002) argue is a defining feature of life in late modernity. In particular, Beck and Beck-Gernsheim argue that being well is an individual obligation, and health is an outcome of the choices and actions made by individuals. The idea that individuals must consciously manage their well-being has been linked by some researchers to the evidence of high rates of anxiety among young people, especially young women (Donald, Dower, Lucke, and Raphael 2000) and with youth suicide (Fullagar 2003). Being well has also been linked with the prominence of consumption in late modernity. For example, Rose (1989, 1999) argues that health and well-being have become a form of consumption – something that individuals choose and purchase. Rose (1999, 87) claims that through media representations and official discourses, individuals are 'offered an image and a set of practical relations of the self and others.' Focusing on the significance of 'self-responsibility' for health and well-being, Rose's work analyses how contemporary society creates a situation where individuals feel they have autonomy and freedom (to choose to be healthy) but are in fact obliged to make particular choices and to achieve particular outcomes.

In addition to our own work, a number of studies have shown that managing to be well is a significant preoccupation of this generation. These include the *Inventing Adulthoods* longitudinal study of UK youth (Henderson et al. 2007) and the *Twenty-07* study in Scotland (West and Sweeting 2002). Being well is linked to a focus on 'becoming' – on building a personal profile and lifestyle that enables young people to successfully navigate their own course through study, work, and personal options. These conditions create opportunities, but they also create pressure and stress for young people.

Drawing on these insights, we highlight the social implications of increasing expectations for educational credentials and the significant role that study plays in the lives of these young people between the ages of eighteen and thirty-something; we also look at the implications of a labour market in which individuals work long hours in full-time work or in several part-time jobs, and in which uncertainty is prevalent. National indicators show that while young people in Canada and Australia are the healthiest group in the population, some health issues are of concern. For example, mental health problems are increasing, and recently there has been concern about drug abuse and obesity (Australian Institute of Health and Welfare 2007; Canadian Institute for Health Information 2006).

Our research informs a policy context in which, despite the increased significance of health and well-being issues in young people's lives, policy frameworks are dominated by education and labour-market concerns. Health and well-being policies have a low profile in relation to young people, especially compared with the emphasis given to education and labour-market policies, which we have discussed in some detail in chapters 3, 5, and 6. In both Canada and Australia, education and labour-market policies are the central elements in policies relating to youth (Betcherman and Leckie 1997; Marquardt 1996). Critiques of this policy framework (for example, Ball, Maguire, and Macrae, 2000; Cohen and Ainley 2000; Wyn 2007) point out that these policies privilege economic development over health and well-being.

This is illustrated by the emphasis in Organisation for Economic Co-operation and Development (OECD) documents on the role of education in developing the capabilities and skills that will ensure the competitiveness of nation states in new global (knowledge and information) economies (OECD 2007). Although officially education is seen as enhancing economic prosperity and competitiveness *as well as* social cohesion, in reality, programs, priorities, practices, and goals related to the latter goal are marginalized (OECD 2007). Most often, health and well-being are subsumed under the categories of non-market or externality-generating effects of education (Haveman and Wolfe 1984). These OECD documents have a significant influence on the ways in which policies affecting young adults are framed in Canada and Australia (Wyn 2007).

The result is that youth health policies tend to be fragmented (focusing on single-issue problems such as alcohol abuse, suicide, and violence) and play a secondary role to education and labour-market policies.

Policies pertaining to young people's health and well-being tend almost exclusively to place the responsibility on individuals to manage their own well-being – however they define this (Henderson et al. 2007; Wyn 2009). For example, attention has been drawn recently to the ways in which public health concerns about rising levels of overweight and obesity in Australia and other Western countries have resulted in school-based and community health campaigns that equate being overweight with lack of personal control and hence with moral weakness (Evans, Evans, and Rich 2003; Gard and Wright 2001; Wright and Burrows 2004). In Canada too, there has been concern about the rising incidence of being overweight and obese (Shields 2006).

Finally, we note that health and well-being are not the same thing, yet the terms are often used interchangeably because they address dimensions of life that are closely related. Health tends to be used to refer to objectively measured indices of morbidity and mortality and is generally identified and discussed as a deficit state of individuals – *ill* health. There are many objective measures of ill health, including the 'burden of disease,' 'quality of life-years (QALYs),' 'disease adjusted life-years (DALYs),' and hundreds of indicators of discrete conditions (for example, depression, anxiety disorders, respiratory diseases, and heart disease) (Australian Institute of Health and Welfare 2007; Manderson 2005). By contrast, well-being is widely regarded as a subjective state of positive health from a holistic perspective. Over the last twenty years well-being has emerged as an increasingly visible issue in the popular media and as a significant area of self-help and individual endeavour (Sointu 2005). Well-being is less often measured than health, although there are attempts to develop measures of dimensions of well-being, such as individual capabilities (Nussbaum 2005; Robeyns 2003; Sen 1993) and community well-being (Brasher and Wiseman 2007; Wiseman 2006). Both health and well-being tend to be seen as the property of individuals, as an individual characteristic. However, both can also be regarded as the product of social relations and hence as a social or community measure. For example, community well-being indicators measure levels of social provision (schools, parks, health centres) and relationships (engagement in decision making) that are regarded as enabling the well-being of local populations (Wiseman 2006). The field of health promotion also takes a social approach to health, focusing on the measurement of indicators such as levels of engagement in economic activity and a sense of belonging (VicHealth 2005).

In chapter 4 we gained a perspective on the subjects of health and well-being from our young people's answers to a wide range of questions about how their lives have progressed. At different points in time, participants have been asked to assess how happy or satisfied they are with their progress and with different elements of their lives. We have also asked direct questions about their physical and mental health, gaining their subjective assessments of these things. Also, participants were asked about anxiety, fitness, and physical and mental health. Their responses to these questions have enabled us to see how health and well-being have emerged as a significant theme in their lives. In order to discuss this, we revisit some of the themes and findings presented in chapter 4 and as we further explore health and well-being. This present chapter provides a sense of how the realities of life over fifteen years have had an impact on the hopes and dreams they held when they were on the threshold of leaving secondary school – and of the hopes they continue to hold for their futures, as well as for their own children and the next generation.

Striving for a Balanced Life

At the outset, participants in both cohorts revealed an awareness of the need to manage their health and well-being. The early surveys and interviews with the Australian cohort focused on their educational pathways, their experiences of work, and their hopes for the future. As they negotiated these aspects of their lives, we began to see evidence that they found it quite difficult. As documented in chapter 4, in 1996, when the Australian cohort was aged twenty-two, 15 per cent of males and 21 per cent of females said that they often felt anxious. Overall, 71 per cent said they sometimes felt anxious. Men who had earned or would eventually earn university credentials were the least anxious (13 per cent), whereas women with the same educational levels were the most anxious (23 per cent). At this early stage the Australian cohort expressed a preference for achieving a balance in life between the competing demands of study, work, and personal life. In 1997, when they were aged around twenty-three, 49 per cent of young men and 41 per cent of young women said that their main priority was to have a balance or 'mixture' of study, work, and family life. Differences by post-secondary-completion status are evident only for men. Fifty-three percent of those who had not completed university wanted a mixture of priorities. Somewhat fewer (46 per cent) of those with university-level credentials shared these views as a higher proportion of this group placed greater weight on their studies.

In 1993, when they were around twenty-three years old, the vast majority of the Canadian sample strongly agreed (47 per cent of females and 40 per cent of males) or agreed (33 per cent and 32 per cent, respectively) that 'given the way things are, it will be much harder for people of my generation to live as comfortably as previous generations.' Women who had graduated from university were the most likely to strongly agree with this statement (49 per cent), compared to 39 per cent of university-educated men, and 44 per cent of women and 40 per cent of men without university credentials.

A few years later, when they were aged twenty-six to twenty-seven, both sets of surveys offered participants the opportunity to write to us about their lives. The theme of achieving a balance was a frequent source of reflection. One Australian young woman felt that her generation faced a wider range of choices than had the previous generation and also faced new kinds of stress:

Adulthood is a very confusing time. We see so many more opportunities and challenges today than our parents did. Too many opportunities/choice[s] creates a new kind of stress. Today is moving so fast that I feel too many of us don't take time out, and this is a concern. It may be a contributing factor to our suicide rates. Society gives higher expectations today than fifty years ago.

The most positive comments by Australian young people at this time were those reflecting on how they had managed to achieve 'the balance.' For example, a young women said, 'I love my life, I enjoy a balance between work, family, and other activities.' However, for many others, this balance was something they hoped to achieve in the future. The following quotes provide an illustration:

Career-driven, direct line through study all the way to future career, on the same path and on-track to get there . . . AND for the first time I am starting to seriously consider other aspects of life and make sure I don't get buried in work, because I am starting to realize (mainly by observation of others) that other things (hobbies, relationships, friends, family) are really important to overall life satisfaction. Not such a scientist-nerd after all! (female)

Well, I think I've done the full circle: got an education, got a job I was less than happy with, got a job I was more than happy with, but now I'm looking to other areas for fulfilment. (male)

The most important aspect affecting my adult life is the choice of occupation. At times the choice of career has been detrimental to general enjoyment of life and left me wondering whether I chose the correct decision for
my life. At present I am enjoying life but looking to change careers in the
near future. (male)

Similarly, in 1998, when they were around twenty-eight years old,
the Canadian sample were asked to comment on their lives. One hundred and one individuals commented on the education-work-family
nexus. Although a few were very positive (for example, 'I am happy
to say I have little time to comment due to excellent lifestyle my career
and family have provided me'), almost all of the others describe either
a lack of balance or the compromises required to achieve their goals.
Women, in particular, wrote long thoughtful quotes that were laden
with their frustration at the challenges they faced.

My personal life, in regards to marriage and children, is not at all where I
thought it would be at this point in time. I virtually traded it for other life
experiences. They are still things I want, things I think about more and
more (especially as all my friends are married and are now starting families of their own, and as the age of thirty is only a couple years away). But
my life, at this point in time, is going down other roads. (female)

I would rather not work so much now with my children being young, but
I feel I need to keep my foot in the door for later. (female)

Although we want to start a family, we have waited because of this issue.
Neither of us will give up our jobs to stay home and raise kids like our
parents' generation. We feel we are not financially secure enough to do so.
If we were, I suppose the other argument would be who would give up
their job. (female)

Moreover, the ability to afford a moderate lifestyle was a constant theme.
As these young people explained, even the most careful approach to
financial stability proved to be challenging:

My husband and I both hold professional degrees, and yet we do not have
the high standard of living that people in our position had thirty years
ago. We own a home and both work full-time, but at the end of the month
there is little left. We do not spend money carelessly and have a financial

planner working with us. We both lived at home until we married to save money, even though we worked full-time. This was the only way we were able to buy a home. When we have children, I will not be able to stay home with them because of the high cost of living. (female)

I think that because of the failing economy, both parents in a household are forced to work full-time in order to have a decent lifestyle, which in turn is causing a breakdown of family values. I feel it is very important to have a parent available at all times, but this goal is unattainable for our family at this time. (female)

These views are matched by the young Australians at age twenty-six (in 2000) in comments that were written in the open sections of the survey by around four hundred participants. The difficulty of achieving the work-life balance was beginning to sink in, and the following quote is typical of their dawning awareness of the difficulties ahead.

It seems over the past two years there has been a greater focus on the work-life balance in the workplace. A plus to this is that you work from an organization that seems to value a nine-to-five lifestyle, but in reality, in my experience, managers of departments don't look upon this favourably. If you want to get somewhere in my work, you need to put in the long hours to show your commitment. (male)

For others, working has provided a sense of identity and well-being that was previously lacking.

Finding a job at which I am very successful has been absolutely key to my sense of satisfaction, security, self-esteem, and optimism. Aspects of life that I previously considered would be instrumental in achieving fulfilment and happiness (for example, marrying, having children, good health) have now assumed the character of 'optional extras' in my outlook. Working full-time in the area in which I was trained has released a pres-sure valve of angst that built up when I had no outlet for recognition or contribution. Working has given me a sense of identity and status that I struggled for as a student. (male)

But the opposite was true for many more.

Life has become much more complex as I realized that work would never be the only thing necessary to truly enjoy life . . . In the past five years my jobs have been to sustain me through uni. Now I have started in a career. It's just four years later than I expected when I finished high school. That's what I learned after leaving school – be flexible. Life is full of twists and turns. (male)

The views of both cohorts can be summed up by the comment of this young Canadian man:

I think that we are living in a time of great change which is at once both frightening and rewarding. I believe the greatest skill for my generation is the ability to embrace change.

All Work and No Play

At the ten-year point, Canadian and Australian young adults were asked about their levels of satisfaction with their lives (figures 1a to 1h). For the most part, over 80 per cent of both female and male respondents from both countries reported that they were 'satisfied' or 'very satisfied' with most dimensions of their lives, which in some ways contradicts their written comments. It may be that answers to forced choice questionnaire items provoke more euphemistic yea-saying responses, which are betrayed when they put pen to paper to describe their lives as lived. However, these figures also reveal that the balance they sought was not always easy to manage. Australian women and men were most dissatisfied about their levels of health and fitness. More men than women from both countries expressed higher levels of dissatisfaction with their level of education, and those who had not earned university degrees were the most dissatisfied. Over a quarter of Australian men reported being dissatisfied with their personal relationships.

Overall, Canadians were more likely than Australians to indicate that they were 'strongly satisfied' with the various dimensions of their lives. Although around 80 per cent indicated that they were satisfied or very satisfied with their personal lives, family lives, and work or careers, a sizable proportion from all groups except women without university degrees reported that they were dissatisfied regarding the more abstract question about career opportunities for their generation. Although 76 per cent of women and only 69 per cent of non-university-educated men were satisfied with the educational opportunities for their generation, 41 per cent of women in this category, compared to 27 per cent of men, voiced their dissatisfaction about their own educational attainments.

Written comments on the surveys at the seven-year point when the Australians were aged twenty-nine and at the ten-year point when the Canadians were aged twenty-eight illuminated the extent to which well-being issues were at the forefront of their concerns. As one Australian young woman who was working full-time in a management position put it,

> I think my generation is deeply concerned with attempting to attain a better work-life balance. This seems to be the catch cry of my friends and is certainly a reason for why I am looking for another job.

Similar sentiments were expressed by Canadians, as these comments indicate:

> Definitely a lot of stress – we really have to make a point of 'stopping to smell the flowers.' Life is what you make it. (female)

> I feel we are the first generation that really has options. These options come with a price, however. We have the right to education or travel or work and the money to choose to do any of them. But since we don't have role models for a balance of the three, we are floundering. There aren't the jobs or opportunities available that there were in my parents' days. No longer does a degree guarantee you work. In fact, we are actually competing with our parents' generation for jobs – we are overeducated and underexperienced. So we look around and see our workaholic parents and decide we don't want that life. The problem is ... there are few guides to what is healthy and 'doable' in our society. Especially since our parents don't know any other way than to work. (female)

As we documented in chapter 4, young people preferred to spend most of their time with family, followed by personal relationships, and then in activities associated with health and fitness. However, in their subjective estimation, work and family life took up most of their time, and the elements that were squeezed out were leisure and recreation and time for health and fitness.

Given the opportunity to write comments about their progress at this time, the theme of finding a balance persisted. As would be expected by the age of twenty-eight, many Australian young adults were 'finding

Figures 1a.–1d. Satisfaction with life, at age 28, in Canada, 1998.

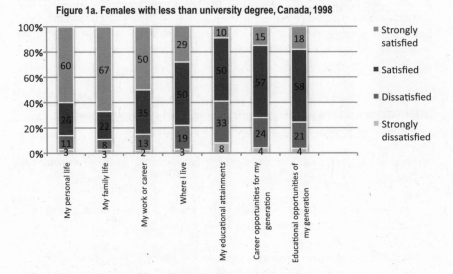

Figure 1a. Females with less than university degree, Canada, 1998

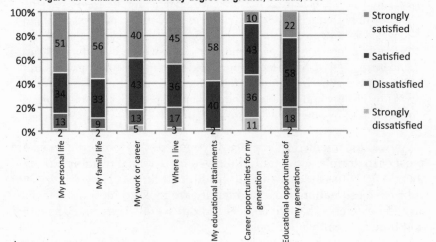

Figure 1b. Females with university degree or greater, Canada, 1998

Figures 1a.–1d. *(Continued)*

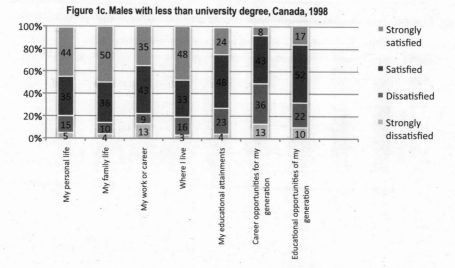

Figure 1c. Males with less than university degree, Canada, 1998

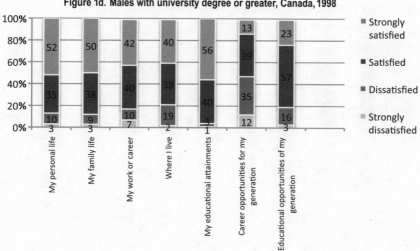

Figure 1d. Males with university degree or greater, Canada, 1998

Figures 1e.–1h. Satisfaction with life, at age 28, in Australia, 2002

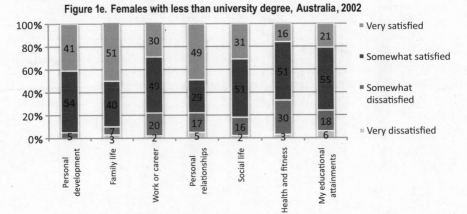

Figure 1e. Females with less than university degree, Australia, 2002

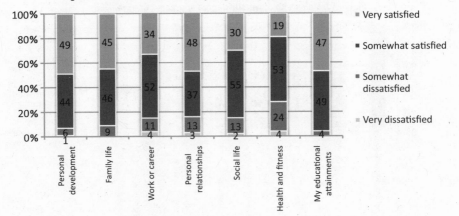

Figure 1f. Females with university degree or greater, Australia, 2002

Figures 1e.–1h. *(Continued)*

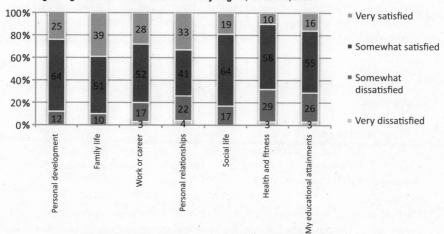

Figure 1g. Males with less than university degree, Australia, 2002

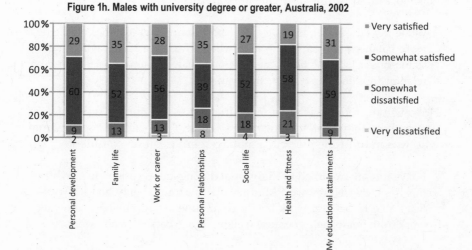

Figure 1h. Males with university degree or greater, Australia, 2002

their feet' and reported feeling 'lucky' that they had made the right choices, or feeling surprised that they had been successful in finding the right mix for themselves. Some were also very proud of what they had achieved, as this young woman in a full-time professional job illustrates:

> I believe I have achieved a great deal for my age, and much of this is because of my continued commitment to study. It takes time, however, to complete initial studies and commence work related to my field of study. I have just changed jobs.

Another young woman who was solely employed in unpaid home duties said:

> I am extremely happy with my life at the moment. My job is very fulfilling and challenging. I am continuously studying short courses to increase my skill set. I am very lucky to have a flexible job that allows me to be a foster parent as well.

Participants who were feeling positive about their lives emphasized the role that having a balance played. For example, a young woman who was working full-time as a salesperson said:

> While my current job is not a career position or high-paying, my life is more balanced and satisfying than when I was in a high-paying, high-status career job. The hours and stress of that position impacted on my relationships and personal life in a way.

However, even those who were feeling successful made a point of mentioning how they achieved the right balance. For example, a young man who was in full-time work in a management position commented:

> I have recently returned to study, undertaking an executive MBA. Whilst this has increased my work/study hours to about seventy hours a week, I am able to balance work-family commitments. Technology (allowing work from home) helps because it allows me to come home to work.

A young woman who was working in a professional full-time job provided a rationale for a change in career directions:

I have recently taken a new job in rural Victoria. I wanted more free time for recreational activities because my job in Melbourne was becoming too demanding. I hope this new position will be less time-demanding, but so far it doesn't appear to be better.

Another young woman, who was working casually in clerical work, expressed her frustration:

I have found the need to rebalance my life as career is less important to me now. I would rather focus on more fulfilling activities and friends than overwork and not take holidays. Next step is to own my own business or study in an area unrelated to my current work.

When they were also aged twenty-eight, the Canadian sample were invited to comment specifically on 'the lives and times of your generation.' As these comments illustrate, they describe their lives as 'hard,' 'uncertain,' 'unstable,' and 'heavy,' which corresponds with Bauman's (2001) term *Unsicherheit*. As these three respondents argue, their quality of life was not what they had expected and for which they strove:

For my generation, times are hard. Hard in that it's difficult to save money for a down payment of a house, difficult to find work that is both challenging and rewarding, and hard to maintain a lifestyle I am accustomed to. (male)

I think my generation has a heavier burden to carry than previous generations because job markets are so tight. It's rarely feasible that a one-income family can make it today, and our children are the ones who suffer. They see less of us than they should, and oftentimes when families are together, the parents have little left to give because the effort just to survive is so huge. Yet, without monumental effort, the future for my generation would be bleak. It makes me afraid for my children. I mean, we work so hard and have less than our parents (lifestyle wise). What can our kids expect? Will they be able to obtain an education at all? And will it help them if they do? (female)

[It is] confusing because the package [we were] sold, i.e., education, travel, world access, does not correspond to perceptions given as a child, i.e., family, $, house, kids. So how do you do all of it? . . . So it's hard to live up to life dreams...No real advances by humanity. We're the same stupid people but more aware. (female)

Even those who were satisfied with their choices expressed some level of concern about the future:

I keep hearing that my generation needs to be flexible. I guess that's true. For me, that involved borrowing an absurd amount of money for my education. I have no regrets and would do the same thing over again. For others who haven't had the same good fortune, it could be a bit trying. (male)

Although I feel fairly secure in terms of my job and family, there does seem to be a feeling of instability in general. It's hard to tell where I or members of my generation will be twenty or even ten years from now. This is a scary but exciting thought. (female)

One young woman articulated very clearly the contractions of the times:

I feel that, by and large, we as a generation are mostly satisfied with our lives, careers, and relationships, however non-traditional they may be. We have many more choices today, particularly us women. We are led to believe that we might be 'missing something' if we 'settle' for the traditional. I generally think that it's terrific to feel you could go anywhere or do anything, but what do you feel if you aren't taking full advantage of it? Perhaps we are a little spoiled for choice. I wonder who is more satisfied in the end – someone who doesn't know what they're missing or someone who does?

The themes arising from the open-ended comments were remarkably similar – and similar over time – for the Australian and Canadian sample, which provides evidence for a generational unity around issues of education, work, personal relationships, and family.

Mental and Physical Health Concerns

Ten years out of high school, both the Australian and the Canadian respondents were also asked to comment more specifically on their physical and mental health. The same questions were asked of both groups, which makes the contrast between the two samples both dramatic and highly troubling. As table 45 clearly portrays, a large proportion of the Australian sample consider themselves neither physically nor mentally well. On average, 57 per cent claim they are physically 'healthy' or 'very healthy'; in contrast, 78 per cent of Canadians describe themselves as 'healthy' or better. In terms of mental health, 39 per cent of Australians describe themselves as less than 'healthy,' whereas only 25 per cent of Canadians make the same claim. That said, the fact that almost 50 per cent of Australian and 25 per cent of Canadian young adults at age twenty-eight do not describe themselves as mentally healthy should be a wake-up call for government officials and educational and labour-market policymakers who promote economic prosperity over the health and well-being of its citizens.

A few of the interviewees, such as this Canadian woman and Australian man, shared their experiences with mental health and related problems:

The life and times of my generation: High stress and burn out. I feel somewhat disillusioned at the age of twenty-eight. Have been on antidepressants for four months. I am OPTIMISTIC, though. (Canadian female)

Even though I had two university degrees and a well-respected job, my life was turned on its head because of heroin addiction. I spent most of 1999 in residential rehabilitation and am now in the process of rebuilding my life. My priorities are now completely different from what they were; career and studies are not important at all. It is finding inspiration in the small things that matters now. (Australian male).

Our data enable us to go beyond the usual broad population-based statistics to look at the question of which groups are managing well and which are not. We have analysed our participants' responses by comparing post-secondary-completion status between Australia and Canada, and the results reveal that Australians are faring worse. For example, 21 per cent of women and 14 per cent of Australian men who had never attended post-secondary institutions described themselves as physically unhealthy or very unhealthy. The comparable figure for Canadian women and men is 5 per cent. Australians who had earned university credentials were almost 20 per cent more likely than Canadians were to describe themselves as less than physically healthy. Across all categories, Canadians asserted that they were more mentally healthy, with the greatest difference occurring between women with university degrees. Whereas 75 per cent of Canadian women in this category considered themselves to be mentally healthy or better, only 58 per cent of Australian women in the same category made such claims.

Although these figures are concerning, in fact the young people's subjective assessments of their mental health, when aggregated, reveal a lower proportion of mental health problems than do the official Australian statistics. Twenty-five percent of young Australians aged eighteen to twenty-four years in 1997 experienced a mental health disorder (Australian Institute of Health and Welfare 2007) 10 percent of this age group were diagnosed with depression, and a total of 14 per cent experienced anxiety disorders (Australian Institute of Health and Welfare 2007). Concern about mental health has continued to be an issue for young Australians. A recent study of young Australians aged twenty to twenty-four years identified depression as the issue of most importance to young people (34 per cent) (Mission Australia 2007). The mental health of young Canadians has also emerged as an issue of concern (Canadian Institute for Health Information 2006). A comprehensive study of the mental health of the Canadian population in 1994–5 showed that 7 per cent of twenty- to twenty-nine-year-olds were depressed, 38 per cent experienced high levels of distress, and 17 per cent of this latter group said that this affected their lives (Stephens, Dulberg, and Joubert 2000). This study showed that 72 per cent of Canadians aged twenty to twenty-nine in 1994–5 were happy and interested in life. It also showed that (across all age groups) those with higher levels of education were the most likely to be mentally well; 33 per cent of those with less than a high school education experienced high levels of distress, compared with 23 per cent of those with a university education; and Canadian men had slightly better mental health levels than did Canadian women.

It needs to be remembered that, overall, young people are the healthiest group of the population (Australian Institute of Health and Welfare 2007; Canadian Institute for Health Information 2006), and we acknowledge the finding by other studies that increased educational participation generally correlates with improved health outcomes (World Health Organization 2004). Given that this cohort of young Australians and Canadians was the most highly educated generation yet, their subjective concerns about their health and well-being and the objective evidence that some health problems, especially mental health, are on the increase appear to represent a paradox.

Table 45

Physical and mental health, by post-secondary-completion status and sex, in Australia and Canada

Physically healthy, age 28, Australia, 2002

	Females			Males			
	No PS %	Non-univ. %	Univ. %	No PS %	Non-univ. %	Univ. %	Total %
Very unhealthy	0	4	3	7	1	0	2
Unhealthy	21	13	12	7	6	5	11
Neutral	21	34	28	40	33	32	31
Healthy	38	35	36	27	52	39	39
Very healthy	21	15	21	20	9	24	18
N	29	136	194	15	89	62	525

Mentally healthy, age 28, Australia, 2002

	Females			Males			
	No PS %	Non-univ. %	Univ. %	No PS %	Non-univ. %	Univ. %	Total %
Very unhealthy	0	4	4	0	3	0	3
Unhealthy	17	15	11	13	7	10	12
Neutral	14	23	28	20	26	19	25
Healthy	48	39	40	40	44	50	42
Very healthy	21	18	18	27	20	21	19
N	29	137	195	15	89	62	527

Physically healthy, age 28, Canada, 1998

	Females			Males			
	No PS %	Non-univ. %	Univ. %	No PS %	Non-univ. %	Univ. %	Total %
Very unhealthy	0	3	0	5	1	2	2
Unhealthy	5	10	6	0	5	2	6
Neutral	5	18	16	0	15	14	15
Healthy	57	41	37	43	43	40	40
Very healthy	33	28	38	52	36	42	37
N	21	181	233	21	116	152	724

Mentally healthy, age 28, Canada, 1998

	Females			Males			
	No PS %	Non-univ. %	Univ. %	No PS %	Non-univ. %	Univ. %	Total %
Very unhealthy	5	3	0	0	2	0	1
Unhealthy	5	9	8	10	8	6	8
Neutral	14	18	18	14	16	12	16
Healthy	38	37	45	24	43	50	43
Very healthy	38	33	30	52	31	32	32
N	21	181	233	21	116	152	724

Although health and well-being may be experienced by young people as the outcome of their own efforts, the evidence shows that young people's health and well-being is directly related to the quality of the social and material resources upon which they are able to draw. Recent Australian data show that as socio-economic status decreases, there is a parallel increase in mortality and morbidity and in smoking, poor exercise, and diet. The likelihood of a young person being a victim of physical or threatened assault also increases with social disadvantage (Australian Institute of Health and Welfare 2007). Young people who are living in families or communities that are fragmented, unsupportive, and badly resourced are the most likely to experience a range of health problems. Parents with young people aged twelve to twenty-four years, living in the most disadvantaged areas of Australia, were twice as likely to report their health as fair or poor (22 per cent) than those living in the least disadvantaged areas (11 per cent); about one-third of parents in the most disadvantaged areas (30 per cent) were estimated to have poor mental health, compared with 18 per cent of those living in the least disadvantaged areas (Australian Institute of Health and Welfare 2007, 99). It is acknowledged that the absence of positive social factors, or their breakdown (for example, marital discord between parents; social isolation; bullying; physical, sexual, and emotional abuse; and socio-economic disadvantage), contribute to mental health problems (Australian Institute of Health and Welfare 2007, 23). Canadian data mainly support the Australian evidence. Stephens, Dulberg, and Joubert, who conducted a comprehensive analysis of Canadians' mental health in the years 1994–5, found that poor mental health was associated with stress; those who were stressed were four times more likely to be depressed than those who were not stressed (Stephens, Dulberg, and Joubert 2000). This study also showed that as the number of 'significant life events' in a person's life increased, so did the likelihood of having mental health problems. Their research is very relevant to the situation of the young people in our study because of the extent to which our young people (and especially the Australians) said that they felt stressed. Also, the impact of uncertainty is that, inevitably, young people face 'significant life events' such as moving their place of residence, experiencing a relationship breakdown, and changing employment.

Unlike the findings of Stephens, Dulberg, and Joubert (2000), however, our data show that mental health issues are more likely to affect those who are more highly educated. The competing demands of family, work, and striving for a lifestyle that continually slips through their fingers are likely to have fuelled mental and physical health issues. Our research reflects an emerging understanding of the connectedness of health, work, and social relationships. Conditions such as social support, safety, community investment, and trust are the key elements of social relations that support well-being. Our study shows the impact of differential access to these resources on young people's health and well-being.

Assessing Life Priorities

In chapter 4, we used Australian 2004 data and Canadian 2003 data to reveal our respondents' priorities and goals. As we reported in table 4, when they were aged twenty-four, Australians placed a high priority on financial security, personal relationships, and family. The Canadian sample at around age twenty-eight also placed a high priority on having time for family and personal relationships, living a healthy lifestyle, and achieving a balance between work and non-work activities. There are two important and related points here. First, it is significant that in their early thirties both groups continued to place a positive value on family relationships, and we know that this included parents, grandparents, and siblings as well as their own partners and children. Second, their priorities and goals show that they associate having time with family (in its widest sense) with being well. Physical and mental health were high priorities (especially for the women) (see table 5, chapter 4). The Canadian cohort, like their Australian counterparts, placed a higher priority on the aspects of life that related to well-being (relationships and living a healthy lifestyle) than on those elements of life that related to success in work or to regular involvement in organized learning activities.

After the years of establishing themselves in workplaces, when many were quite positive about work, the realities of work had begun to sink in. As they got older, they were more aware of the ongoing tensions involved in managing work and family life. In 2003, when they were around thirty-three, only a minority of Canadian young adults 'strongly agreed' that they looked forward to coming to work (14 per cent of males and 15 per cent of females), and nearly a quarter found their work psychologically stressful (22 per cent). Just over a quarter of the women felt their work enabled them to balance work and personal life, but only 18 per cent of males felt they could manage this balance.

This perception is important – when we consider that 70 per cent of women and 60 per cent of men said that achieving a balance between work and non-work activities was very important – because it indicates a disjunction between their values and the realities of their lives.

Despite the challenges of getting 'the balance' right, overall our participants appear to be happy. When asked about the extent to which they were satisfied with their lives at fifteen and thirteen years following high school graduation, again our respondents were overwhelmingly satisfied with their personal lives and development, family lives, careers, and educational attainments (see pages 216–19). However, when we explore the patterns of satisfaction, a slightly different picture emerges. We found important differences in levels of satisfaction by gender and post-secondary-completion status.

Around 20 per cent of Canadian women and men who had achieved less than a university degree continued to be dissatisfied with their educational attainments, reflecting the significance of education in the labour market, and perhaps also reflecting difficulties in re-engaging with education. This group of Canadians were also 10 per cent more likely than their university-educated counterparts to say that they were dissatisfied about educational opportunities for today's children. When asked to comment about their educational attainments, this group of Canadian respondents were somewhat more dissatisfied than were their Australian counterparts. Earlier we noted that a high proportion of the Australian cohort *eventually* undertook further education; therefore, their level of satisfaction with their educational attainments may reflect the fact that they were able to access some form of post-secondary education as adults.

However, attitudes towards health and fitness reveal a different pattern. Australians in all categories, and particularly women with university degrees, continued to be the most dissatisfied with their health and fitness, reflecting the greater challenges they faced in managing the work-life balance as discussed in chapter 7.

A relatively high proportion of women and men from both countries were dissatisfied with their fitness levels. Also, only around 60 per cent reported being satisfied with the amount of time they had to spend on activities they enjoyed. Around 20 per cent of university-educated men in Australia were not satisfied with their personal relationships or social lives; this proportion is considerably higher than that of all the other groups. We have discussed, in chapters 6 and 7, the relatively harsh workplace laws during the 1990s and the expectations of long working hours that affected the Australian cohort. It is very likely that the low satisfaction levels of university-educated Australians reflects the personal costs they have borne in achieving their work and career goals. As many have commented, balance in life has been difficult to achieve.

Are We There Yet?

In 2003 (Canada) and 2006 (Australia) respondents were again invited to write to us about their lives and experiences. A total of 183 Australians, who were now aged around thirty-two, commented on two themes, both of which are central to this chapter: 'How satisfied are you with the way things have turned out?' and 'If you were giving advice to young people leaving school in 2006, what advice would you give them?' A small minority expressed positive views or felt that they had 'arrived':

> Life kicks ass! (male)

> I have reached a time in my life where everything I have worked for is paying off. I am getting married in January, and both work and personal life is at a peak at present. (female)

> It took turning thirty and being in the same job since leaving uni for me to realize that I had worked ridiculously hard and become very successful but it was time to make a change for myself and to get a life. Moving to [a large city in another country] was a drastic change, but has been amazing and is the best decision I have made in years. I now understand what work-life balance means. (female)

Most (around 70 per cent) wrote comments that indicated that they were 'generally' or 'overall' feeling satisfied with their lives, but most of these were hedged with a sense that they were not able to get the right balance:

> Overall I'm very satisfied. However, some things have been much harder than I had imagined – a previous relationship breakdown. With work and study going so well, I'm really busy and often feel worn out – run off my feet with not enough time for fitness, health, or social life. But the outcomes give me lots. (female)

Generally I am very happy. I just need more time to keep fit and some time to myself, I am very busy. (female)

I would like to be in a relationship but am happy with my life in general. Health and fitness are improving. (female)

A number of participants were clearly not satisfied, and felt they had some way to go:

My life sucks! (female)

Further studies took a long time to complete whilst working. Health and fitness suffered due to imbalance in work and study. Balance is important, but balance will only shift if priorities change. (male)

At this stage in my life, the difficulty of finding interesting but manage-able part-time work and an employer who really understands work-life balance is the challenge. (female)

Work taking too many hours of the week. As a result all else suffers. (male)

In total, 154 Canadian respondents, who were aged thirty-three in 2003, commented on themes addressed in this chapter. Of these, like the Australians, a small proportion were exuberant about their lives and their futures:

The prospects for my (future) children are bright as my wife and I are both well educated and earn a reasonable income. I have grave con-cerns for the options available to children born in a less comfortable environment. (male)

I am grateful for the educational opportunities my husband and I received in British Columbia. We can now afford to live our desired lifestyle and provide a great future for our children. (female)

For others, expressions of satisfaction had undertones of resignation:

I have always wanted to have a professional degree, but roads/paths I have chosen have brought me in a different direction. I have no guilt or regret in the direction I have chosen as I have a wonderful and supportive family. My lifestyle, I could have not asked for anything better. My family and myself are away every weekend at the lake where we stay during the summer months. My children are active in sports during the rest of the months. My career has given me the flexibility to do so. I could always make more money, but there is always a price to pay, i.e., time, which seems to be on a decrease. (male)

In the city, I see so many of us struggling to balance cost of living (home debt) with needs of family, difficulty in finding good affordable childcare, work demands, and anxieties about aging parents and health care. We also carry the tax burden. (female)

Several Canadian and Australian respondents voiced concerns – and hope – for future generations, including their children:

I'll have to work hard for my children to train them to be balanced, capable, good, and reasonable people. (Canadian male)

I have many fears for the accessibility/affordability of post-secondary education for my children and wonder what their world is like. I feel that we are the first generation to not pass our parents' standard of living. People generally need a 'boost' of some sort to get ahead now, and I wonder what it'll be like for my children. (Canadian female)

The future is bright for kids who live in Canada; even if they don't choose post-sec. education right away, there are still a lot of opportunities if you look. (Canadian female)

My aim is to get my children through school. Have healthy relationships. Find out more to support my autistic child. (Australian female)

To me young people are in a terrible position today; expected to become, almost from birth, calculating, work-ethic-obsessed, 'New Right' subjects. I can't stress highly enough the value of 'making mistakes' and to make decisions for yourself. (Australian male)

The acceleration of today's society was clearly on the minds of a considerable proportion of respondents. Their comments echo Rosa's writings (1998, 2003) on the relationships among production, consumption, and the acceleration of time.

Figures 2a.–2d. Satisfaction with life, at age 33, in Canada, 2003

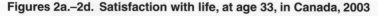

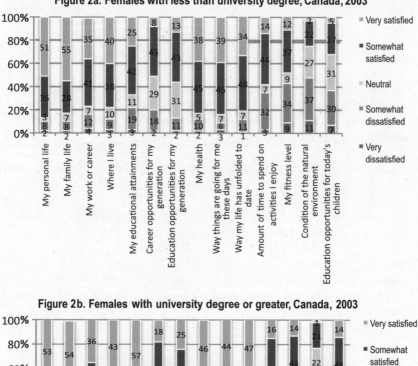

Figure 2a. Females with less than university degree, Canada, 2003

Figure 2b. Females with university degree or greater, Canada, 2003

Figures 2a.–2d. *(Continued)*

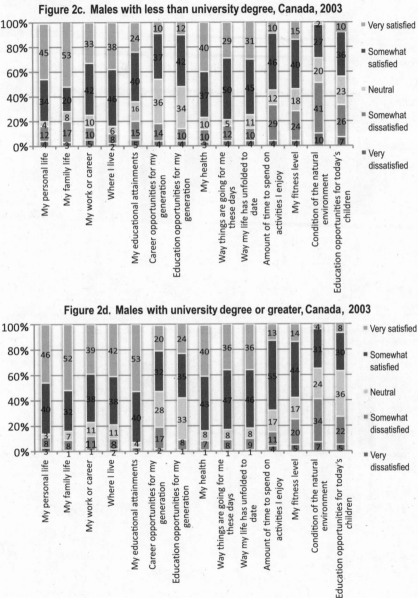

Figure 2c. Males with less than university degree, Canada, 2003

Figure 2d. Males with university degree or greater, Canada, 2003

Figures 2e.–2h. Satisfaction with life, at age 30, in Australia, 2004.

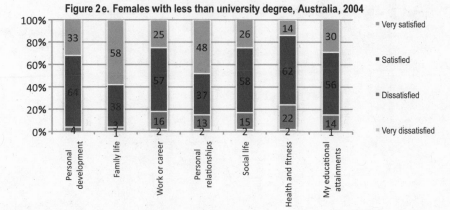

Figure 2 e. Females with less than university degree, Australia, 2004

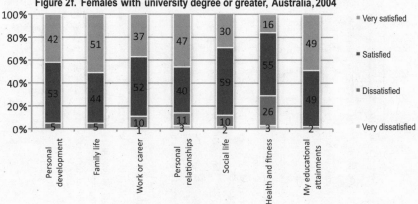

Figure 2f. Females with university degree or greater, Australia, 2004

Figures 2e.–2h. *(Continued)*

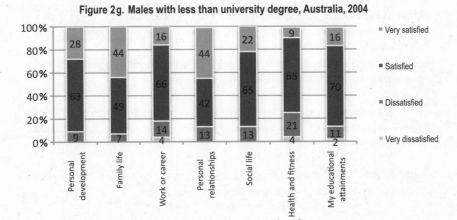

Figure 2g. **Males with less than university degree, Australia, 2004**

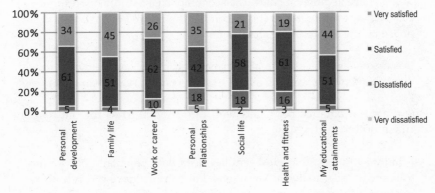

Figure 2h. **Males with university degree or greater, Australia, 2004**

You can't teach common sense and family values, and both seem to be suffering in the new 24-hr world we are creating. Commercialism and materialism have taken their toll on moral values and relationships and well-being. People need to stop and smell roses and put balance back in their lives. I also believe physical fitness = mental fitness, so get outside and play! (Canadian male)

I find today's world so fast paced that some of today's families don't spend enough time together. A lot of families have to have two incomes to survive, which can take away from the family time. Now families have to schedule time together, which, I guess, is better than nothing, but it is sad that it has changed over the years. (Canadian female)

Life for me seems to be in fast-forward. Everything is happening faster than I expected – but I am also happy with how it's going. (Australian female)

Others described their lives, at least in terms of family, as 'on hold' until societal conditions became more favourable:

Currently, like many other couples we know, it seems the only possible way for both of us to be employed at the level we desire in our careers, we must live in different cities. The econom[y has] reduced opportunities, etc., has all contributed to this becoming the norm. We have also postponed family as a result. (Canadian female)

It is extremely difficult to make financial headway, and I am concerned that it is interfering with my ability to start a family. (Canadian male)

The theme of balance persisted well into their thirties for the respondents in both countries:

I find it sad to see that most families need both parents to be working full-time in order to live in Vancouver. I'm delaying having kids until we can be in a financial place to support a family on 1.5 incomes. (Canadian female)

Today most families need to have both parents working, therefore leaving limited time for family life. I question if education always makes for better family life. In our situation my husband and I have eleven years post-secondary combined, and both have stressful jobs with lots of responsibility. (Canadian female)

Trying to find a balance between family and work, while doing a good-to-excellent job at both, is my daily struggle. I hate having my child in day care, even though it is great, but it is our only option financially. I would love to stay at home and raise my children full-time. I think lack of parenting in general is responsible for the huge changes in today's youth. (Canadian female)

My expectations at school were to marry and have children and possibly my own business. I have a great business, which I enjoy, but little time to socialize and therefore no marriage/children. (Australian female)

I am becoming more aware of needing to be adaptable career-wise. The importance of family and a stable relationship and remaining informed about everything in order to make better work, life, and financial decisions is now a priority. (Australian male)

Women raised specific concerns regarding their attempts to achieve fulfilment. Men's voices did not come through in the same way, which suggests that for the Canadians and the Australians in our studies women were more strongly affected by competing demands, as the following comments by women illustrate:

At this point in my life the challenges are about the options I have: to have / not to have children; work and save money / downsize and relax. I have many more options than ever before. (Australian)

I would like to comment on the aspect of being a woman and 'having it all' – but at a cost. I am a mother of two small children, own my own (very small) company, and [am] currently enrolled in a graduate degree. I am the primary caregiver and home maker, plus have work and schoolwork, so I am constantly juggling my life. I am happy, but it can get overwhelming. I believe this is a uniquely female issue. I know if my spouse went back to school, he wouldn't (expect to) do anything other than schoolwork. (Canadian)

I could write an epic on the particular dilemmas of this generation's women of childbearing age and related value conflicts (i.e., 1. the servitude of motherhood vs. 'getting recognized/paid for your labour'; 2. 'mother as tireless and faultless child-educator/psychologist' vs. Oprah-esque responsibility of mother to 'take care of herself'; 3. the social isolation of mothering (being home) with small children while most of the community is at work; 4. the pressure of the societal idealization of child-rearing and family life vs. the grunt-work reality and immense challenge and lack of perfection). I could go on, but my children are arguing. I can't maintain a coherent line of thought, and I'm afraid I'll never get this to you. Ask me in five years! (Canadian)

In many of the comments, there is a sense that the 'good life,' as envisioned fifteen years earlier, is eluding them:

Never thought I would be terminally single. Plus, also assumed youthful fitness would last. (Australian female)

The cost of living nowadays has resulted in us having only two children and not three as originally planned. We would need more space, and with interest rates rising we are not willing to take the risk (especially on one wage). (Australian female)

I believe that today's family will not have what our parents or grandparents had, i.e., house, cottage, boat, pool, etc. Or that we necessarily want all that. We (or at least my wife and I) believe in quality of life. Quality time together, time for ourselves (i.e., fitness, relaxation). (Canadian male)

In order to afford a house big enough for a family I have to . . . commut[e] back and forth to work, [which] takes too much time out of my day – especially with the limitations of full-time childcare; as a result my quality of life is lower than I would like. I have no immediate family in the area to help with childcare, as is not uncommon in today's society, and no sense of community, I am suffering from an extreme lack of time, which is why I haven't filled this out. (Canadian female)

I'm not where I feel that I 'should be' in my life. I'm dissatisfied that I am single, unmarried, and childless at age thirty-three. I also have anxieties over an aging mother (my father is already deceased) and other family responsibilities. I fear not being financially self-sufficient and potentially being homeless. (Canadian female)

A few individuals were very candid about the ongoing mental health issues that they faced:

People need to slow down – we are going too fast + not getting enough time to think and reflect. I'm working 50 per cent teaching; I've found a wonderful partner teacher – I've gone through counselling for depression, anxiety, stress, and gambling addiction. I'm still on meds for depression – will be until Sept. 2004. I'm getting married Feb. 2004, and we are planning a family to start 2004. I feel great now and am only working P/T to keep a balance in my life. I am much more positive about the future, and we are more financially secure. Things look good right now. (Canadian female)

Occasionally, respondents experienced grave tragedy in their lives. The stories of these three respondents must be seen in light of all the comments above, as tragedy adds another layer of burden on already unbalanced, insecure, and demanding lives.

I hope my wife beats cancer so we can grow old together. My kids to stay healthy, and to be able to retire at fifty-five, not sixty-five. Also to buy a summer house in [a rural area] or move there full-time. (Canadian male)

It hasn't been easy to live my life. I can't and won't compare it to anybody else. I have a great husband, but he is only human. I have two great children, a house to keep us dry and warm, most of the time. If I looked at my history, it could be looked at as tragic (my son ill, daughter needing heart surgery, father dies unexpectedly, farming become more difficult, mother getting cancer (still alive), both sisters getting depression. Not becom[ing] a teacher like I would have liked to have; son getting bone marrow transplant; friend (my husband's best friend) killing himself; another being crushed at work but survived; other friend, four children + wife, he died in tragic work accident). Life can and will in many cases be difficult, but don't lose hope. Ask for help at school, home or wherever you feel lost or confused. Life is about learning, and you can learn in the most unexpected places. You don't always need a certificate to be educated. (Canadian female)

My battle with cancer has severely hurt my hopes and aspirations. I feel that I am far behind in all areas of my life because of illness. It's easy to feel deprived or bitter over a life that is hard or frustrating, but that is useless.

Hope for future goals is imperative. I hope to be free of cancer, to regain my old self-image, spend more time working but also with friends – just to be well! (Australian female)

Most of our participants have 'arrived,' not at a place or status but at a point of relative satisfaction, a personal space where they feel comfortable with their lives. Most have developed strategies for continuing to invent and reinvent themselves as they negotiate the continually changing landscape of their worlds.

Conclusion

In their late teens the young people in our studies shared the hopes they had for their futures and the goals they had for their lives. As we have shown in chapter 4, these hopes were relatively unremarkable and mostly quite modest: job security, fulfilling employment, and good, stable personal relationships, including, for many, marriage and having children. By the time they were in their early thirties, most had achieved their original goals, some had changed their goals, and the majority of our participants felt a genuine sense of satisfaction about what they had achieved. We feel that it is important to acknowledge the success of this generation, especially given the tendency within the wider literature to problematize young adulthood. The stories of our participants serve as a reminder that the majority of young people do manage to live fulfilling and satisfying lives.

However, this chapter makes visible the extent of the struggle to achieve their modest goals in the conditions of the 1990s and early 2000s in Canada and Australia. Our work supports other research and especially statistical reports that show that educational credentials have been this generation's most significant tool for ensuring labour-market success. However, we have felt the need to go beyond these ways of representing young people's pathways. The lines of association between education and employment drawn in statistical tables are always straight and smooth, even when the associations for different groups (based on parental-educational levels and on gender, for example) are not the same. The texture of real life trajectories, however, even for the successful, as witnessed in the narratives of our participants, are rough, wobbly, and multidirectional. Our data have enabled us to explore in depth, through the use of both statistical representations and narratives, the nature and quality of young people's lives in the

1990s. In this chapter our analysis of their health and well-being adds an important dimension to the understanding of their experiences of education and employment and the significance of personal relationships; these dimensions are constantly intertwined.

This chapter has raised two significant issues. First, it has reinforced the extent to which this generation has had to manage, invent, and negotiate new territory. Their narratives convey a powerful sense of living through change, of managing choices, coping with stress, balancing competing demands, and striving to reach that elusive state – a balanced life. We sum up the tone of this process as *Unsicherheit*, emphasizing the weight that this generation has borne in the form of individual struggle to live well. In this sense, striving to be well, and managing well-being, has indeed been a defining characteristic of this generation.

Second, the chapter has presented in stark detail the costs of this struggle for a significant group. Our Australian participants have found it especially difficult to manage their well-being, physically and mentally. Their concerns about their mental and physical health are supported by official statistics showing that today one in five young Australians, regardless of their levels of education, experience mental health problems. We believe that, through our detailed comparison of young people in both countries, across many of the key dimensions of life (education, work, and relationships or family), our analysis provides a unique insight into how social conditions make people unwell. The high levels of physical and mental health concerns among the Australian cohort, and the dissatisfaction felt in this regard across all groups, including those who are university educated, reveal the personal costs of the mismatch of social and economic goals.

Although the Canadian participants have not experienced the same levels of physical and mental health concerns as have their Australian counterparts, their narratives reveal exactly the same struggles to manage their well-being, and they face the same challenges (albeit on a lesser scale) to ensure physical and mental well-being. Like the Australians, they needed to learn balance. The conclusions drawn in this chapter raise important policy issues that are taken up in chapter 9.

9   Implications: Generation and Inequality

At moments of change,
you need to step back into your life from another direction.
Life isn't a straight line, it's more like a dance.
And you have to know the moves.[1]

In this chapter we reflect on the implications of the evidence we have presented thus far. Social science too can benefit from stepping back into our thinking from another direction. Social scientists some-times know 'the moves' of their practice too well, and this can result in 'interpret[ing] reality and world views based on past experiences' (Inglehart 1990, 422). Our approach to making meaning of the patterns within our data and the narratives and attitudes of the young people is to open up new lines of questioning. We have attempted to avoid mak-ing young people's lives 'more real, more orderly and more predictable' than they are (Ball 2006, 4). Working across the two academic fields of higher education and youth studies has made it necessary for each of us to engage with unfamiliar conceptual frames, such that when we have returned to more familiar theoretical territory, it has indeed come from another direction. One of the consequences of this is that we do not present a tidy summary of the making of this generation, neatly bound with conceptual string. In this chapter we reflect on what we have found and step back to reflect on this project for the final time in the book, to share our thoughts about the implications of our work.

This study has analysed the interrelated nature of social change and individual biographies in detail. It captures the dynamics of social change

---

1 Opening frame of the Australian television show *Secret Life of Us*.

at a particular historical period including an education revolution and the labour-market deconstruction of the 1990s. It shows how these two social changes exerted a powerful force on the subjectivities and biographies of the young people – as they learned and practised the 'moves' that would enable them to achieve their hopes and live their dreams.

In reflecting on the evidence and its implications, we aim here to push as far as we can to explore the significance of the research. We return to the questions that informed this book. We conclude, first, that economic and social conditions and global processes have had a significant impact on the lives of this generation. We also find evidence of distinctive attitudes and priorities. In the following sections we summarize the main ways in which conditions have affected their lives to create distinctive generational approaches to life. We then reflect on the role of government policies in shaping this generation, exploring both intended and unintended consequences, and on the interrelationship of local conditions on global processes. This enables us to highlight some significant features of the comparison between Canada and Australia. Finally we offer some reflections on the practical role of theory in our research. In chapter 2 we outlined the main conceptual frameworks that informed our analysis, and they have been expanded on in the chapters that followed; here we provide some reflections on the practical role of theory as a 'conceptual toolbox and means of analysis and a system of reflexivity' (Ball 2006).

Young Adulthood in the 1990s

The individual trajectories and stories that are traced through our analysis have revealed some clear patterns that enable us to tell a story about this generation. Here we share the strong themes to emerge from the data presented in the chapters of this book, as well as some of the important divergences from these themes. In a snapshot, our understanding of the story of this generation is told through its five interrelated themes: reluctant change makers, an education generation, generating new patterns of family life, a generation in search of work-life balance, and a diverse generation. We address each theme in turn.

Reluctant Change Makers

This generation was remarkable. In many countries their lives were so different from those of the previous generation that they spawned the term *Generation X* and precipitated an industry that has contributed an ever-expanding vocabulary to describe social generations, names that ranged from those that reinvented the past (for example, *baby boomers, the Silent Generation, Generation X, Generation Me, Millennials*, and many others) to those that reframed contemporary youth. Yet this generation did not set out to make history. Their hopes were unremarkable, even modest. They wanted security and enough money to live comfortably and own a home; they wanted to have good relationships, including 'settling down' and marrying. For many, these hopes were not to be; for others, they have been achieved through struggle; and for many, in the end, their priorities have been changed to embrace a new adulthood. They have been thrust into a world in which change is the norm and in which they have had to play roles for which they were often unprepared. Life has not been 'in a straight line' for many, and they have struggled to know 'the moves' of a dance in which they have been forced to participate but which they do not necessarily understand. As our data show in stark figures as well as in more nuanced narratives, some have never learned the moves and have remained on the sideline.

An Education Generation

Education has played a pivotal role in the lives of these young people. Both the Australians and the Canadians overwhelmingly believed that post-secondary education would benefit their lives and open up opportunities. Education was seen as a personal investment, a tool for personal development, and as necessary for achieving employment security. They were in the vanguard of a shift towards universal post-secondary education, establishing a trend that continues today. However, the context in which they negotiated their first and subsequent steps in their educational careers was different. First, the Canadians were more likely to come from families in which at least one parent had a post-secondary-school qualification than were the Australians, giving them cultural resources that assisted them in making decisions about education. Second, the British Columbian education system had more effective articulation between secondary and post-secondary education than did the Victorian system. This meant that the young Australians had a more chaotic experience because they were forced to rely on their own resources to make decisions about their education. Despite these differences, the expansion of the proportion of the population who

entered post-secondary education at that time did open up opportunities for sections of the population that had previously not accessed
further education. Despite this equalizing trend, older patterns of
inequality in educational participation – and in the returns on investment in education – have largely been replicated.

Generating New Patterns of Family Life

This generation has forged new patterns in relation to families, which
has yet to be recognized in policies (Esping-Andersen 2009). They
set the trend for young people to remain living with, and financially
dependent on, their parents for longer than the previous generation
had. Contrary to the established orthodoxies about youth being a time
of independence, our research found that this generation forged strong
interdependent relationships with their parents. It was notable that
many of the young people said that their parents were a source of support and were valued and enjoyed for their company. Although there
was a trend across both countries for later marriage, this was accentu-
ated in the Australian cohort. The Australians tended to marry later
and less, and have children later and less, than did the Canadians. The
national patterns show that there are strong local differences in the
ways in which generational patterns are played out.

A Generation in Search of Life-Work Balance

At the outset the young people in both countries saw their investment in education as holding out the promise of benefits in the labour
market. While this is accurate in the broadest sense, it is difficult to
say with any clarity that any one group has benefited. This is partly
because work conditions have such a significant impact on all other
areas of life. University-educated women have, on the face of things,
benefited most in the sense that they have better job security (and, in
Canada, benefits) than has any other group. However, they have borne
the cost in their personal lives, with lower rates of marriage and childbearing than those of other groups. As the Australian and Canadian
economies recovered from the economic recession of the early 1990s,
most groups in our study managed to gain a foothold in the labour
market, and we conclude that their investment in education did protect many from the worst effects of the economic transformation occurring in both countries. By the time they were in their early thirties, the

overwhelming majority had achieved a great amount. We also note that their achievements were frequently hard won as they charted new territory. We have especially highlighted the extent to which these young adults felt pressure, were stressed, and struggled to manage their lives in a context of changing work expectations. The Australians especially show the effects of living with workplace conditions that compromised their personal lives, health, and well-being, especially when compared with their Canadian peers. These effects are reflected in poor mental and physical health and in their ongoing struggle to achieve a balance in life.

A Diverse Generation

Perhaps the most significant finding of this study is the diversity of their lives, despite the trends that we have identified above. Our analysis has enabled us to identify the groups that do not fit in with the broader patterns and to explore the implications of diversity and of inequality. Our analysis has revealed (a) the complexity of outcomes right across the group in terms of the extent to which education paid off as an investment in labour-market security and success, and (b) the very different experiences and outcomes created by inequalities based on social class and gender. Our findings demonstrate that risk does indeed 'stem from multiple sources' and that all groups do 'face risks' (Esping-Andersen 1999, 175). In each of the chapters we arrive at the conclusion that young men from low socio-economic backgrounds – and especially those who have not participated in post-secondary studies – have fared the worst of any group. It is not clear which group has fared the best, but social class is significantly implicated in the outcomes of our young women and men.

Policies Matter

Our research offers a powerful evidence base for reflection on the role and impact of policies. It has several features that distinguish it from conventional policy-oriented research. Extending for fifteen years, our analysis provides a rare view of the ways in which policy initiatives reverberate in individual lives through the years, offering in-depth reflection on the medium- and long-term outcomes of policies. The project has a relatively wide frame of reference, aiming to understand young adults' lives holistically, and it is complex enough to take in several policy domains at the same time. For example, we are able to reflect on the policy areas of higher education; labour and the workplace; health; and family. Comparing the lives of young people in two countries that share a great amount economically, politically, and socially enables us to focus on points of divergence in their outcomes and to explore the ways in which different policy approaches may have contributed to this. We have recorded and analysed their views, the reasons for their decisions, and their subjectivities as well as their behaviour. This means that, unlike large population studies, our analysis does not need to rely on conjecture to understand the reasons for decisions about patterns of employment, fertility, marriage, or other trends.

Our research shows unequivocally that policies do have a significant impact on individual lives. However, these effects are not necessarily intended. Policy effects accumulate over time to have an impact on the very nature of a generation and on the social fabric. Indeed, as we have seen from our analysis of higher education policy in the 1990s in both Canada and Australia, it was the explicit goal of governments to create wholesale change in the educational levels of the young population in order to ensure global competitiveness and national prosperity through economic change (see chapter 3). Although policy domains are discrete, real lives do not correspond to these abstractions. Education and labour policies have an impact on other areas of life in ways that are unintended but inevitable. We would add our voice to the extensive literature already advocating for greater collaboration in policy and program development between government jurisdictions, in order to ensure that unintended outcomes are minimized and to bring a broader, more realistic perspective to policy development (Tett, Crowther, and O'Hara 2003).

We are in agreement with Esping-Andersen's argument (2009) that it is time for a new, more holistic approach to policies that acknowledges the importance of personal relationships, family life, and the possibility of having children. We would go further than Esping-Andersen, however, and argue that alongside family policies are needed policies that address health and well-being. Our findings are, in some respects, quite disturbing because they reveal the rapidity with which inequalities based on socio-economic status have become entrenched, and they reveal the failure of contemporary policy frameworks to adequately address the direct results of previous policies. Although there is an increasing awareness of the need to generate new policy frameworks, and especially of the need for more holistic approaches, education and labour-market policies continue to dominate the policy domain in both Australia and Canada.

To illustrate this, we highlight two examples of the unintended consequences of education and labour policies on the lives of our participants: low fertility and poor mental health. Our analysis is sharpened by the comparison of the different policy approaches in Canada and Australia that were aiming to address the same basic issue: ensuring global competitiveness and economic prosperity by increasing human capital through education.

Fertility rates across all OECD countries have been falling since the 1970s, and studies show a very similar pattern for Canada and Australia (Lattimore and Pobke 2008) with the rate of childbirth dropping quite steeply in the 1970s, reaching its lowest point in 2000–2001, and then increasing slightly. Researchers of these broad trends acknowledge that it is difficult to find clear 'causes' for fertility patterns, based on statistical research (for example, econometric analysis of patterns), but a clear association exists between women's wages and fertility. Population studies consistently link increases in women's income with decreases in fertility (Drago, et al. 2009; Lattimore and Pobke 2008). The complexities are exposed by considering the greater difficulty that the Australian participants experienced, compared with the Canadian participants, in establishing conditions under which they could make the decision to become parents (as we discussed in chapter 7). Both countries had higher education policies that meant many young people deferred full-time entry into the labour market, and both countries were undergoing changes to the nature of work and workplace conditions (O'Connor, Orloff, and Shaver 1999). These changes extended the period of their lives in which young people were working part-time and led to increases in personal debt. At the same time, labour-market policies that were designed to give employers greater flexibility in their employment practices inevitably created greater uncertainty for employees and greater precariousness of employment and ensured that individuals worked longer hours. In both countries there were concerns about the erosion of work-life balance (Duxbury and Higgins 2003). Yet the effects of these changes were felt especially strongly in Australia, reflected in lower rates of marriage and childbearing compared with the Canadians (see chapter 7). We link this outcome directly to the Australian government labour policies, enshrined in the Workplace Relations Act of 1996. This act meant that the young Australians in our study encountered particularly family-unfriendly working conditions. In their own words, increases in working hours and insecure employment made it difficult to form stable long-term relationships and to consider starting a family. Indeed, the rate of childbearing dropped so low in 2001 that the Australian government introduced a new policy measure to counter the (unintended) effects of previous policies, by offering a bonus payment of $3000 to each Australian woman who gave birth or adopted a child from 1 July 2004. This initiative was associated with a modest increase in fertility (Drago et al. 2009). Despite more family-friendly working conditions, the young Canadian women and men in this study also stressed the difficulty of juggling the overwhelming and competing demands of career, relationships, and family.

Many respondents commented that children were simply unaffordable. Esping-Andersen (1999, 181) points out that 'if young families are to be encouraged to have children it is obviously tantamount that these children not grow up in poverty. His work emphasizes that (over) reliance on family dependencies places families and children at risk. He asserts that 'minimalising family dependencies implies a radically recast welfare state' because 'contemporary welfare states can no longer count on the availability of housewives and full-time mothers' (Esping-Andersen 2009, 70).

Concerns about mental health also emerged in Canada and Australia over the period of our study (Tempier et al. 2009). Our analyses based on self-reported data show that the Australians were more likely than the Canadians were to report concerns about their mental (and their physical) health. Their subjective assessments line up remarkably well with data generated through large-scale epidemiological studies. A comparative analysis of mental health data for Canada in 2002 and Australia in 1997 found that Australia had a higher proportion of the population living with 'low distress' mental disorders than had Canada (29 per cent compared with 18 per cent) and higher rates of anxiety disorders (32 per cent in Australia compared with 21 per cent in Canada) (Tempier et al. 2009, 67). Given that mental health problems are most likely to occur during young adulthood (Australian Institute of Health and Welfare 2007; Statistics Canada 2002), the levels of self-reported mental health concerns in our study align well with more objective measures.

Taking their views seriously, we see a link between mental health and the two areas of life that they consistently returned to in interviews: (a) decision making associated with the changing education – labour market nexus of the 1990s and (b) the struggle to achieve a reasonable balance between work, study, and life. Both of these areas were associated with pressure and stress that many struggled to manage effectively (see chapters 5, 6, and 8).

Mental health problems are an example of the risks (and costs) that individuals have borne as a direct outcome of education and labour policies. As we have already discussed in depth, the shifts towards universal post-secondary education and flexible labour conditions have placed pressures on individuals to manage personal outcomes within very complex and uncertain processes. Willing participation in the government's agenda to increase levels of human capital through post-secondary education, by a proportion of both Canadians and Australians in order to be employed in demanding jobs, has been at the expense of equally important areas of their lives – relationships and well-being. The more adverse mental health picture for the Australians directly reflects the more adverse social conditions imposed on young people through government policies.

The comparison with Canada enables us to see that the costs borne by the Australians (high rates of mental illness, poor physical health, and low rates of marriage and childbirth compared with the Canadian cohort) were not *necessary*. Canada's economic prosperity was not jeopardized by having (relatively) more socially just workplace conditions and more effective articulation from secondary to post-secondary educational pathways. Esping-Andersen (1999, 126) points out that de-industrialization in Australia and a few other countries 'occurred on the backdrop of an unusually large stock of unskilled workers.' However, whereas some countries (for example, Sweden) embraced retraining policies for such vulnerable workers, this was not the case in Australia. Hence, those who were at higher risk of being unemployed remained so.

These two examples highlight the processes that create adverse outcomes for individuals. It is important to remember that individuals are 'vulnerable' or 'at risk' (to use contemporary policy buzzwords) because they are positioned in this way by policies. Government policies, combined with conditions that are not under the control of governments (for example, global financial and economic processes), make some groups of people vulnerable. As Bennett (2006, 239) argues, 'social exclusion and inequality are not an exception to the rules that operate differently "within the mainstream"' but should be seen as an example of 'the ways in which cultural and economic capital – education and occupational class – also work to produce cultural inequalities within the mainstream.' Each of the chapters of this book reveals different dimensions of the struggles that some groups – especially those whose parents do not have post-secondary-educational qualifications – have endured to achieve their goals in life. We suggest that young people who are without strong family support to sustain the long years of gaining educational qualifications are the most in need of systematic, long-term, sustained support through government programs. In our studies, in both countries, those who found it most difficult to achieve their goals were young men from lower socioeconomic families. They found it difficult to learn 'the moves' of a dance routine to which they did not relate. Educational programs that focus on skills and academic outcomes do not provide them with the capacity to live within a subjective domain in which reflexivity (stepping back into life from a different direction) is routine. It also needs to be recognized that policies promoting personal debt (for example, Australia's Higher Education Contribution Scheme and the Canada Student Loans Program – see chapter 5) place young people in this group in double jeopardy. The risks of debt for them are greater than for any other group because they have fewer resources in the first place (both material and cultural) to enable them to respond to changing circumstances. Investment is always a risk, but when the line between education and employment is far from 'straight,' investment in education is indeed risky, especially for those who are already disadvantaged. 'Entrapment in inferior life chances' (Esping-Andersen 1999, 42) was not merely a possibility for some of our study respondents; it was a reality. We agree with Esping-Andersen that the new marginal strata do 'herald the arrival of a bundle of new social risks, and signal the possibility that many find themselves sidelined and even trapped in some kind of underprivilege' (2009, 150).

Unless new approaches to welfare systems are developed, the disjunctures and inequalities that are identified in our study will increase for future generations, as identified by Esping-Andersen (2009). Our longitudinal research has turned out to be a powerful tool for demonstrating exactly the extent to which the different policy spheres of education, work, health, and family are connected. It is time for policymakers to connect the dots. More important, it is time to develop new welfare approaches that enable all groups to participate in family life and economic activity and to be well. This means developing much stronger family-friendly, health-promoting policies in workplaces, thereby ensuring that domestic labour is shared by men and women. It also means considering the ways in which governments can invest

more effectively in children and young people. Providing stronger support for them and those who care for them makes sense.

The Relevance of Theory

The central conceptual idea in this book is the interrelatedness of
social change and biography. As we discussed in chapter 2, we have
drawn on conceptual frameworks that enabled us to understand how
Canadian and Australian society changed during the 1990s and to
explore the implications of these changes for young people, whose
lives were also in transition. In a number of chapters we have drawn
on Bourdieu's work to highlight the ways in which individuals draw
on cultural and material resources, reproducing but also changing patterns of inequality. We have also drawn on theorists of social change
(for example, Ulrich Beck, Zygmunt Bauman, and Hartmut Rosa) to
understand how the processes of individualization and the emergence of reflexive biographies have framed the lives of our research
participants. We reiterate the point that we have tried not to impose
theoretical schemas on our evidence that would give a false impres-
sion of order and predictability. Hence, in this final chapter we take
the opportunity to reflect on our use of concepts and theories and
to expose some of the questions that remain and the gaps that have
emerged. We offer some reflections on the dynamics of social change
and biographical construction in order to generate questions for further research within the fields of educational policy, higher education,
and youth studies.

   At a conceptual level this book contributes to two main theoretical domains. It has traced the history of *inequality* in Canada and
Australia through the 1990s and early 2000s, and it has documented
the making of a *social generation*. These two dimensions stand in a
productive tension with each other throughout the book. On the one
hand, understanding inequality invites a perspective on difference and
social processes that distinguish groups from each other, identifying
processes that disadvantage some and advantage others. On the other
hand, the idea of social generation involves a focus on processes that
all groups share and on dynamics that they experience in common.
Yet they are not mutually exclusive theoretical domains. In the following discussion we show how both of these conceptual ideas can be
used productively to build an understanding of the lives of our young
adults.

Inequality

Each of the chapters of this book reveals the ways in which processes of gender and class have been manifested in the lives of our participants. We have used the very basic measure – levels of education (parental and their own) – which reveals how powerfully class underlines the patterns of their lives. Young men without educational credentials, almost universally from families with low or no post-secondary education, have found it the most difficult to achieve employment stability (and, in Australia, personal happiness) and have struggled through all the years of the study to keep a foothold in the labour market. The group that most effectively accessed educational opportunities were young women who came from families with educational credentials. These young women achieved educational success and were subsequently the most likely to achieve stable, well-paid jobs. However, their educational careers did not necessarily prepare them for employment careers. Although they initially tended to gain professional jobs with a level of permanency, their longer-term patterns were patchy as they bore the brunt of employment policies that were not family friendly. Their male peers, young men whose parents had post-secondary qualifications, have, in the long term, fared the best. Workplace dynamics and personal politics have enabled them to maximize their educational investments. The overwhelming majority of young men with parental responsibilities did not see their work status change when they became parents. The personal politics of child-rearing have remained highly gendered.

One of the central questions our research raises with regard to education, given the expansion of higher education in the early 1990s and the subsequent opening up of opportunities for new groups of young people through the gaining of educational qualifications, is what processes led to some groups accessing education more effectively than others. Our interest in these aspects of education aligns our research closely with Bourdieu's work. Bourdieu's concept of field as a structured social space is useful for us because our study tracks young people's movement through the different and overlapping structured social spaces of post-secondary education, work, family, and intimate relationships (Bourdieu 1991, 1998). The idea of habitus invokes the world views and dispositions that provide the frame through which they perceive choices. Young people's views, recorded through interviews and replies to open-ended questions on our surveys, have given us insights into their subjectivities. According to Bourdieu (1991), the position in the social space occupied by a given individual is defined by the position that she or he occupies in the different fields (for example, education, work, family) and the distribution of powers that are active in each field. The powers of cultural and social capital that are eventually converted into educational attainment and occupational status produce differences in knowledge and dispositions that lead to different ways of operating in the world, or different lifestyles, based on the capacity to classify and differentiate everyday practices and products (Ball et al., 2002). As Ball et al. (2002, 51) argue, young people's 'choices' about higher education are embedded in different kinds of biographies and institutional habitus and different 'opportunity structures.'

Our research supports the significance of habitus as a 'socialised subjectivity' through which identities are formed (Webb, Schirato, and Danaher 2002). Indeed, our data show the strong effect of parental education on the longer-term outcomes for young people's lives. Parental educational levels continue to correlate with the different patterns of young people's lives approximately fifteen years after they have left secondary school. The significance of educational qualifications is reinforced by the correlation between their own levels of education and their labour-market situation.

Bourdieu's theories have been used to highlight the importance of cultural and material resources to young people's trajectories and patterns of life. In our data, and that of many others (Adkins 2000; Andres 1994; Ball et al. 2002; Kenway and Bullen 2004), the ideas of habitus and field serve largely to show how inequality is reproduced. The broad aggregations of statistics on the labour-market outcomes of our two cohorts broadly reinforce the reproduction of class structures. However, the meaning of this changes when we look more closely at the fine grain of their lives. We would argue that there are subtleties in the ideas of habitus and field and the related concepts of cultural capital that the longitudinal and comparative nature of our project highlights, and these relate to temporal dimensions that are seldom exposed.

Previously we have highlighted the significance of the vanguard of young women who took advantage of the expansion of post-secondary and higher educational opportunities and, in doing so, changed the patterns of low educational participation experienced by the previous generation of women. They tended to come from families whose educational backgrounds included at least some post-secondary education, although this was not universally so, especially for the Australian cohort. Nevertheless, we have reason to assume that their educational success was supported by families who believed that educating girls (as well as boys) was important. The survey data support this, and their comments in interviews emphasize the importance of family support in gaining their educational credentials. Capital and habitus were in alignment for them to find themselves within the educational field; we can see how their reflexive subjectivities, their capacity to be proactive, and their ability to draw on appropriate cultural and material resources enabled them to achieve success, given the way that education operates as a structured space. However, as time progressed and they entered a different field (work), we suggest that the alignment between field and habitus was less apparent. Although these women were remarkably successful in the early years following graduation, their engagement in the workforce began to weaken compared to that of their male counterparts. In chapter 6 we noted that breaking the gender barriers was not without ongoing challenges.

Drawing on Bourdieu's concepts of habitus and field, we can see how ultimately the privilege that has come with class background has worked quite effectively for some groups of women within the field of education, but less so outside of this field. In workplaces, many found a lack of support, not directly in an interpersonal sense but within the structures of workplaces that presume a male lifestyle. The necessity to work long hours and the difficulty of achieving a work-life balance were remarked on by both men and women, but ultimately it was the women who adjusted their own lives. Also, we have commented on the pattern for males of high socio-economic status to continue living with their parents for longer than any other group. We have suggested that this may be an indicator of their success in accessing parental support, long after their female peers have left home. If this is the case, then our longitudinal research poses interesting questions about the processes of habitus and field and the ways in which particular groups are able to mobilize support and resources in order to maintain an alignment between their sense of self and the structured social relations within which they move (both at home and at work). We agree with Ball (2006) that within educational research (and, we would add, youth research), studies of class seem 'crude and ineffectual.' Our research suggests that short-term longitudinal research and snapshot studies are particularly prone to reinforcing overly deterministic understandings of class. We suggest that in the spaces between 'fields' as people move from one domain to another (for example, education, work, and parenthood) we see the complex operation of class, gender, and other processes of inequality.

A second important dimension in the study is the dramatic increase in educational levels for our participants compared with those of their parents, particularly in Australia. Given the strong pattern for young people in our studies (especially the more educated) to continue living in their parents' homes during their early and mid twenties, this means that the flows of resources between generations have been two-way. It is generally assumed within the educational literature that cultural capital is vested in parents and accessed and mobilized by their children. However, in periods of rapid social change, as in the 1990s in Australia and Canada, cultural resources can flow the other way. Young people are able to interpret the world for their parents and provide valuable cultural resources that contribute to the quality of life of both generations. We have noted the extent to which many of the young people liked living with their parents and enjoyed their parents' company. It would be interesting to see an analysis of intergenerational uses of resources made through the concepts of habitus (parents' and children's) and field (the family) and not assuming a one-way interchange.

Although our study supports the use of Bourdieu's concepts, it has also exposed some areas for further exploration in the new and old ways in which inequalities are structured, experienced, and reproduced. We suggest that, because the short-term studies that track young people's trajectories during school or over the first years after leaving secondary school (McLeod and Yates 2006), or that examine higher education choices (Ball et al. 2002), focus on fewer dimensions of individuals' lives, they may provide stronger evidence of social reproduction than do longer-term studies. Our analyses show that over the longer term the clear class differences become less vivid and gender becomes inscribed 'in new but old ways' (McLeod 2005).

Social Generation

The world changed in significant ways at the same time that these young people left secondary school. As we have argued in chapter 2 and throughout the book, it is important to recognize the historical specificity of this generation. We have found it useful to use the term *generation* in the sense of a 'social generation' as a conceptual framework for understanding their lives. The use of this framework foregrounds social change at the same time that we explore their personal trajectories through individual lives. In this way our project has witnessed the making of a generation.

Our use of the term *social generation* has a number of conceptual implications. First, it keeps open the future; it does not presume a timeline or
natural sequence (for example, a life course) that spreads ahead of them.
Instead, the use of the concept of social generation holds onto the idea
that circumstances have an impact on lives and that individuals also
shape their lives, so the course of biography is indeed co-constructed
(through habitus and field). The use of the term *social generation* also
enables us to encompass broad dimensions of life, in contrast to the
more limited idea of youth as a period of transition (for example, from
school to work or from dependence on parents to independence).
Indeed, it is fundamental to our understanding that a social generation
is forged across a wide span of life areas. Our research also highlights
the importance of understanding that transitions occur throughout life
and that adulthood is not a destination but a process. The dominance
of the term *transition* within educational and youth research (especially
with reference to fifteen- to twenty-four-year-olds) obscures the significance of individual responses to social change throughout life. Our
longitudinal research has followed this generation into their thirties,
revealing multiple points of transition – as they manage parenthood,
review their life goals, experience unemployment, or manage their
own or a loved one's illness. All of these transitions involve engagement with structured spaces (in Bourdieu's terms) that have an impact
on individuals' sense of self.

In utilizing the idea of a social generation, we draw on a long sociological tradition that seeks to understand the relationship between
biography and social *change*, not simply social *relations*. For both conceptual and policy-related reasons we argue that it is important to
understand how a generation is made. Mannheim argued that social
generations should be distinguished from biological generations. He
argued that culture is developed through the experiences and practices
'of individuals who come into contact anew with the accumulated heri-
tage' (Mannheim 1970, 383). Taking a social psychological approach,
Mannheim posited that meeting something anew created a form of
distance and a novel approach in 'assimilating and using' social realities. He argued that a social generation is forged through common
experience of significant change and is 'similarly located' within broad
social processes. He elaborates:

> The fact that people are born at the same time, or that their youth, adult-
> hood and old age coincide, does not in itself involve similarity of location;

what does involve a similarity of location is that they are in a position to experience the same events and data, etc. and especially that these events impinge on a similarly 'stratified' consciousness. Only where contemporaries are definitely in a position to participate as an integrated group in certain common experiences can we rightly speak of community of location of a generation. Mere contemporaneity becomes socially significant only when it involves participation in the same historical and social circumstances. (388–9)

It is notable that it was this generation – born just after 1970 – that initiated the flurry of so-called generational naming in the mass media. We would argue that they encountered historical and social circumstances that did indeed constitute them as a social generation in Mannheim's sense. We suggest that as a social generation this cohort has set trends and established dispositions that continue to shape the lives of subsequent age cohorts. In essence, the conditions that the participants in our studies encountered have not changed significantly enough to forge a new social generation. Instead, subsequent age cohorts work within the 'new' realities.

These 'new' realities have been described by a range of theorists as involving a societal shift away from traditions and institutional processes towards de-traditionalization, fragmentation, and unpredictability (Bauman 2001; Beck and Lau 2005). We argue that these conditions constitute historical and social circumstances that create a new social generation. Our work has especially resonated with the idea of individualization (that is, the way in which individuals experience a sense of personal responsibility for risks and options that are structurally produced). It has also resonated with the shift towards reflexive biographies (Beck and Beck-Gernsheim 2002) and the ideas of new temporalities involving the acceleration of time (Rosa 2005).

When the young people in our studies embraced the government's agenda of increasing educational participation, they also embraced new ways of thinking about young people and new ways of conceptualizing and managing youth as a period of life. It should be emphasized that the notion of youth as a form of capital for economic development, an explicit concept within the policies of the late 1980s and early 1990s (OECD 1996), had a defining impact on their lives. It meant that government policies focused almost exclusively on the education-employment nexus, to the detriment of broader policies that also recognized health, well-being, and social cohesion. This positioning of young people had

an impact on the entire generation – even on those who did not participate fully in post-secondary education. Our research has documented
the distinctive nature of the dispositions and subjectivities they practised. It reveals the invisibility of structural processes (such as class
and gender) to them. The conditions that this generation encountered
'anew' did not affect all young people in the same way. As our discussion above reveals, some groups were able to mobilize more effectively
to reinforce the practice of reflexivity and entrepreneurial dispositions.
Young women from more privileged backgrounds were especially able
to draw on both class and gendered resources to take advantage of new
educational opportunities and to gain a foothold early in professional
jobs in the new and emerging economies. However, not all groups were
able to produce the kinds of dispositions that were rewarded within
these times. Although the entire generation experienced the same conditions of change, not all were positioned to thrive.

Our use of the concept of social generation underlines the importance of understanding social conditions, broad social patterns across
populations, and subjectivities and dispositions. These three sources of
data enable an analysis of the ways in which social change and individual trajectories intersect. In our analysis it has enabled us to recognize
the personal effort taken by individuals to 'become' functioning, successful, and well members of this new generation. It has enabled us to
understand young people's lives relatively holistically, so that personal
relationships, lifestyle, and well-being have been emphasized alongside the more traditional duo of education and employment. Most
significantly, our analysis using these conceptual tools has enabled us
to highlight the ways in which young adults in this generation have
brought their own meaning to all areas of life.

Conclusion

The persistence of inequality and the reality of generation pose particular challenges for Canadian and Australian policies. Our research has
illustrated how a generation is made through structured processes of
inequality. Indeed, we have shown that some groups become outsiders within their own generation because they cannot access or mobilize
the resources necessary to achieve success. Educational participation
has become a powerful proxy for class, and those without educational
qualifications have little in the way of protection from the risks of societies in which individuals *must* be proactive, reflexive, and motivated.

Given the crucial importance of education, it is not sufficient any longer for educational policies to frame education as simply a private choice. However, taking into account the nature of this social generation, policies can no longer simply require compliance to outmoded conceptions of age-related transitions. For example, while it would be simple to force all young people to remain in secondary school until they had acquired the educational qualifications to enable them to progress to post-compulsory education, the realities of new generational attitudes and dispositions are that compulsion risks simply alienating those it is intended to benefit. Instead, flexible options and post-secondary structures that allow individuals to more easily gain educational qualifications are more likely to benefit the full range and diversity of young people. Higher education options too would be more rewarding for young people if higher education institutions reflected the flexibility that young people themselves have had to develop, offering more effective articulation across sectors and disciplines.

Policies aimed at addressing inequalities through educational participation via the use of user-pay approaches (for example, higher education contribution schemes) may in fact play into the (re)production of inequalities by failing to recognize the full extent of the material and cultural resources that young people from privileged class locations can access. In this sense, the meaning and risks of debt are not evenly spread across the population.

The realities of social generational change also need to be taken into account in the structuring of policy domains. It appears to be outmoded for policy fields to remain so tightly and artificially constrained within narrow confines (for example, education, labour, health) when young people's own understandings of the key elements in their lives show how these areas intersect and overlap in reality. We have drawn attention to the policy domain of health and well-being in order for it to be brought into a closer partnership with the dominant policy areas of education and labour markets. Despite the processes of individualization that characterize these times, with their attendant trends towards fragmentation and the weakening of institutional processes, policies still have an impact on lives, and good policies can contribute to the making of generations that are able to live well.

Appendix A

Table A.1
Mail-out survey data collection points in Canada and Australia

Canada

Original sample size	Year	Years out of high school	Age	No. surveyed	% of original sample
10,000	1989	1	19	5345	53
	1993	5	23	2220	22
	1998	10	28	1055	11
	2003	15	33	733	7

Australia

Original sample size	Year	Years out of high school	Age	No. surveyed	% of original sample
29,155	1991	0	17	10985	
	1992	1	18	4079	37
	1995	3	21	1925	18
	1996	4	22	1314	12
	1997	5	23	1410	13
	1998	6	24	1293	12
	1999	7	25	1109	10
	2000	8	26	774	7
	2002	10	28	625	6
	2004	12	30	334	3
	2006	14	32		

Table A.2
Interview data collection points in Canada and Australia

| | Canada | | | Australia | |
Year	Age	N	Year	Age	N
1989 Grade 12 (October)	18	51	1997	23	59
1990 Grade 12 (May)	19	46	1998	24	100
1990 (October)	19	44	1999	25	48
1993	22	39	2000	26	51
1998	27	32	2002	28	22
2003	32	30	2004	30	15
			2006	32	10

Table A.3
Questionnaire response rates in relation to key 1989 variables, by sex, in Canada, 1989–2003

	Females (%)				Males (%)				Total (%)			
	1989	1993	1998	2003	1989	1993	1998	2003	1989	1993	1998	2003
Total post-secondary participants, 1989	78	82	83	85	73	76	78	79	76	77	78	81
Total post-secondary non-participants, 1989	22	18	17	15	27	24	22	21	26	22	22	20
Father's occupational status, 1989												
(low)	27	28	27	27	28	26	27	28	27	27	27	28
(high)	32	32	35	34	32	35	35	34	32	33	35	34
Mother's educational level, 1989												
(low)	50	48	45	43	51	50	44	45	50	48	44	44
(high)	39	41	43	44	39	41	44	44	39	41	44	44
Geographic location, 1989												
(metro)	34	32	32	32	34	36	33	36	34	34	32	33
(urban/rural)	39	39	42	43	39	37	40	36	39	38	41	40
(remote)	28	29	26	26	27	27	27	28	27	28	26	27
Responses by gender	57	59	59	60	43	41	41	40				

Table A.4
Questionnaire response rates in relation to key 1989 variables, by sex, in Australia, 1992–2006

	Females (%)						Males (%)						Total (%)					
	1992	1996	1999	2002	2004	2006	1992	1995	1999	2002	2004	2006	1992	1995	1999	2002	2004	2006
Total post-sec. participants, 1992	71	77	84	85	85	85	64	72	78	81	83	87	68	75	82	83	84	86
Total post-sec. non-participants, 1992	29	23	16	16	15	15	36	28	22	19	17	13	32	25	18	17	16	15
Father's occupational status, 1996																		
(low)	–	21	20	23	23	22	–	19	20	21	19	17	–	21	20	22	22	21
(high)	–	57	58	58	58	59	–	54	54	55	54	54	–	56	57	57	57	57
Mother's educational level, 1996																		
(low)	–	67	64	62	66	62	–	67	65	66	68	73	–	67	64	63	67	65
(high)	–	15	17	17	15	17	–	14	14	14	14	11	–	15	16	16	15	15
Geographic location, 1996																		
(metro)	–	66	65	66	66	66	–	66	66	66	67	69	–	66	65	66	66	67
(urban/rural)	–	18	18	17	17	16	–	19	18	18	16	14	–	18	18	18	17	15
(remote)	–	16	17	17	17	18	–	16	17	16	17	18	–	16	17	17	17	18
Responses by gender	56	65	65	67	68	69	44	35	35	33	31	31						

References

Aapola, S., M. Gonick, and A. Harris. 2005. *Young femininity: Girlhood, power, and social change*. New York: Palgrave/Macmillan.

Adkins, L. 2000. Objects of innovation: Post-occupational reflexivity and re-traditionalisations of gender. In *Transformations: Thinking through feminism*, ed. S. Ahmed, J. Kilby, C.M. Lury, M. McNeil, and B. Skeggs, 258–272. London: Routledge.

Ainley, J., and P. McKenzie. 1999. The influence of school factors. In *Australia's young adults: The deepening divide*, ed. D. S. Forum. Sydney: Dusseldorp Skills Forum.

Akyeampong, E.B. 2002. Unionization and fringe benefits. *Perspectives on Labour and Income* 3(8), 5–9.

Akyeampong, E.B., and D. Sussman. 2003. Health-related insurance for the self-employed. *Perspectives on Labour and Income* 4(5), 1–7.

Alberta. 1984. Committee to Examine Participation Trends of Alberta Post-secondary Students. *Participation patterns study: Report of the committee to examine participation trends of Alberta post-secondary students*. Edmonton: Alberta Advanced Education, Planning Secretariat.

Allen, S. 1968. Some theoretical problems in the study of youth. *The Sociological Review* 16 (3), 319–331.

Andres, L. 1992. *Paths on life's way: Destinations, determinants, and decisions in the transition from high school*. Vancouver: University of British Columbia.

– 1993. Life trajectories, action, and negotiating the transition from high school. In *Transitions: Schooling and employment in Canada*, ed. P. Anisef and P. Axelrod, 137–157). Toronto: Thompson Press.

– 1994. Capital, habitus, field, and practice: An introduction to the work of Pierre Bourdieu. In *Sociology of education in Canada*, ed. L. Erwin and D. MacLennan, 120–135. Toronto: Copp Clark Pitman Ltd.

– 1999. Multiple life sphere participation by young adults. In *From educa-tion to work: Cross-national perspectives*, ed. W. Heinz, 149–170. Cambridge: Cambridge University Press.

– 2002a. *Paths on life's way: Base line study (1988) and first follow-up (1989)*. Vancouver: Department of Educational Studies, University of British Columbia.

– 2002b. *Paths on life's way: Phase II follow-up survey,1993, five years later (revi-sed)*. Vancouver: Department of Educational Studies, University of British Columbia.

– 2002c. *Paths on life's way: Phase III follow-up survey of 1998, ten years later*. Vancouver: Department of Educational Studies, University of British Columbia.

– 2005. *Social capital, perceptions and experiences of work and learning: A fifteen year perspective*. Paper presented at the 4th International Conference on Researching Work and Learning, Sydney, Australia, 10–15 December.

Andres, L., and M. Adamuti-Trache. 2006. *Gender segregation and university degree completion: Evidence from Canada, United States and Australia*. Paper pre-sented at the American Educational Research Association, San Francisco, 6 April.

– 2007. You've come a long way, baby? University enrolment and comple-tion by women and men in Canada, 1979–2004. *Canadian Public Policy* 33(1), 93–116.

– 2008. Life course transitions, social class, and gender: A fifteen year per-spective of the lived lives of Canadian young adults. *Journal of Youth Studies* 11(12), 115–145.

– 2009. University attainment, student loans, and adult life course activities: A fifteen year portrait of British Columbia young adults. In *Who goes? Who stays? What matters? New empirical evidence on participation in post-secondary education in Canada*, ed. R. Finnie, R. Mueller, A. Sweetman and A. Usher. Montreal: McGill-Queen's University Press.

Andres, L., and A. Licker. 2005. Beyond brain drain: The dynamics of geogra-phic mobility and educational attainment of B.C. young women and men. *Canadian Journal of Higher Education* 35(1), 1–36.

Andres, L., and E.D. Looker. 2001. Rurality and capital: Educational expec-tations and attainment of rural, urban/rural, and metropolitan youth. *Canadian Journal of Higher Education* 31(2), 1–46.

Andres, L., and J. Wyn. 2008. *Theory, policy, structure, and agency and the con-struction of Canadian and Australian young adults*. Paper presented at the International Sociology Association (ISA) Forum of Sociology, Sociological Research and Public Debate, Barcelona, Spain, 5–8 September.

Anisef, P. 1980. *Is the die cast? Educational achievements and work destinations of Ontario youth.* Toronto: Ministry of Colleges and Universities.

– 1985. *Accessibility to post-secondary education in Canada: A review of the literature.* Ottawa: Department of the Secretary of State of Canada.

– 2000. *Opportunity and uncertainty: Life course experiences of the Class of '73.* Toronto: University of Toronto Press.

Anisef, P., and L. Andres. 1996. Dropping out in Canada: The construction of a crisis? In *Debating dropouts,* ed. D. Kelly and J. Gaskell, 84–100. New York: Teachers College Press.

Arnett, J.J. 2005. Emerging adulthood: Understanding the new way of coming of age. In *Emerging adults in America: Coming of age in the 21st century,* ed. J.J. Arnett, 8–19. Washington, DC: American Psychological Association.

Ashton, D., and G. Lowe. 1991. School-to-work transitions in Britain and Canada: A comparative perspective. In *Making their way: Education, training and the labour market in Canada and Britain,* ed. D. Ashton and G. Lowe, 1–14. Buckingham, UK: Open University Press.

Australian Bureau of Statistics. 2005. *Australian Social Trends, 2005.* Catalogue no. 4102.0. Canberra: Commonwealth of Australia.

– 2009. *A picture of a nation, 2006.* Catalogue no. 2070.0. Canberra: Australian Bureau of Statistics.

Australian Education Council (AEC). 1991. *Review committee: Young people's participation in post-compulsory education and training.* Canberra: Australian Government Publishing Service.

Australian Institute of Health and Welfare. 2007. *Young Australians, their health and well-being 2007.* Catalogue no. PHE 87. Canberra: Australian Institute of Health and Welfare.

Bagnall, N., ed. 2005. *Youth transition in a globalised marketplace.* New York: Nova Publishers.

Ball, S.J. 2003. *Class strategies in the educational market: The middle classes and social advantage.* London: Routledge/Falmer.

– 2006. The necessity and violence of social theory. *Discourse: Studies in the Cultural Politics of Education* 27(1), 3–10.

Ball, S.J., J. Davies, M. David, and D. Reay. 2002. 'Classification' and 'Judgement': Social class and the 'cognitive structures' of choice of higher education. *British Journal of Sociology of Education* 23(1), 51–72.

Ball, S.J., M. Maguire, and S. Macrae. 2000. *Choice, pathways and transitions post-16: New youth, new economies in the global city.* London: Routledge/Falmer.

Bauman, Z. 2000. *Liquid modernity.* Cambridge: Polity Press.

– 2001. *The individualized society.* Cambridge: Polity Press.

Beaudry, P., T. Lemieux, and D. Parent. 2000. What is happening in the youth labour market in Canada? *Canadian Public Policy* XXVI, 26 (Supplement 1), S59–83.

Beck, U., and E. Beck-Gernsheim. 2002. *Individualization*. London: Sage.

Beck, U., and C. Lau. 2005. Second modernity as a research agenda: Theoretical and empirical explorations in the 'meta-change' of modern society. *British Journal of Sociology of Education* 56(4), 525–557.

Bennett, T. 2006. Postscript: Cultural capital and inequality; refining the policy calculus. *Cultural Trends* 15(2), 239–244.

Betcherman, G., and N. Leckie. 1997. *Youth employment and education trends in the 1980s and 1990s*. Working Paper No W/03. Ottawa: CPRN.

Beutell, N.J., and U. Wittig-Berman. 2008. Work-family conflict and work-family synergy for generation X, baby boomers, and matures. *Journal of Managerial Psychology* 23(5), 507–523.

Bills, D.B. 1988. Educational credentials and promotions: Does schooling do more than get you in the door? *Sociology of Education* 61(1), 52–60.

Blackwell, L., and J. Bynner. 2002. *Learning, family formation, and dissolution*. London: Centre for Research on Wider Benefits of Learning, Institute of Education.

Bourdieu, P. 1976. Marriage strategies as strategies of social reproduction. Trans. E. Forster. In *Family and society*, ed. R. Foster and O. Ranum, 117–144. Baltimore: John Hopkins University Press.

– 1979. *The inheritors*. Trans. R. Nice. Chicago: University of Chicago Press (Original work published in 1966).

– 1986. The forms of capital. Trans. R. Nice. In *Handbook of theory and research for the sociology of education*, ed. J.E. Richardson, 241–258. New York: Greenwood Press.

– 1987. What makes a social class? *Berkeley Journal of Sociology* 32(1), 1–17.

– 1988. *Homo academicus*. Cambridge: Polity Press.

– 1991. *Language and symbolic power*. Trans. G. Raymond and M. Adamson. Cambridge: Harvard University Press.

– 1998. *On television*. New York: The New Press.

– 2000. *Pascalian meditations*. Trans. R. Nice. Cambridge: Polity Press.

Bourdieu, P., J.C. Chamboredon, and J.-C. Passeron. 1991. *The craft of sociology: Epistemological preliminaries*. Berlin: de Guyer.

Bourdieu, P., and J.-C. Passeron. 1977. *Reproduction in education, society, and culture*. Trans. R. Nice. London: Sage Publications.

– 1979. *The inheritors: French students and their relation to culture*. Chicago: University of Chicago Press.

Bourne, L.S., and R. Damaris. 2001. The changing face of Canada: Uneven geographies of population and social change. *Canadian Geographer* 45(1), 105–119.

Bowen, H.R. 1977. *Investment in learning.* San Francisco: Jossey-Bass.

Boyd, M., and D. Norris. 1999. The crowded nest: Young adults at home. *Canadian Social Trends,* Spring, 2–5.

Boyd, M., and E.T. Pryor. 1989. The cluttered nest: The living arrangements of young Canadian adults. *Canadian Journal of Sociology* 14(4), 461–477.

Brasher, K., and J. Wiseman. 2007. *Community well-being in an unwell world: Trends, challenges and opportunities.* Policy Signpost 1. Melbourne: The McCaughey Centre.

Brint, S., and J. Karabel. 1989. *The diverted dream: Community colleges and the promise of educational opportunity in America, 1900–1985.* New York: Oxford University Press.

British Columbia. 1988a. Ministry of Advanced Education and Job Training. *B.C. post-secondary enrolment statistics, 1987/88.* Victoria, BC: Funding and Analysis Division.

– 1988b. Provincial Access Committee. *Access to advanced education and job training in British Columbia: Report of the Provincial Access Committee.* Victoria, BC: Ministry of Advanced Education and Job Training.

– 1988c. Royal Commission on Education. *A legacy for learners.* Victoria, BC: Queen's Printer.

Bynner, J. 2001. British youth transitions in comparative perspective. *Journal of Youth Studies* 4(1), 5–23.

– 2005. Rethinking the youth phase of the life course: The case for emerging adulthood? *Journal of Youth Studies* 8(4), 367–384.

Canada. 1983. *Report of the Royal Commission on the Economic Union and Development Prospects of Canada.* Ottawa: Information Canada.

– 1987. Standing Senate Committee on National Finance. *Federal policy on post-secondary education.* Ottawa: Minister of Supply and Services Canada.

– 1988. Department of the Secretary of State. *Access to excellence: Being Canadian . . . . Working together for post-secondary education.* Ottawa: Minister of Supply and Services.

– 1990. Department of the Secretary of State. *Federal and provincial support for post-secondary education in Canada, 1988–89.* Ottawa: Minister of Supply and Services.

Canadian Council on Learning. 2007. *Report on learning in Canada, 2007: Post-secondary education in Canada; strategies for success.* Ottawa: Canadian Council on Learning.

Canadian Institute for Health Information. 2006. *Improving the health of Canadians: An introduction to health in urban places.* Ottawa: CIHI.

Clarke, A., and L. Edwards. 1980. The Williams committee of inquiry into education and training in Australia: Recommendations for universities. *Higher Education* 9(3), 495–528.

Coffield, J., C. Borrill, and S. Marshall. 1986. *Growing up on the margins: Young adults in the north east.* London: Open University Press.

Cohen, P. 1997. *Rethinking the youth question: Education, labour, and cultural studies.* London: Macmillan.

Cohen, P., and P. Ainley. 2000. In the country of the blind? Youth studies and cultural studies in Britain. *Journal of Youth Studies* 3(1), 79–95.

Coleman, J.S., and T. Husén. 1985. *Becoming adult in a changing society.* Paris: OECD.

Commonwealth of Australia. 1988. *Higher education: A policy statement.* Canberra: Australian Government Publishing Service.

– 1991. Report of the Australian Education Council Review Committee. *Young people's participation in post-compulsory education and training.* Canberra: Australian Government Publishing Service.

– 1993. Department of Employment Education and Training. *National report on Australia's higher education sector.* Canberra: Department of Employment, Education and Training, Higher Education Division.

Commonwealth of Australia Department of Employment Education and Training, and National Board of Employment Education and Training. 1990. *A fair chance for all: National and institutional planning for higher education.* Canberra: Department of Employment, Education and Training and the National Board of Employment, Education, and Training.

Côté, J., and A. Allahar. 1994. *Generation on hold: Coming of age in the late twentieth century.* New York: New York University Press.

Coupland, D. 1991. *Generation X.* New York: St. Martin's Press.

Crompton, S. 1995. Employment prospects for high school graduates. *Perspectives on Labour and Income* 7(3), 8–13.

Currie, D., D. Kelly, and S. Pomerantz. 2009. *'Girl power': Girls inventing girlhood.* New York: Peter Lang.

Davies, B. 2004. Identity, abjection and otherness: Creating the self, creating differences. *International Journal in Equity and Innovation in Early Childhood Education* 2(1), 58–80.

Davies, S. 2005. A revolution of expectations? Three key trends in the SAEP data. In *Preparing for post-secondary education: New roles for governments and families,* ed. R. Sweet and P. Anisef, 149–165. Montreal: McGill-Queen's University Press.

Delors, J. 1996. *Learning: The treasure within.* Report to UNESCO of the International Commission on Education for the Twenty-first Century. Paris: UNESCO.

Dennison, J.D., and P. Gallagher. 1986. *Canada's community colleges: A critical analysis* Vancouver: University of British Columbia Press.

Donald, M., J. Dower, J. Lucke, and B. Raphael. 2000. *The Queensland young people's mental health survey.* Brisbane: University of Queensland.

Drago, R., K. Sawyer, K. Sheffler, D. Warren, and M. Wooden. 2009. *Did Australia's baby bonus increase the fertility rate?* Melbourne Institute Working Paper Series, 1/09. Melbourne.

du Bois-Reymond, M. 1998. 'I don't want to commit myself yet': Young people's life concepts. *Journal of Youth Studies* 1(1), 63–79.

Dusseldorp Skills Forum. 2006. *How young people are faring: 2006 key indicators.* Sydney: Dusseldorp Skills Forum.

Duxbury, L., and C. Higgins. 2003. *Work-life conflict in Canada in the new millennium: A status report.* Ottawa: Health Canada.

Dwyer, P., G. Poynter, and D. Tyler. 1997. *Participant pathways and outcomes in vocational education and training, 1992–1995.* Melbourne: Youth Research Centre.

Dwyer, P., G. Smith, D. Tyler, and J. Wyn. 2005. *Immigrants in time: Life-patterns 2004.* Melbourne: Youth Research Centre.

Dwyer, P., B. Wilson, and R. Woock. 1984. *Confronting school and work: Youth and class cultures in Australia.* Sydney: Allen and Unwin.

Dwyer, P., and J. Wyn. 2001. *Youth, education and risk: Facing the future.* London: RoutledgeFalmer.

Economic Council of Canada. 1990. *Good jobs, bad jobs: Employment in the service sector.* Ottawa: Supply and Services Canada.

Edmunds, J., and B. Turner. 2005. Global generations: Social change in the twentieth century. *British Journal of Sociology* 56(4), 559–577.

Elder, G. 1974. *Children of the great depression.* Chicago: University of Chicago Press.

Esping-Andersen, G. 1990. *The three worlds of welfare capitalism.* Princeton, NJ: Princeton University Press.

– 1999. *Social foundations of postindustrial economics.* Oxford: Oxford University Press.

– 2009. *Incomplete revolution: Adapting welfare states to women's new roles.* Cambridge: Polity Press.

Evans, J., B. Evans, and E. Rich. 2003. 'The only problem is, children will like their chips': Education and the discursive production of ill-health. *Pedagogy, Culture and Society* 11(2), 215–240.

Evans, K. 2002. Taking control of their lives? Agency in young adult transitions in England and the New Germany. *Journal of Youth Studies* 5(3), 245–269.

Finch, J. 1986. 'Age'. In *Key variables in social investigation*, ed. R. Burgess. London: Routledge, Kegan, Paul.

Finnie, R. 2004. The school-to-work transition of Canadian post-secondary graduates: A dynamic analysis. *Journal of Higher Education Policy and Management* 26(1), 35–58.

Foot, D.K. 1996. *Boom, bust, and echo: How to profit from the coming demographic shift*. Toronto: Macfarlane, Walter, and Ross.

Forsyth, A., and A. Stewart, eds. 2009. *Fair work: The new workplace laws and the Work Choices legacy*. Annandale, NSW: Federation Press.

Fortin, M. 1987. *Accessibility to and participation in the post-secondary education system in Canada*. Saskatoon: National Forum on Post-Secondary Education.

Foucault, M. 1988. Technologies of the self. In *Technologies of the self: A seminar with Michel Foucault, L.H. Martin, H. Gutman, and P. Hutton*, ed. M. Foucault, L.H. Martin, H. Gutman and P. Hutton. London: Tavistock Publications.

Frost, L. 2003. Doing bodies differently? Gender, youth, appearance, and damage. *Journal of Youth Studies* 61(1), 53–70.

Fullagar, S. 2003. Wasted lives: The social dynamics of shame and youth suicide. *Journal of Sociology* 39(3), 291–307.

Furlong, A., and F. Cartmel. 2007. *Young people and social change: Individualisation and risk in late modernity*. 2nd ed. Buckingham, UK: Open University Press.

Furlong, A., F. Cartmel, A. Biggart, H. Sweeting, and P. West. 2003. *Youth transitions: Patterns of vulnerability and processes of social inclusion*. Edinburgh: Scottish Executive Social Research.

Gard, M., and J. Wright. 2001. Managing uncertainty: Obesity discourse and physical education in a risk society. *Studies in Philosophy and Education*, 20, 535–549.

Gayo-Cal, M. 2006. Leisure and participation in Britain. *Cultural Trends* 15(2), 175–192.

Giddens, A. 1984. *The constitution of society*. Berkeley, CA: University of California Press.

– 1991. *Modernity and self identity: Self and society in the late modern age*. Oxford: Polity Press.

Gillies, V. 2000. Young people and family life: Analysing and comparing disciplinary discourses. *Journal of Youth Studies* 3(2), 211–228.

Goldscheider, F., and C. Goldscheider. 1994. Leaving and returning home in 20th-century America. *Population Bulletin* 48(4), 1–35.

Guppy, N. 1984. Access to higher education in Canada. *Canadian Journal of Higher Education* 14(3), 79–93.

Harris, A. 2004. *Future girl: Young women in the twenty-first century.* London: Routledge.

Haveman, R.H., and B.L. Wolfe. 1984. Schooling and economic well-being: The role of nonmarket effects. *Journal of Human Resources* 19(3), 377–407.

Hays, S. 1999. Generation X and the art of the reward. *Workforce*, November, 45–48.

Heath, S., and E. Cleaver. 2003. *Young, free, and single? Twenty-somethings and household change.* Basingstoke, UK: Palgrave/Macmillan.

Heiman, R. 2001. *Childhood.* London: Sage.

Heinz, W. 1996. Status passages as micro-macro linkages in life course research. In *Society and biography: Interrelationships between social structure, institutions, and the life course,* ed. A. Weymann, 51–65. Weinheim FRG: Deutscher Studien Verlag.

– ed. 1999. *From education to work: Cross-national perspectives.* Cambridge: Cambridge University Press.

Heisz, A. 2007. *Income inequality and redistribution in Canada, 1976 to 2004.* Ottawa: Statistics Canada, Business and Labour Market Analysis Division.

Henderson, S., J. Holland, S. McGrellis, S. Sharpe, and R. Thomson, with T. Grigoriou. 2007. *Inventing adulthoods: A biographical approach to youth transitions.* London: Sage.

Holdsworth, C. 2000. Leaving home in Britain and Spain. *European Sociological Review* 16(2), 201–222.

Howe, N., and W. Strauss. 2000. *Millennials rising: The next great generation.* New York: Vintage Books.

Inglehart, R. 1990. *The role of culture in social change.* Princeton, NJ: Princeton University Press.

James, R., J. Wyn, G. Baldwin, G. Hepworth, C. McInnis, and A. Stephanou. 1999. *Rural and isolated students and their higher education choices: A re-examination of student location, socioeconomic background and educational advantage and disadvantage.* Canberra: Australian Government Publishing Service.

Jones, G. 1995. *Leaving home.* Buckingham, UK: Open University Press.

Jones, G., and C. Wallace. 1992. *Youth, family, and citizenship.* Buckingham, UK: Open University Press.

Jurkiewicz, C. 2000. Generation X and the public employee. *Public Personnel Management* 29(1), 55–74.

Kelly, P. 2006. The entrepreneurial Self and 'youth at-risk': Exploring the horizons of identity in the twenty-first century. *Journal of Youth Studies* 9(1), 17–32.

Kenway, J., and E. Bullen. 2004. Subcultural capital and the female 'under-class'? A Feminist response to an underclass discourse. *Journal of Youth Studies* 7(2), 141–153.

Kilmartin, C. 2000. Young adult moves: Leaving home, returning home, relationships. *Family Matters*, 55, 36–40.

Krahn, H. 1996. *School-work transitions: Changing patterns and research needs.* Consultation paper prepared for Applied Research Branch, Human Resources Development Canada, Ottawa.

Krahn, H., and J. Hudson. 2006. *Pathways of Alberta youth through the post-secondary system into the labour market, 1996–2003.* Ottawa: Canadian Policy Research Networks, Inc.

Krahn, H., and G. Lowe. 1999. School-work transitions and post-modern values: What's changing in Canada? In *From education to work: Cross-national perspectives,* ed. W. Heinz, 260–283. Cambridge: Cambridge University Press.

Lattimore, R., and C. Pobke. 2008. *Recent trends in Australian fertility.* Canberra: Productivity Commission Staff Working Paper.

Learning well . . . living well. 1991. Ottawa: Minister of Supply and Services Canada.

Leccardi, C., and E. Ruspini, eds. 2006. *New youth? Young people, generations and family life.* Aldershot, UK: Ashgate.

Lehmann, W. 2005. 'I'm still scrubbing the floor': Experiencing high school based youth apprenticeships. *Work, Employment, and Society* 19(1), 107–129.

Lennards, J. 1980. Education. In *Sociology,* ed. J. Hagedorn, 30. Toronto: Holt, Rhinehart, and Winston of Canada.

Lerner, A.J., and F. Loewe. 1956. Wouldn't it be loverly.

Lesko, N. 2001. *Act your age! A cultural construction of adolescence.* London: Routledge/Falmer.

Levin, I., and J. Trost. 1999. Living apart together. *Community, work and family* 2(3), 279–294.

Lewchuk, W., A. de Wolff, A. King, and M. Polanyi. 2003. From job strain to employment strain: Health effects of precarious employment. *Just Labour,* 3, 25–35.

Looker, E.D. 1993. Interconnected transitions and their costs: Gender and urban/rural differences in the transition to work. In *Transitions: Schooling and employment in Canada,* ed. P. Anisef and P. Axelrod, 43–64. Toronto: Thompson Educational Publishing.

MacDonald, J.B. 1962. *Higher education in British Columbia and a plan for the future.* Vancouver: University of British Columbia.

Mahler, V., and D.K. Jesuit. 2006. Fiscal redistribution in the developed countries: New insights from the Luxemborg Income Study. *Socio-Economic Review,* 4, 483–511.

Malcolmson, J., and M. Lee. 2004. *Financing higher learning: Post-secondary education funding in BC*. Vancouver: Canadian Centre for Policy Alternatives.

Manderson, L., ed. 2005. *Rethinking well-being*. Perth: API Network and Academy of the Social Sciences in Australia.

Mannheim, K. 1970. The problem of generations. *Psychoanalytic Review* 57(3), 378–404.

Marquardt, R. 1996. *Youth and work in troubled times: A report on Canada in the 1990s*. Ottawa: Canada Policy Research Networks.

Marshall, K. 2003. Benefits on the job. *Perspectives on Labour and Income* 4(5), 5–12.

McLaughlin, M. 1999. Comparing learning and work for young adults in Australia and Canada. In *Australia's young adults: The deepening divide*, ed. Dusseldorp Skills Forum. Sydney: Dusseldorp Skills Forum.

McLeod, J. 2005. Feminists re-reading Bourdieu: Old debates and new questions about gender habitus and gender change. *Theory and Research in Education* 3(1), 11–30.

McLeod, J., and L. Yates. 2006. *Making modern lives: Subjectivity, schooling and social change*. Albany, NY: State University of New York Press.

Mensik, J. 2007. A view on generational differences from a Generation X leader. *JONA* 37(11), 483–484.

Mills, M., and H.-P. Blossfeld. 2003. Globalization, uncertainty, and changes in early life courses. *Zeitschrift für Erziehungwissenschaft* 6(2), 188–218.

Mission Australia. 2007. *National survey of young Australians, 2007*. Sydney: Mission Australia.

Mitchell, B.A. 2006. *Boomerang age*. New Brunswick, NJ: Aldine Transaction.

Mizen, P. 2004. *The changing state of youth*. New York: Palgrave.

Morehead, A., M. Steele, M. Alexander, K. Stephen, and L. Duffin. 1997. *Changes at work: The 1995 Australian workplace industrial relations survey; a summary of the major findings*. Canberra: Australian Department of Workplace Relations and Small Business.

Myles, J., G. Picot, and T. Wannell. 1988. The changing wage distribution of jobs, 1981–1986. *The Labour Force* (Statistics Canada Catalogue 71-001), October.

Nayak, A. 2003. Review Symposium 2: Generation, culture and society. *British Journal of Sociology of Education* 24(4), 530–532.

Nova Scotia. 1985. *Report of the Royal Commission on Post-secondary Education, Province of Nova Scotia*. Halifax, NS: The Commission.

Nussbaum, M.C. 2005. Well-being, contracts, and capabilities. In *Rethinking well-being*, ed. L. Manderson. Perth: API Network and Academy of the Social Sciences in Australia.

O'Connor, J.S., A. Orloff, and S. Shaver. 1999. *States, markets, families: Gender, liberalism and social policy in Australia, Canada, Great Britain, and the United States*. Cambridge: Cambridge University Press.

Ontario. 1984. Commission on the Future Development of the Universities of Ontario. *Ontario universities: Options and futures*. Toronto: Queen's Printer.

Organisation for Economic Co-operation and Development (OECD). 1976. *Review of national policies in Canada*. Paris: OECD.

– 1996. *Lifelong learning for all*. Paris: OECD.

– 2001. *Knowledge and skills for life: First results from PISA 2000*. Paris: OECD.

– 2006. *Education at a glance: OECD indicators*. Paris: OECD.

– 2007. *Education at a glance: OECD indicators*. Paris: OECD.

– 2009. *Education at a glance: OECD indicators*. Paris: OECD.

Ortner, S.B. 1998. Generation X: Anthropology in a media-saturated world. *Cultural Anthropology* 13(3), 414–440.

Pike, R. 1986. *Social goals and economic constraints: Issues in accessibility to Canadian higher education during the 1980s*. Newcastle, NSW, Australia: Department of Economics, University of Newcastle.

Pilcher, J. 1994. Mannheim's sociology of generations: An undervalued legacy. *British Journal of Sociology* 45(3), 481–495.

Pocock, B. 2003. *The work/life collision: What work is doing to Australians and what to do about it*. Sydney: Federation Press.

Pomerantz, S. 1999. *This is (not) a generation: Deconstructing X*. Unpublished master's thesis. University of New Brunswick, Fredericton.

Porter, M., and G. Jasmin. 1987. *A profile of post-secondary students in Canada*. Ottawa: Minister of Supply and Services Canada.

Psacharopoulos, G. 1986. Links between education and the labour market: A broader perspective. *European Journal of Education* 21(4), 409–415.

Radwanski, G. 1987. *Ontario study of the relevance of education, and the issue of dropouts*. Toronto: Ministry of Education.

Reay, D. 2004. 'It's all becoming a habitus': Beyond the habitual use of habitus in educational research. *British Journal of Sociology of Education* 25(4), 431–444.

Redpath, L. 1994. Education-job mismatch among Canadian university graduates: Implications for employers and educators. *Canadian Journal of Higher Education* 24(2), 89–114.

Rhoades, G., and S. Slaughter. 1998. Academic capitalism, managed professionals, and supply-side higher education. In *Chalk lines: The politics of work in the managed university*, ed. R. Martin, 33–68. Durham, NC: Duke University Press.

Robeyns, I. 2003. Sen's capability approach and gender inequality: Selecting relevant capabilities. *Feminist Economics* 9(2–3), 61–91.

Rosa, H. 1998. On defining the good life: Liberal freedom and capitalist necessity. *Constellations* 5(2), 201–214.

– 2003. Social acceleration: Ethical and political consequences of a desyn-
chronized high-speed society. *Constellations* 10(1), 3–33.

– 2005. The speed of global flows and the place of democratic politics. *New
Political Science* 27(4), 445–459.

Rose, N. 1989. *Governing the soul*. London and New York: Routledge.

– 1999. *Powers of freedom*. Cambridge: Cambridge University Press.

Rothman, S., and K. Hillman. 2008. *X and Y: Three decades of education, employment and social outcomes of Australian youth*. Paper presented at 'Touching
the future: Building skills for life and work' conference. Melbourne:
Australian Council for Educational Research.

Saunders, R. 2003. *Defining vulnerability in the labour market*. Ottawa: Canadian
Policy Research Networks.

Schwartz, T.T. 2008. Family capital and the invisible transfer of privilege:
Intergenerational support and social class in early adulthood. In *Social class
and transitions to adulthood: New directions for child and adolescent development,
no. 119*, ed. J.T. Mortimer, 11–24.

Science Council of Canada. 1988. *Winning in a world economy. University-
industry interaction and economic renewal in Canada*. Ottawa: Minister of
Supply and Services.

Sen, A. 1993. Capability and well-being. In *The quality of life*, ed. M. Nussbaum
and A. Sen, 30–53. Oxford: Clarendon Press.

– 2008. Violence, identity, and poverty. *Journal of Peace Research* 45(1), 5–15.

Shannon, M., and M.P. Kidd. 2001. Projecting the trend in the Canadian gender wage gap, 2001–2031: Will an increase in female education acquisition
and commitment be enough? *Canadian Public Policy* 27(4), 447–467.

Sheahan, P. 2005. *Generation Y: Thriving and surviving with Generation Y at work*.
Melbourne: Hardie Grant.

Shields, M. 2006. Overweight and obesity among children and youth. *Health
Report (Statistics Canada)* 17(3), 27–42.

Skeggs, B. 2005. The re-branding of class: Propertising culture. In *Rethinking
class: Culture, identities and lifestyle*, ed. F. Devine, M. Savage, J. Scott, and
R. Crompton. New York: Palgrave/Macmillan.

Sointu, E. 2005. The rise of an ideal: Tracing changing discourses of well-
being. *The Sociological Review* 53(2), 255–274.

Statistics Canada. 1989a. *Canada's youth: A profile of their 1986 labour market
experience*. Catalogue 71-207. Ottawa: Minister of Supply and Services
Canada, March.

- 1989b. *Income distributions by size in Canada 1988*. Catalogue 13-207. Ottawa: Minister of Supply and Services Canada, November.
- 2001. *Profile of Canadian families and households: Diversification continues*. Catalogue No. 96F0030XIE2001003. Ottawa: Statistics Canada.
- 2002. *Canadian community health survey: Mental health and well-being. The Daily*. http://www.statcan.gc.ca/daily-quotidien/030903/dq030903a-eng.htm (accessed on 25 May 2008).
- 2003. Update on families. *Canadian Social Trends*, Summer (69), 11–13.
- 2005. University tuition fees. *The Daily*, 1 September 2005. http://www.statcan.ca/Daily/English/050901/d050901a.htm (accessed 21 September 2007).
- 2006a. *Families, Households and Housing*.
- 2006b. University tuition fees. *The Daily*, 1 September 2006. http://www.statcan.ca/Daily/English/060901/d060901a.htm (accessed 21 September 2007).
- 2006c. *Women in Canada: Work chapter updates*.
- 2007. *Average undergraduate tuition fees for full-time students, by discipline, by province*. http://www40.statcan.ca/l01/cst01/educ50a.htm?sdi=tuition per cent20fees per cent20provinces (accessed 21 September 2007).
Stephens, T., C. Dulberg, and N. Joubert. 2000. Mental health of the Canadian population: A comprehensive analysis. *Chronic Diseases in Canada* 20(3), 118–126.
Stephenson, B. 1982. Closing address. In *Council of Ministers of Education, Canada: Post-secondary issues in the 1980s*, proceedings of the CMEC Conference on Post-secondary Education, Toronto, Ontario.
Stobert, S., and A. Kemeny. 2003. Childfree by choice. *Canadian Social Trends*, Summer (69), 7–10.
Stokes, H., A. Wierenga, and J. Wyn. 2004. *Preparing for the future and living now*. Melbourne: Youth Research Centre.
Sweet, R., and P. Anisef. 2005. *Preparing for post-secondary education: New roles for governments and families*. Montreal: McGill-Queen's University Press.
Teese, R. 2000. *Academic success and social power: Examinations and inequality*. Melbourne: Melbourne University Press.
Teese, R., and J. Polesel. 2003. *Undemocratic schooling: Equity and quality in mass secondary education in Australia*. Melbourne: Melbourne University Press.
Tempier, R., G.N. Meadows, H.-E. Vasiliadis, K.E. Mosier, A. Lesage, A. Stiller, et al. 2009. Mental disorders and mental health care in Canada and Australia: Comparative epidemiological findings. *Social Psychiatry and Psychiatric Epidemiology* 44(1), 63–72.

Te Riele, K., and J. Wyn. 2005. Transformations in Youth Transitions in Australia. In *Youth transitions in a globalised marketplace*, ed. N. Bagnall. New York: Nova Science Publishers.

Tett, L., J. Crowther, and P. O'Hara. 2003. Collaborative partnerships in community education. *Journal of Education Policy* 18(1), 37–51.

Todd, S. 2004. *Improving work-life balance: What are other countries doing?* Human Resources and Skills Development Canada.

Trow, M. 1972. The expansion and transformation of higher education. *International Review of Education* 18(1), 61–84.

Twenge, J.M. 2006. *Generation me*. New York: Free Press.

VicHealth. 2005. *Access to economic resources as a determinant of mental health and well-being: Research Summary 4*. Melbourne: Victorian Health Promotion Foundation.

Vosko, L.F. 2003. Precarious employment in Canada: Taking stock, taking action. *Just Labour*, 3, 1–5.

Watts, R.L. 1987. *The challenges and opportunities facing post-secondary education in Canada*. Saskatoon: National Forum on Post-secondary Education.

Webb, J., T. Schirato, and G. Danaher. 2002. *Understanding Bourdieu*. London: Sage.

West, P. 1997. Health inequalities in the early years: Is there equalisation in youth? *Social Science and Medicine* 44(6), 833–58.

West, P., and H. Sweeting. 2002. *A review of young people's health and health behaviours in Scotland*. Occasional Paper 10. Glasgow: MRC Social and Public Health Sciences Unit.

West, P., H. Sweeting, R. Young, and M. Robbins. 2006. A material paradox: Socioeconomic status, young people's disposable income and consumer culture. *Journal of Youth Studies* 9(4), 437–462.

White, R., and J. Wyn. 2007. *Youth and society*. Melbourne: Oxford University Press.

Williams, A., J. Coupland, A. Folwell, and L. Sparks. 1997. Talking about Generation X: Defining them as they define themselves. *Journal of Language and Social Psychology* 16(3), 251–277.

Wilson, B., and J. Wyn. 1987. *Shaping futures: Youth action and livelihood*. Sydney: Allen and Unwin.

Wiseman, J. 2006. Local heroes? Learning from recent community strengthening initiatives in Victoria. *Australian Journal of Public Administration* 65(2), 95–107.

Witz, A. 1995. Gender and service-class formation. In *Social change and the middle classes*, ed. T. Butler and M. Savage, 41–57. London: UCL Press.

Wooden, M. 1998. The labour market for young Australians. In *Australia's youth: Reality and risk*, ed. Dusseldorp Skills Forum. Sydney: Dusseldorp Skills Forum.

Wooden, M., and A. VandenHeuvel. 1999. The labour market for young adults. In *Australia's young adults: The deepening divide*. Sydney: Dusseldorp Skills Forum.

World Health Organization. 2004. *Young people's health in context: Health behaviour in school-aged children (HBSC) study; international report from the 2001/2002 survey*, ed. Dusseldorp Skills Forum. Denmark: World Health Organization.

Wright, J., and L. Burrows. 2004. 'Being healthy': The discursive construction of health in New Zealand children's responses to the National Education Monitoring Project. *Discourse: Studies in the Cultural Politics of Education* 25(2), 11–30.

Wyn, J. 2007. Learning to become somebody well: Challenges for educational policy. *Australian Educational Researcher* 34(3), 35–52.

– 2008. New youth transitions in education. In *Youth and the future: Processes of social inclusion and patterns of vulnerability in a globalised world*, ed. R. Bendit and M. Hahn- Bleibtreu. Farmington Hills, MI: Opladen and Barbara Budrich Publishers.

– 2009. *Youth health and welfare: The cultural politics of education and well-being*. Melbourne: Oxford University Press.

Wyn, J., and R. White. 1997. *Rethinking youth*. Sydney: Allen and Unwin.

Wyn, J., and D. Woodman. 2006. Generation, youth and social change in Australia. *Journal of Youth Studies* 9(5), 495–514.

– 2007. Researching youth in a context of social change: A reply to Roberts. *Journal of Youth Studies* 10(3), 373–381.

Yates, L. 1993. *The education of girls: Policy, research, and the question of gender*. Melbourne: Australian Council for Educational Research.

Zhang, X. 2009. Earnings of women with and without children. *Perspectives on Labour and Income* 10(3), 5–13.

Index

and leaving home, 164–71
and marriage, 175–8
and priorities, 78–81
and social change, 38–40, 91
and well-being, 76–8, 191, 194–8,
206, 208–9, 212, 215–22, 224
Generation, 3, 5, 15, 20, 24, 34, 40, 67,
81, 90–1, 101, 184, 226, 227, 236,
240–4
and change, 18, 23–6, 91, 93,
224–5, 227–30, 236, 242–3
and education, 18, 59–65, 66, 98,
101, 125–7
and family, 17, 159–65, 171, 174,
182, 186–7, 229
generational consciousness, 33,
241–2
Generation X, 5, 23, 32, 33, 35, 228
Generation Y, 32
Generation Z, 32
and the labour market, 128, 156–8
and policy, 16, 42–3, 63, 64, 231
post-1970, 8, 33
stereotypes, 5, 15, 18, 23, 32–3
and subjectivity, 34–5
and transition, 9, 31, 32
and well-being, 17, 190, 191,
224–5, 229
Giddens, A., 9, 28, 125
Gini index, 130, 156
Globalization, 26, 42, 46–7, 66, 128

Habitus, 21, 36, 237–40, 241
and gender, 39
Health, 14, 17, 18, 82, 86, 121, 151,
206–11, 230
and balance, 198–9, 210–11
and class, 210, 217–19
conceptualization, 193

and education, 201–3, 207–9
and gender, 206–8, 212, 217–19,
221
mental, 192, 194, 207–9, 222–3, 230,
232–4
and personal responsibility, 190–1,
193, 194, 210, 225
physical, 194, 207, 230
policy, 43, 144, 192–3
and social change, 26
Higher Education Contribution
Scheme (HECS), 58
Home ownership, 3, 72, 163, 174–7
Human capital, 45, 49, 63–5, 97, 129,
232, 234

Identity, 9, 21, 34, 35, 37, 197
identity work, 27, 28
Individualization, 9, 15, 21, 26–9, 90,
92, 128, 174, 236, 242–4
and health, 190
and labour markets, 128, 158
and policy, 28
and relationships, 159, 189
Inequality, 130, 237–9, 243–4
and education, 59–63
and identity, 37
and individualization, 27
and social change, 21
and social policy, 14, 30, 44, 63, 130,
234, 243
See also Class; Gender; Rurality
Insecurity, 17, 188, 223
in the labour market, 129, 131, 152,
233
Interdependence, 5, 188, 229

Job mobility, 149, 157
Job satisfaction, 140–5, 154–5